Contributions to Economics

For further volumes:
http://www.springer.com/1431-1933

Giorgio Calcagnini · Enrico Saltari
Editors

The Economics of Imperfect Markets

The Effects of Market Imperfections on Economic Decision-Making

Physica-Verlag

Editors
Professor Giorgio Calcagnini
D.E.M.Q
Università di Urbino "Carlo Bo"
Via Saffi 42
61029 Urbino
Italy
giorgio.calcagnini@uniurb.it

Professor Enrico Saltari
Department of Public Economics
Università di Roma "La Sapienza"
Via del Castro Laurenziano, 9
00161 Rome
Italy
Enrico.Saltari@uniroma1.it

ISSN 1431-1933
ISBN 978-3-7908-2130-7 e-ISBN 978-3-7908-2131-4
DOI: 10.1007/978-3-7908-2131-4
Springer Heidelberg Dordrecht London New York

Library of Congress Control Number: 2009932416

Cover design: SPi Publisher Services

Printed on acid-free paper

Physica-Verlag is a brand of Springer-Verlag Berlin Heidelberg

Springer is part of Springer Science+Business Media (www.springer.com)

Preface

This book is one of the final products of a research project on the effects of market imperfections on economic behavior and decisions. The project was put together by four Italian universities (Università di Roma "Tor Vergata" and "La Sapienza" Università Cattolica del Sacro Cuore – Piacenza and the Università di Urbino "Carlo Bo") in 2005 and funded by the Italian Ministry of Higher Education and Research for the period 2006–2007. The research title of the project "Corporate governance, financial systems and firms' performances" was indicative of its agenda: to investigate the role of market imperfections and their interactions on firms' decisions. In 2006 (May 12) the research group held the first conference at the Università di Urbino where intermediate results were first presented and discussed with outstanding scholars from US, UK, and Italian universities, and the European Central Bank.

The book reproduces the papers presented at the Università di Roma "La Sapienza" conference (May 16–17 2008) and is organized in two parts. The first one discusses imperfections that are mainly related to the working of financial markets. The second part includes contributions which focus on different topics of real market imperfections.

We wish to thank Steve Nickell, Philip Vermeulen and all the participants at the Urbino and Rome conferences who made both events extremely productive with their scientific contributions. We are especially grateful to Bob Chirinko who participated in both conferences and constantly encouraged us to carry out our scientific project on the economics of imperfect markets.

Contents

Contributors

Antonio Affuso University of Parma, via Kennedy, 6, 43100-Parma, Italy, antonio.affuso@unimi.it

Corrado Andini Universidade da Madeira, Departamento de Gestão e Economia, 9000 - 390 Funchal Portugal, andini@uma.pt

David Bartolini Osservatorio per le Politiche Economiche Regionali (OPERA), Ancona, Università Politecnica delle Marche, Ancona, Italy, d.bartolini@univpm.it

Giorgio Calcagnini Department of Economics and Quantitative Methods, Università di Urbino, Via Saffi 42, Italy, giorgio.calcagnini@uniurb.it

Adam Gehr Department of Finance, DePaul University, 1 E. Jackson, Chicago, IL, USA, agehr@mozart.depaul.edu

Vivek Ghosal Georgia Institute of Technology, Atlanta, GA 30318, USA

Germana Giombini Department of Economics and Quantitative Methods, Università di Urbino, Via Saffi 42, Italy, germana.giombini@uniurb.it

Enrique Martínez-García Federal Reserve Bank of Dallas, 2200 N, Pearl Street, Dallas, TX 75201, USA, enrique.martinez-garcia@dal.frb.org

Kazuo Ogawa Institute of Social and Economic Research, Osaka University, Osaka, Japan, ogawa@iser.osaka-u.ac.jp

Sílvio Rendon Department of Economics, Stony Brook University, Stony Brook, NY 11794, USA, srendon@ms.cc.sunysb.edu

Enrico Saltari Department of Public Economics, Sapienza, University of Rome, Rome, Enrico.Saltari@uniroma1.it

Jens Søndergaard Monetary Assessment and Strategy Division, Monetary Analysis, Bank of England, Threadneedle Street, London EC2R 8AH, UK, jens.sondergaard@bankofengland.co.uk

Elmer Sterken Department of Economics, University of Groningen, The Netherlands, e.sterken@rug.nl

Roberto Tamborini Department of Economics, University of Trento, Via Inama 5, 38100 Trento, Italy, roberto.tamborini@economia.unitn.it

Ichiro Tokutsu Graduate School of Business Administration, Kobe University, Japan, tokutsu@port.kobe-u.ac.jp

Giuseppe Travaglini Department of Economics and Quantitative Methods, Università di Urbino, via Saffi 42, Italy, giuseppe.travaglini@uniurb.it

Toni M. Whited Simon Graduate School of Business, University of Rochester, Rochester, NY, USA, toni.whited@simon.rochester.edu

Clifford R. Wymer Department of Public Economics, Sapienza, University of Rome, Rome, wymer@mail.com

Alberto Zazzaro Money and Finance Research Group (MoFiR) and CFEPSR, Università Politecnica delle Marche, Ancona, Italy, a.zazzaro@univpm.it

Introduction

This book is a collection of eleven papers concerned with the effects of market imperfections on the decision-making of economic agents and on economic policies that try to correct the inefficient market outcomes due to those imperfections. We may broadly define market imperfections as influences that generate costs that interfere with trades. The Contents table provides a classification between financial and real imperfections of each contribution according to the type of imperfections discussed.

It is clear however that the effects of imperfections do not impact just one market but affect other markets also; therefore, they affect the decision-making of firms and households who operate in those markets. As a consequence, real and financial imperfections are related: economic decisions are simultaneously affected by imperfections present both in real and financial markets. Some of the papers published in this volume provide a detailed description of the way those imperfections interact and jointly affect both investment and labor decisions. In addition, the analysis of the interactions among market imperfections is at the core of a recent strand of the economic literature (Blanchard and Giavazzi 2003; Belke et al. 2005; Wasmer and Weil 2004; Calcagnini et al. 2009).

Notwithstanding the obvious fact that market interdependence is not novel, scholars' interest is typically concentrated on the specific relationship among economic decisions originating from particular imperfections. The most well known example can be found in the economic literature on capital market imperfections and dates back to the 1958 Modigliani–Miller theorem: Financial market imperfections make fixed investment decisions depend on financing decisions even though, according to the traditional theory, real and financial decisions should be independent. Investment by firms depends both on the prices of goods determined in the real market and on the user cost of capital (i.e., the sum of the interest and depreciation rates) determined in the financial market. If markets are perfect, firms react to changes in the user cost of capital, but they do not respond to changes in the mix of financial resources (equity, bonds, bank loans, cash flow). Perfect capital markets imply that different sources of funds are perfect substitutes and then, based on arbitrage reasoning, there should be no differences in their cost. This explains why – in the case of perfect financial markets – we can speak of "the" user cost of capital without any other specification.

G. Calcagnini and E. Saltari (eds.), *The Economics of Imperfect Markets*, Contributions to Economics,
DOI: 10.1007/978-3-7908-2131-4_0, © Springer Physica-Verlag Berlin Heidelberg 2010

In contrast, financial market imperfections imply that diverse sources of funds are not perfect substitutes. Consequently, the arbitrage principle does not work, and the cost of funds is not univocally defined but depends on the firm's capital structure. Thus, investment is affected by the mix of financing sources. As a result, investment decisions are not only determined by demand and technological opportunities but also by the available sources of funds. For instance, according to the financial hierarchy theory, sources of funds can be ordered according to their cost (starting from the cheapest): first, cash flow, then debt and, finally, equity. If firms need to access external sources of funds besides the internal ones, the financing cost increases and investment is lower.

One issue that is still at the core of the economic debate concerns the determination of just how important financial market imperfections are for investment decisions. Indeed, most of the papers included in this book discuss the relationship between the capital structure of firms and their investment decisions. In the following pages, we will briefly review this issue to allow the reader to better appreciate the originality of the papers published in this book.

The theory of investment dates back to the Sixties with the work of Jorgenson (1963). More precisely, we should speak of demand for capital rather than investment. Indeed, Jorgenson assumes that firms are able to instantaneously adjust their capital stock to the desired one (as Jorgenson dubbed it) by equating in each period the marginal product of capital to its user cost. However, models based on the assumption that firms are able to purchase and install new capital instantaneously, or by means of a deterministic time lag function as in the Jorgenson approach, failed to produce significant empirical results. It was almost immediately clear that these models were inadequate as a basis for understanding the investment decisions of firms; therefore, the assumption of costless and instantaneous adjustment of capital stock was dropped and replaced by the adjustment costs hypothesis (Eisner and Strotz 1963; Lucas 1967; Gould 1968; Treadway 1969). The idea behind adjustment costs is a simple one, even though it remains more of an analytical device than an assumption deriving from empirical observations: Increasing (or decreasing) capital stock is expensive and adjustment costs rise with (dis) investment at an ever-increasing rate. In other words, adjustment costs are a convex function of (dis) investment. Therefore, capital stock is a quasi-fixed input: Firms can change it but at an increasing cost; as a consequence, current capital stock differs from desired capital stock. The latter, and the equality between capital marginal productivity and the user cost, is only reached in steady state. Within this framework, firms are unable to control capital, that becomes a state variable while the investment rate (the speed at which the firms increase the capital in each period) becomes the control variable.

Around the same time, Tobin (1969) offered a new investment theory that became known as the Tobin's q theory. In his original paper, Tobin assumes that exists a single good that can be consumed or invested, but the price of existing capital goods and the price of new capital goods (which is equal to their production cost, by definition equal to 1) may be different. Tobin's q is simply the ratio between the prices of existing and the new capital goods. When q is larger than 1, firms find buying new capital goods profitable, i.e., they make investments. Tobin's theory however, has two types of problems: First, it does not explain why the price of already installed capital goods may be different from their production cost; second, it is mainly a static theory. Indeed, Tobin only makes a distinction between the short run, during which q may be different from 1, and the long run when q is necessarily equal to 1.

At the beginning of the Eighties, the 1982 Hayashi model merged the two investment theories, Jorgenson's neoclassical theory and Tobin's Keynesian theory, although Lucas and Prescott (1971) and Abel (1977) had already made steps towards the same theoretical direction. In his contribution to the investment theory, Hayashi notes that q may differ from 1 because of adjustment costs due, for instance, to the installation of new equipment. The presence of adjustment costs explains why – unless we are in steady state – already installed capital offers an economic rent. As the first order conditions of the Hayashi's model show, optimal capital demand is reached when the difference between the price of existing capital goods and the price of new capital goods is equal to the adjustment costs of the planned investment.

The Hayashi dynamic model has not, however, proved to be a very successful attempt to integrate the two investment theories. Hayashi's q is not in general the same as Tobin's. The former is obtained by the Euler equations of the firm's optimization process and, therefore, it is a shadow price obtained as the ratio of the market value of an additional unit of capital to its replacement cost; it is a *marginal* q, as defined by Hayashi (p. 214, 1982), and as such, cannot be observed diversely from Tobin's q. The latter, on the other hand, is an *average* q, that is the ratio of the market value of existing capital to its replacement cost.

There exist technological and market conditions under which *marginal* q and *average* q are the same, specifically where the firm is a pricetaker with constant returns to scale in both production and installation technology. In this case, it is straightforward to obtain a linear please, emphasise linear relationship between investment and q, where the q coefficient is inversely related to the adjustment speed of existing capital to desired capital. Moreover, if stock prices reflect the future profitability of firms (which means that financial markets are efficient), they can be employed to calculate the q and directly used to estimate the investment linear model.

Notwithstanding the stringent assumptions behind its formulation, the linear model of investment shows undoubted theoretical advantages. First, the linear model between investment and q is directly obtained from an intertemporal optimization process where the firm's behavior is explicitly modeled. Second, the relationship between investment and q depends on the production technology and adjustment costs, and can be directly estimated. Finally, q synthesizes all investment opportunities; in other words, q represents a sufficient statistic of the expected profitability of firms.

Given these advantages, it is, thus, not surprising that the linear investment model has been one of the models most often utilized in empirical work. However, empirical results have mostly been disappointing. Two types of problems are typically recurrent with the q linear model. First, the estimated coefficient of q is usually small (in the original 1982 Hayashi paper, the estimated coefficient of q was about 4%), implying that the adjustment costs are unrealistically large. Second, the estimated coefficients of other financial variables, such as cash flow, are statistically significant. Therefore, the hypothesis that q is a sufficient statistic for the investment decisions of firms does not find empirical support.

There is no dearth of reasons for these disappointing outcomes. As for the large adjustment costs, it is sufficient to recall the restrictive nature of the technological and market conditions imposed on the model. As for the empirical significance of variables different from q for investment decisions, scholars refer to financial market imperfections due to the presence of asymmetric information. Costs generated by information imperfections make external funds more expensive than internal resources; indeed, sometimes these costs may be so large as to induce the firm not to invest.

Note, however, that a large value of the estimated cash flow coefficient does not necessarily mean that the firm is financially constrained. This is because, in these models, the variable q always exhibits low descriptive power (small estimated coefficients). Thus, it is natural to expect that the use of the cash flow (given by the sum of current profits and depreciation) as a regressor improves the forecast of the profit expectations of firms, independently of financial constraints.

Perhaps, the most important contribution of the 1988 Fazzari, Hubbard and Petersen (FHP) paper lies in its having found a way to address the second problem by providing an interpretation of the cash flow estimated coefficient. The FHP idea is to split the sample using an a priori criterion (the dividend payout rate in their paper), in order to identify the firms financially constrained. Firms that fall into this category will be likely to show their investment spending, sensitive to cash flow. In other words, the cash flow coefficient of liquidity-constrained firms is expected to be statistically significant or larger anyway than the estimated coefficient of the cash flow for unconstrained firms. The FHP empirical results support their hypothesis: The cash flow coefficient for liquidity-constrained firms is twice as large as that of unconstrained ones. It should be noted, though, that the FHP approach does not solve the other problem of the small estimated coefficient of Tobin's q. Thus, FHP's results are twofold: On one hand, they show that investment decisions depend on financial variables; on the other, they highlight the weakness of the q theory obtained from Hayashi's model. The subsequent empirical papers have been using the FHP approach, even though changes were incorporated into the original model, such as new measures of investment opportunities and new methods to identify liquidity-constrained firms. Most of these papers confirmed the results obtained by FHP.

Until recently, the consensus in favor of the FHP approach was almost unanimous among economists. Empirical studies based on an a priori classification of liquidity constrained and unconstrained firms (identified according to their size, their dividend payout ratio, or their rating) show that financial variables are important to investment. Recently, however, both the FHP approach and its empirical outcomes have been challenged. To keep things simple, we will summarize the criticisms directed at the FHP methodology into two categories:

- The use of linear investment models based on Tobin's q
- The validity and the interpretation of the estimated coefficients of the financial variables within investment models

We want to emphasize that the criticisms do not concern the dynamic investment model with adjustment costs, but the Hayashi linear version where the average q is equal to the marginal q and – in particular – where financial variables are used as regressors.

The first two contributions in this book discuss this recent critical approach to the linear investment model and suggest new research directions. Whited's paper distinguishes itself for the originality of the econometric methodology used to identify liquidity-constrained firms and its empirical results.

Let us assume that financial markets are imperfect, so that sources of funds are not perfect substitutes, and their cost is different. Concluding, as in FHP, that firms are liquidity-constrained only on the basis of the estimated coefficient of the financial variables in the investment equation may be misleading. A statistically significant coefficient of the cash flow variable may just be the result of the difference between the measured average q and the unobserved marginal q. Indeed, measurement errors in variables may produce ordinary least squares (OLS) estimates biased toward zero in the "true" Tobin's q coefficient and statistically significant coefficients for unimportant variables, as may be the case for the cash flow variable. Therefore, measurement errors in variables may cause us to define firms as liquidity-constrained when actually they are not.

Whited correctly states that a firm may be classified as liquidity-constrained if a windfall increase in internal funds determines an increase in investment. The change in internal funds must be unexpected to result uncorrelated with the Tobin's q, i.e., with the profitability expected by the firm. Exactly the opposite of what occurs with the cash flow, which is the sum of current profits and amortization. In other words, if firms react to unexpected changes in internal funds by increasing their investments, it means that internal finance is cheaper than external finance.

But how can we identify exogenous shocks to internal funds? Whited, following Rauh (2006), terms as exogenous shocks the contributions firms are required to make to their defined benefit pension plans in the event that assets backing these plans fall below the estimated liabilities. Although the contributions themselves are clearly endogenously determined together with other real (investment) and financial firm decisions, the contributions are calculated via a rule that entails a discrete shock to the firm's resources if the firm's pension assets fall just below its pension liabilities. In the latter case, firms need to fill the gap between assets and liabilities by cutting back on expenses.

Whited's original contribution is in the use of a regression discontinuity design in which the discontinuity is the point of violation of underfunding of corporate defined benefit pension plans. Specifically, the regression discontinuity allows the identification of the effects of financial frictions by disentangling them from those of investment opportunities. The design only requires the analysis of firms just under or above the threshold beyond which firms are required to re-finance their pension plans and, then, to cut back on the expenses. Indeed, as being just under or above the threshold is a random event, shocks to internal funds may be considered as exogenous.

By applying the regression discontinuity technique to a sample generated by means of a dynamic model, Whited's paper reaches two important results.

First, outcomes from an estimated investment linear equation that uses Tobin's q, the cash flow and the difference between pension assets and liabilities (or the funding gap) as regressors may be biased. Indeed, investment may negatively react to the funding gap even though external finance is not more costly than internal finance. The explanation provided by Whited falls into the first of the two categories of criticisms seen above: Investment linear models are just an approximation, valid only under very restrictive hypotheses, of an optimality condition that is generally non linear.

Second, by applying the regression discontinuity technique to the sample firms whose financial position is close to the threshold beyond which firms are required to re-finance their pension plans, Whited shows that in the presence of an exogenous resource shortfall, firms adjust on the least costly margin. The latter is not necessarily investment. Indeed, the most striking aspect of Whited's results is that even though external financing is costly, for instance if the firm only gets to keep 70 cents of every dollar of external finance raised, investment does not decrease. The intuition is that "this one-time fee, although large, is not as large as the long-run cost of decreasing factors of production."

Rendon's paper raises theoretical issues similar, in some respects, to Whited's. He shows analytically why using Tobin's q within investment linear models may cause more problems than solve them. Indeed, as we have seen above, because the marginal q is unobservable, the researcher makes use of a calculated average q to estimate investment models. But, by doing this, she introduces into the econometric model measurement errors, the presence of which reduces its ability to describe investment decisions and makes the statistical significance of financial variables dubious.

Therefore, the use of Tobin's q as an explanatory variable in investment models should not be pursued as it is "a variable that summarizes information about the future, that is, future state or choice variables is an intermediate object, helpful in the process of solving the dynamic programming problem, but cannot be an argument of the solution itself." The simple but rigorous model developed by Rendon shows the advantages of modeling investment decisions by means of a Bellman equation, with and without financial constraints.

Giving up the use of Tobin's q also provides econometric advantages as researchers are induced to switch to the General Method of Moments (GMM) procedure that directly tests the Euler equation, i.e., the equation that must be satisfied along the optimal path.

The issue of imperfect financial markets is also at the core of the Calcagnini, Gehr and Giombini paper. They analyze the cash holdings of firms in the presence of financial market imperfections and study how cash holdings affect a firm's market value. If markets were perfect, and firms may switch from one source of funds to another without costs, holding cash would be economically worthless. Instead, with market imperfections, internal finance is valuable because, like in the pecking order theory, it is less costly than external finance.

The pecking order theory is only one of several theories that provide motives for firms to hold cash. Calcagnini et al. take into consideration two more theories: the agency cost theory and the transaction cost theory. The former claims that managers hold cash to avoid using external funds because doing so would subject them to the market discipline. The latter holds that by having an optimal level of cash holdings (defined as the point where marginal benefits of holding cash are equal to marginal costs), firms are able to avoid the costs of raising external finance or liquidating existing assets to finance growth opportunities.

One of the purposes of the Calcagnini et al. paper is to test the three previous theories by estimating European firms' demand for cash holdings by means of a set of explanatory variables among which are firm size and investment. It is worth noting that in their paper, the liquidity of firms increases with labor market imperfections, as measured by the OECD EPL index.

Overall, the estimates of Calcagnini et al. show that the cash holdings of firms are more consistent with the pecking order theory than with the trade off and the agency cost theories. Further, the cash holdings of firms are a positive function of labor market imperfections: more rigid labor markets increase the financial fragility of firms which, consequently, have an incentive to strengthen their liquidity position. As for the effect of cash holdings on the market value of firms, the authors show that financial markets attach a positive value to firms' cash holdings, but that the contemporaneous presence of labor market imperfections decreases firm valuation. In other words, financial markets recognize, and consistently value the fact that stricter employment protection laws determine less internal funding of investment and higher cash flow volatility.

In their paper, Ogawa, Sterken, and Tokutsu concentrate on the role that single- and multiple bank relationships may play to guarantee funding to firms in the presence of financial market imperfections. Relationship banking is one of the "missing explanatory variables" in the Calcagnini et al. model of firms' cash holdings and, therefore, the paper fills a gap in the description of desired liquidity by firms. Indeed, the existence of relationship banking may reduce the need to hold large amounts of unproductive cash due to the presence of asymmetric information between lenders and borrowers in financial markets. More specifically, the authors try to understand what caused Japanese firms to establish single and multiple bank relations.

The theme of the single-bank relationship is also known as the theme of the main-bank relationship; firms may find it convenient to operate with a single bank because the latter, by holding a large share of loans of affiliated firms, has a strong incentive to collect information about the firms' prospects and to monitor them. Moreover, single-bank relations help to mitigate problems caused by asymmetric information that lead to adverse selection and/or moral hazard: Close monitoring helps identify the types of distress their clients face and thus reduce the cost of this distress. However, the authors also note that concentration of information about client firms by a main bank is a double-edged sword that creates monopoly exploitation (the hold-up problem) and, consequently, leads to the search for other banks.

In their analysis of Japanese small- and medium-sized firms, by taking the length of a main bank relation as a measure of the severity of the hold-up problem, Ogawa et al. find that the longer the main bank relation, the more severe the hold-up problem, so that the main bank extracts a monopoly rent from the affiliated firm.

In this paper, bank monopoly rents take the form of higher loan interest rates and the request to pledge personal guarantees. Therefore, to prevent informational exploitation, firms increase the number of bank relations. The authors also find that the firm whose main bank has a low capital ratio, increases the number of bank relations and that the effect becomes greater as the capital ratio approaches the minimum level. The reason is the need firms have to diversify liquidity risk by increasing transactions with other banks in the event of a deterioration of bank capital ratios, as observed in Japan during the late Nineties and the early years of the present decade.

Three more chapters of this volume are concerned with the (mal) functioning of the financial system and its effects on the working of the economy. Affuso's paper analyzes the working of a credit market with asymmetric information, while Tamborini's paper analyzes the macroeconomic consequences of information imperfections in financial markets. Finally, Andini's paper is an empirical analysis of the relationship between the development of financial systems and economic growth. We will discuss them in turn; we suggest that they be read in this order. Unlike the previous chapters in which imperfections are assumed as givens, Affuso's, Tamborini's and Andini's papers investigate the origin of market imperfections and then discuss, theoretically and empirically, their effects on the economy.

In Affuso's paper firms plan new investment that requires external financing in the form of bank loans. Indeed, by assumption, firms do not have internal finance, only illiquid assets. In turn, banks have to handle an asymmetric information problem (which assumes the form of adverse selection) as they are unable to distinguish between good firms, that will repay their debt in prosperity as well as in depression, and bad firms, that will repay their bank loan only in prosperity.

Banks handle the adverse selection problem by trying to separate the two types of firms. To this end, banks offer two types of loan contracts: The first requires the repayment of the initial loan together with the firm's assets as collateral; the second requires no collateral but a repayment larger than the initial loan. The interesting outcome of Affuso's model is that the possibility of reaching a separating equilibrium, and thus avoiding credit rationing, depends crucially on the number of bad firms.

The explanation for this result is simple: When a bad firm goes bankrupt, its assets are sold in the market and are likely bought by good firms. Therefore, the collateral provided by firms depends on the market value of their assets. If there are "too many" bad firms, and therefore, the supply of assets is high, asset prices are low, and all firms will decide to provide collateral. Conversely, if there are "too few" bad firms and the asset supply is low, asset prices are high and no firms will be willing to provide collateral. In order to reach a separating equilibrium, the asset price must be within these two prices (high and low).

The malfunctioning of financial markets, of which Affuso's model is an example, is not the only effect caused by the presence of asymmetric information. As we know, financial market imperfections affect investment and, consequently, may generate macroeconomic problems originating from savings and investment imbalances. Tamborini's paper deserves credit for focusing on the possibility that financial market imperfections may potentially be the foundations for a new macroeconomics alternative to the traditional New Neoclassical Synthesis, according to which sticky prices are the main cause of imbalances and business cycles.

Tamborini's contribution has two dimensions: (1) a microeconomic one along which the author provides a brief, but extremely useful guide of how asymmetric information creates adverse selection, moral hazard and agency problems that, in turn, are at the root of the malfunctioning of the financial market. (2) a macroeconomic one that focuses on the role of financial market imperfections in investment, namely credit rationing and trading at false prices. Starting from the trading-at-false-prices issue, Tamborini builds a simple model where the banking industry guarantees the equilibrium in the capital market even in the presence of a savings-investment imbalance – a gap which is filled by firm loan expansions and contractions. Within this Wicksellian economy, the interest rate set in the capital market may diverge from the "natural" interest rate, that is from the interest rate at which saving equals investment, thus ensuring the intertemporal general equilibrium. Indeed, when this divergence between the effective and the natural rate persists, it affects production and employment and, therefore, the imbalance between savings and investment does not clear in the current period, but continues to persist in future periods, as well.

Obviously, there are interest-rate mechanisms such as a central bank's rule of inflation targeting that are able to eliminate intertemporal imbalances between savings and investment. However, Tamborini shows that these mechanisms are effective only if they avoid targeting the natural interest rate, given that the latter is subject to unobservable shocks and fluctuations.

The issue of the positive relationship between financial market efficiency and investment is important both for the study of business cycles and for the economic growth. As long as financial markets are able to value firms correctly, i.e., on the basis of their "fundamentals," they will force firms to operate more productively, thereby acting as a stimulus for investment and consequently, for economic growth. Diversely, if imperfect financial markets inefficiently allocate resources, they will hinder economic growth. However, as is well known, economists are divided into two groups about the relationship between financial markets and economic growth. On the one hand, there are those, such as Schumpeter, who think that the development of financial markets accelerates economic growth; on the other, we find those, such as Lucas, who think that the importance of financial markets is overemphasized.

The attempt to find an empirical answer to this question has, in most cases, favored the financial markets, meaning that several variables measuring the degree of financial development (such as stock market liquidity or the amount of bank loans) are good predictors of GDP per capita growth rate and capital accumulation, once we control the effects of other variables considered potential sources of economic growth.

Levine is certainly one of the economists who has more than others contributed with his work to supporting the latter interpretation. Andini's paper analyzes the most well-known and recent of Levine's papers (Levine et al. 2000) to show that the evidence in favor of the importance of financial markets for economic growth is biased by the presence of outliers. Specifically, Andini underlines the influential role on the econometric analysis of countries such as Korea and Taiwan that, in the Nineties, contemporaneously exhibited higher GDP per capita growth rates and higher values of variables measuring financial development than those of the other countries included in Levine's sample. Indeed, once Korea and Taiwan are removed from the sample, as is done in Andini's paper, the empirical evidence in favour of the positive effect of financial development on economic growth vanishes. It should be noted that there exists a strand of economic literature showing how the economic growth of countries such as Korea and Taiwan (the Asian tigers), besides the development of financial markets, was mainly determined by a government-administered system of credit allocation that played an important role in allocating resources towards the most productive investments (see Zhu et al. 2004, and the references therein). This system was subsequently dismantled during the Asian financial crisis at the end of the Nineties.

Turning now to "real" imperfections, three papers of this book focus on adjustment costs. The first two aim at discussing the role of adjustment costs in the context of macroeconomic models, while the third paper uses adjustment costs to describe the entry and exit dynamics of firms.

Saltari, Travaglini and Wymer built a model incorporating two types of adjustment costs to describe the employment and investment dynamics of the Italian economy during the last 25 years (1980–2006). The first type of adjustment costs applies to changes in the capital-labor ratio at the firm level; the second one applies to changes in the productive capacity at the industry level as measured by the investment level.

The starting point of their analysis is the model of Saltari and Travaglini (ST) (2007, 2009) which was originally designed to provide an interpretation of the three main changes that have occurred in the Italian economy over the last fifteen years. Indeed, recent years have witnessed an increase in the contribution of labor to GDP growth; but this favourable event has been accompanied by a reduction in the contribution of labor to productivity, and capital accumulation to growth. The ST model permits a rigorous discrete time analysis of this trade-off, focusing on the role of technological and non technological shocks in affecting the short and long run properties of the economy.

In this light, the contribution by Saltari et al. presented in this volume aimed at widening that original model to the case of continuous time. In their paper there are three models that are empirically tested in continuous time. The first is an extension at the macroeconomic level of Saltari and Travaglini (2007, 2009) that incorporates the two types of adjustment costs discussed above, a Cobb–Douglas production function, and where wages, even if sticky, adjust to the marginal product of labor. The second model maintains the same adjustment cost structure of the first model, but with a CES technology and wages determined by a non-tatonnement process that depends on excess demand. The third model incorporates a more general specification of adjustment costs where a two step optimization procedure is employed: The firm first optimizes an objective function to find the optimal medium to long-run levels of capital and labor and then minimizes a cost function to take into account the firm's deviation from its optimal position.

What is the main result of their analysis? It was found that when the core model was estimated in continuous time it was not accepted by the data. Nonetheless, the augmented forms of this core model improved the original estimates. The best results are obtained with the third model. With this adjustment process, the estimation improves meaningfully, implying that rigidities and frictions affect the dynamic evolutions of the economy in a more complex way than the one usually assumed in the standard model of investment.

Martínez-García and Søndergaard's paper contains an experiment similar to Saltari et al.'s, but it focuses on the effects of adjustment costs on international trade dynamics. Specifically, the authors use a two-country Dynamic Stochastic General Equilibrium (DSGE) model with adjustment costs to replicate some of the stylized facts concerning investment and international trade that show countercyclical net exports.

The relationship between investment and net exports is easily explained: When a productivity shock hits an economy, its investment increases by much more than the increase in foreign consumption; so, the domestic country draws more resources from abroad and its trade deficit widens at the same time as the domestic output shows a rise. Hence, the trade balance is countercyclical. The traditional Real Business Cycle (RBC) models that are able to replicate the stylized fact concerning investment and trade balance, show theoretical investment volatility higher than that observed in the data, and, symmetrically, lower consumption volatility. The introduction of adjustment costs, by making investment less reactive to shocks, should decrease investment volatility and, at the same time, increase consumption volatility.

Martínez-García and Søndergaard discuss three models. The first model has flexible prices and no adjustment costs in the tradition of the International Real Business Cycle (IRBC) models. The other two models belong to the International New Neoclassical Synthesis (INNS) class of models because they assume sticky prices set by a mechanism *à la* Calvo. In the second model, adjustment costs are related to the investment growth rate (measured as the ratio of current investment over lagged investment) while in the third model, adjustment costs are related to the accumulation rate, i.e., the ratio between investment and capital stock.

Estimates of INNS models with adjustment costs are mixed. Adjustment costs make investment and consumption volatility closer to the observed one, but at the same time they also make net exports pro-cyclical and not countercyclical. The explanation for the latter result is simple: As investment is slowed down by adjustment costs, the country will experience a smaller resource inflow and accordingly, net exports will improve.

Ghosal's paper is the last of the three papers that focus on adjustment costs. Unlike the two previous papers, Ghosal follows a microeconomic or industry approach, and adjustment costs take the form of sunk costs.

Previous work by Dixit (1989) and Dixit and Pindyck (1994) shows that the joint presence of irreversibility and uncertainty creates an option value that affects both the entry and exit decisions and investment by firms. The option value approach provides very plausible outcomes concerning industry structures. According to theory, the presence of an option value makes the industry trigger entry price larger, and an exit price lower than the traditional Marshallian threshold values. Consequently, an increase in uncertainty, and thus a larger option value, increases the trigger entry price and decreases the trigger exit price. Note, however, that the former increases more than the latter decreases. It follows that the number of firms that enter the industry is lower than the number leaving the industry, and the overall number of firms decreases when uncertainty increases. In other words, the net entry is negative. Likewise, the option value in the presence of irreversibility has a negative effect on investment when uncertainty increases.

By taking a large sample of US industries, Ghosal tests both predictions concerning the effects of uncertainty on the number of firms within an industry and on investment in the presence of investment irreversibility. Empirical results support the author's predictions. An increase in uncertainty, as measured by profit volatility, increases firm concentration within industries given that the number of firms that find it more convenient to leave the industry is larger than the number of firms with an incentive to enter. Therefore, net entry is negative indeed.

This result is confirmed both in the case of a cross-industry analysis and a within-industry analysis (i.e., looking at the time series of net entries). Further, estimates show that the effect of uncertainty is positively correlated with the importance of irreversibility within each industry. The latter result should be taken cautiously because estimates show that small-sized firms are those most affected by an increase in uncertainty, while uncertainty seems to have no significant effect on large-sized firms (i.e., firms with more than 500 employees). In other words, only small firms' plants are shut down when uncertainty increases, not those of large-sized firms.

A possible explanation for the latter result is that irreversibility, i.e., the reduction in the plant value in secondary markets, should be measured relative to the firm size. Therefore, Ghosal's outcomes seem to show that irreversibility is *relatively* larger for small than for large-sized firms.

The conclusion that an increase in uncertainty brings about a higher industry concentration matters for antitrust policy programs, even though the latter are not traditionally concerned with the effects of uncertainty on market structures. The last paper published in this volume discusses the issue of antitrust policies.

Bartolini and Zazzaro's paper shows how the interaction of market imperfections and institutions (antitrust agencies and policies) may lead to unexpected results. By an updated review of the literature on antitrust policies, they show that it might be optimal for society (consumers and producers) to tolerate some degree of collusion among firms, given the costs of enforcing antitrust policies. The introduction of antitrust penalties or leniency programs can have the understandable effect of stabilizing cartels and increasing their size, as these policies may raise the costs of deviating and/or renegotiating a collusive agreement. In other words, the presence of market imperfections could cause antitrust interventions to be detrimental for market competition.

As regards penalties, this is intuitive because a monetary fine tends to reduce competition by making the collusive agreement easier to sustain, given that the fine increases the costs of deviation and/or the cost of renegotiating the original agreement. In the case of leniency programs, a generous one can succeed in breaking collusive agreements, as it makes the threat of self-reporting more credible. Moreover, leniency policies reduce the duration of collusive agreements, which is good for markets where a cartel would have formed in any case.

The policy implications of the Bartolini and Zazzaro paper are not in favor of the abrupt elimination of any antitrust policy, but rather they suggest paying more attention to the design of policies that should produce the desired effects. Specifically, the authors suggest that only very strong monetary and non-monetary sanctions can discourage firms from colluding. However, they conclude that in a world of uncertainty – where the exact penalty levels that induce more collusion are not known to the Anti-trust Authority – a large penalty makes cartel deterrence more likely, but also increases the risk of fostering broader and tougher collusive agreements.

There are at least three main lessons that we, as editors, learnt from our own reading of the eleven papers in this volume. First, investment theory has gained new momentum, as Whited's and Rendon's papers clearly demonstrate. In particular, Whited's contribution has not only shown us the flaws of the empirical approach, which "simply" adds financial variables on the right-hand side of the investment equation, but her innovative paper has also indicated the cure: The regression discontinuity technique tells us how to tackle the endogeneity issue that always hangs over the financial variables, such as the cash flow.

The second lesson has mainly a negative flavor. We have seen, both in a domestic and in an international context, that the traditional quadratic adjustment costs do not perform well when it comes to passing empirical tests. We need something new in this respect, but the problem is that we do not know what exactly it is. It is clear that the process of adjustment is slow. But it is far less clear what kind of adjustment process best characterizes firm investment decisions.

Finally, we want to emphasize an aspect of market imperfections already underlined at the beginning of this introduction. In our opinion, the best approach to market imperfections is to address them jointly, analyzing, for instance, how labor and financial market imperfections jointly influence investment. This aspect has been touched upon in some of the papers presented in this volume. But it is largely an unresolved issue and remains a topic for future research.

References

Abel AB (1977) Investment and the value of capital. Ph.D. thesis, Massachusetts Institute of Technology

Belke A, Gocke M, Hebler M (2005) Institutional uncertainty and European social union: Impacts on job creation and destruction in the CEECs. J Pol Model 27:345–354

Blanchard OJ, Giavazzi F (2003) Macroeconomic effects of regulation and deregulation in goods and labor markets. Q J Econ 118(3):879–907

Calcagnini G, Giombini G, Saltari E (2009) Financial and labor market imperfections and investment. Econ Lett 102:22–26

Dixit A (1989) Entry and exit decisions under uncertainty. J Polit Econ 97:620–638

Dixit AK, Pindyck RS (1994) Investment under uncertainty. Princeton University Press, New Jersey

Eisner R, Strotz RH (1963) Determinants of business investment. In: Impacts of Monetary Policy. Prentice-Hall, New Jersey
Fazzari S, Hubbard G, Petersen B (1988) Financing constraints and corporate investment. Brookings Papers Econ Activ (1):141–195
Gould J (1968) Adjustment costs in the theory of investment of the firm. Rev Econ Stud 35:47–55
Hayashi F (1982) Tobin's marginal q and average q: A neoclassical interpretation. Econometrica 50:213–224
Jorgenson D (1963) Capital theory and investment behavior. Am Econ Rev 53:247–259
Levine R, Loayza N, Thorsten B (2000) Financial intermediation and growth: Causality and causes. J Monetary Econ 46:31–77
Lucas RE (1967) Adjustment costs and the theory of supply. J Polit Econ 75(1):321–334
Lucas RE, Prescott EC (1971) Investment under uncertainty. Econometrica 39:659–682
Rauh J (2006) Investment and financing constraints: evidence from the funding of corporate pension plans. J Finance 61:33–71
Saltari E, Travaglini G (2007) Sources of productivity slowdown in European countries during 1990s. Department of Economics, University of York
Saltari E, Travaglini G (2009) The productivity slowdown puzzle. Technological and non technological shocks in the labor market. Int Econ J (forthcoming)
Tobin J (1969) A general equilibrium approach to monetary theory. J Money Credit Bank 1:15–29
Treadway A (1969) On rational entrepreneurial behavior and the demand for investment. Rev Econ Stud 36:227–240
Wasmer E, Weil P (2004) The macroeconomics of labor and credit market imperfections. Am Econ Rev 94:944–963
Zhu A, Ash M, Pollin R (2004) Stock market liquidity and economic growth: a critical appraisal of the Levine/Zervos model. Int Rev Appl Econ 18(1):63–71

Part I
Imperfections in Financial Markets

Chapter 1
What Can Cash Shortfalls and Windfalls Tell Us About Finance Constraints?

Toni M. Whited

Abstract This paper examines the relative magnitude of financial versus real frictions by looking at how firms react to quasi-exogenous cash shortfalls to pension assets. To answer the question theoretically, we examine a dynamic model of financing and exogenous cash shortfalls. We find that when financing costs are high, firms adjust on real margins and vice versa. We find that firms optimally avoid costly cash shortfalls, only experiencing these events after serious negative shocks to profits. We also find that commonly used regression tests for the presence of finance constraints can produce false positives. In contrast, regression discontinuity techniques can provide an accurate method for uncovering the existence and magnitudes of finance constraints.

Introduction

Dating back to the influential work of Fazzari et al. (1988), researchers have used the sensitivity of investment to cash flow as a metric for gauging the severity of finance constraints. The intuition behind this test is straightforward. If a firm cannot obtain outside finance, then its investment should respond strongly to movements in internal funds. Implementing this idea requires controlling for investment opportunities; otherwise, cash flow might capture movements in investment opportunities instead of movements in internal funds. This idea has spawned an enormous literature that examines regressions of investment on a proxy for investment opportunities (usually Tobin's q) and cash flow. Surveyed in Stein (2003), this body of work almost always finds that the sensitivity of investment to cash flow is higher for a priori constrained firms.

More recently, two strands of the literature have questioned both the existence and the meaning of these findings. For example, Erickson and Whited (2000) find that cash flow sensitivity is an artifact of measurement error in q, and that correcting

---

T.M. Whited
Simon Graduate School of Business, University of Rochester, Rochester, NY, USA,
e-mail: toni.whited@simon.rochester.edu

G. Calcagnini and E. Saltari (eds.), *The Economics of Imperfect Markets*, Contributions to Economics,
DOI: 10.1007/978-3-7908-2131-4_1,

for this measurement error leaves no cash flow sensitivity at all for any groups of firms, even those deemed to face financial constraints. Even if cash flow sensitivities can be found, it is not clear what they mean. Gomes (2001) attributes cash flow sensitivity in part to decreasing returns to scale; Moyen (2005) finds that cash flow sensitivity decreases with the severity of finance constraints; and Hennessy and Whited (2007) show that the relation between cash flow sensitivity and financial frictions depends on the type of friction.

One type of investment-cash flow sensitivity has been argued to be immune to these criticisms: the sensitivity of arguably exogenous cash windfalls and shortfalls. Because these movements in internal resources are already disentangled from investment opportunities, investment can only respond if external finance is more costly than internal. Otherwise, the firm would have used external finance.

In an intriguing recent article, Rauh (2006) uses as exogenous shocks the contributions firms are required to make to their defined benefit pension plans if assets backing these plans fall below the estimated liabilities. Although the contributions themselves are clearly endogenously determined with other real and financial firm decisions, the contributions are calculated via a rule that entails a discrete shock to firm resources if the firm's pension assets fall below its pension liabilities. One can exploit this discontinuity to deal with the endogeneity problem. In so doing, Rauh (2006) (Rauh, hereafter) find that firms cut their capital expenditures almost 70 cents for every dollar of mandatory pension contributions. The finding is important because it demonstrates that external finance is more costly than internal finance. However, the finding is also puzzling inasmuch as firms do face substantial costs of adjusting both the capital stock and the rate of investment. For example, Cooper and Haltiwanger (2006) estimate that the former are economically important on a microeconomic basis, and Christiano and Eichenbaum (2005) demonstrate that the latter are important for explaining aggregate business cycle dynamics. The findings in Rauh are therefore perplexing because it seems plausible that firms would prefer to adjust assets and liabilities with low adjustment costs.

We attempt to explain this puzzle from a theoretical angle. We start with an intuitive description of econometric technique used in Rauh – regression discontinuity. Suppose one observes only firms close to the point where pension assets equal pension liabilities. Intuitively, firms on each side of this point are not much different from one another on the dimension of pension funding status, and they can therefore be thought of as randomly assigned to paying the mandatory contributions. Then if one finds a difference in investment between the near violators and near escapees, one can attribute a causal effect of pension funding violations on investment. Although Rauh discusses identification around the discrete jump in the function relating mandatory contributions and underfunding, he includes the whole sample in his estimation. Because this function is public knowledge, firms optimize subject to the existence of these discontinuities and endogenously choose whether they want to be close to point of a funding violation. This clear source of endogeneity questions whether regressions can uncover the presence of finance constraints in this context.

We use a dynamic model to better understand when using a full sample regression provides the same answers as a purely local regression around a discontinuity. The model features a firm with an infinite horizon and a stochastic production technology that employs factors that are both costless and costly to adjust. This firm is burdened with an inherited pension plan subject to mandatory contributions, its pension assets are subject to random shocks to value, and it can only raise external finance at a premium to the opportunity cost of internal funds. It chooses external finance, fixed and variable factors, distributions, and pension contributions endogenously. In this setting we find that firms do optimally anticipate and overfund their pension liabilities. Further, we find that misleading results can be produced by testing for the effects of mandatory contributions on firm decisions using firm-year observations away from the point of a funding violation. In particular, we find that one can find a response of real decisions even when external finance is costless.

Our paper fits into the prior literature that has tried to understand the relation between finance and investment by studying how firms respond to arguably exogenous shocks to cash flow. Clearly, Rauh fits into this category. In addition, Blanchard et al. (1994) study legal settlements; and Lamont (1997) studies the reaction of the non-oil subsidiaries of oil firms to the dramatic drop in oil prices in the mid-1980s. Our paper is similar in spirit to Gomes (2001) in that it examines the behavior of reduced-form regressions using data simulated from a dynamic model.

The paper proceeds as follow. Section Regression Discontinuity introduces regression discontinuity; Section A Model of Pention Funding, describes the model; Section Simulations presents the model simulations; and Section Conclusion concludes.

Regression Discontinuity

We wish to identify the margins on which firms respond to changes in their resource base. The main empirical challenge is finding a source of independent variation in internal funds. To this end we borrow the useful and novel insight in Rauh that one can use mandatory pension contributions, even though they are clearly endogenously determined with other firm decisions. The key institutional feature of these contributions that allows identification is that they occur when a continuous variable, net pension assets, falls below zero.

To see how this discontinuity aids in identification, it is useful to consider an ideal experimental setting in which one would flip a coin to assign a pension funding violation to a group of firms at random and then compare treated and control groups. Clearly, this sort of experiment is infeasible, but one can obtain a quasi-experimental setting because the firms that have barely violated the pension funding rules are not much different from those that have barely escaped a violation. Therefore, the near-escapees and near-violators can be thought of as close-to-randomly assigned to a violation, and by calculating the average differences between characteristics of these two groups of firms, one can estimate what is called a local average treatment effect, or LATE. This idea of regression discontinuity is originally from Thistlethwaite and Campbell (1960).

More formally, let y_i be a variable of interest, such as investment, employment, liquid assets, or external financing. Let ϕ_i be a violation indicator, and let s_i be the funding surplus. We are interested in estimating the regression

$$\begin{aligned} y_i &= \beta + \alpha\phi_i + u_i \\ \phi_i &= \phi(s_i) = 1\{s_i \leq 0\}, \end{aligned} \tag{1.1}$$

in which α is the average treatment effect from "treatment" with a funding violation. If one were to try estimating this on a sample of firms with wide variation in funding surpluses and deficits, assignment is not random; so $E(u_i|\phi_i) \neq 0$, and OLS produces biased coefficients.

As we have argued informally, however, we can use a restricted sample to estimate a LATE, which we define formally as

$$LATE = \lim_{s\downarrow 0} E(y|s) - \lim_{s\uparrow 0} E(y|s). \tag{1.2}$$

Why does this expression identify the treatment effect, α? To see why, note from (1.1) that

$$\begin{aligned} \lim_{s\downarrow 0} E(y|s) - \lim_{s\uparrow 0} E(y|s) &= \alpha(\lim_{s\downarrow 0} E(\phi|s) - \lim_{s\uparrow 0} E(\phi|s)) \\ &\quad + \lim_{s\downarrow 0} E(u|s) - \lim_{s\uparrow 0} E(u|s) \\ &= \alpha(1-0) + \lim_{s\downarrow 0} E(u|s) - \lim_{s\uparrow 0} E(u|s) \end{aligned}$$

If we assume that $E(u|s)$ is continuous in s, then the last term goes to zero and we have

$$\alpha = \lim_{s\downarrow 0} E(y|s) - \lim_{s\uparrow 0} E(y|s).$$

The assumption that $E(u|s)$ is continuous in s is crucial, and it is therefore important to understand what it means in economic terms. If one takes the regression (1.1) seriously, it implies that the only variable that should determine firm investment or employment or external financing or any other variable we consider is whether a firm's pension assets are greater than its pension liabilities. This interpretation is, of course, absurd, but it points out that many determinants of our variables of interest are omitted from (1.1) and are therefore implicitly contained in the error term, u_i. The continuity assumption then implies that none of these variables exhibits a discontinuity at the exact point of a pension funding violation. This assumption is from an intuitive standpoint likely to hold at least approximately. For example, even though Tobin's q capitalizes information about funding violations, the impact is small because Tobin's q also capitalizes all other information about investment opportunities, both now and in the indefinite future.

One difficulty with estimating a LATE is that one cannot necessarily extrapolate one's inferences to the rest of the sample. It is possible to do so, however, by using the concept of a control function from Heckman and Robb (1985). Suppose that the only determinant of a pension funding violation is the difference between pension assets and liabilities. Then one can write the regression error, u_i, as

$$u_i = E(u_i|s_i) + e_i, \tag{1.3}$$

in which e_i is, by definition, orthogonal to $\phi_i = \phi(s_i)$. Substituting (1.3) into (1.1) then gives

$$\begin{aligned} y_i &= \beta + \alpha\phi(s_i) + E(u_i|s_i) + e_i \\ &= \beta + \alpha\phi(s_i) + k(s_i) + e_i \end{aligned} \tag{1.4}$$

in which $k(s_i) \equiv E(u_i|s_i)$. In general, $k(s_i)$ will be a smooth function of s_i, although it will only be linear if $u_i|s_i$ is normally distributed, which is an implausible assumption in this instance. For example, investment is highly skewed. Nonetheless, if we are willing to swallow the assumption that s_i is the only determinant of ϕ_i, we can estimate this regression by including smooth functions of the distance between pension assets and pension liabilities in the regression.

Clearly, this assumption is hard to swallow, but thinking about the assumption points out the key difficulty with estimating (1.4) on a sample with wide variation in pension funding status. The regression must be very well specified in order for this technique to work. If not, then if $\phi(s_i)$ is correlated with anything that is left out of the regression, its coefficient will be biased. Van der Klaauw (2002) puts the point slightly differently by noting that estimating (1.4) requires strong assumptions to achieve identification. In particular, one has to assume that the effects of s_i (the pension funding gap) on y_i are adequately controlled for by other variables in the regression.

This condition may be violated for a variety of reasons. For example, if y_i is the rate of investment, then the regression (1.4) should contain a measure of investment opportunities. As pointed out in Erickson and Whited (2000), the usual measure of investment opportunities, Tobin's q, only captures about fifty percent of the variation in true investment opportunities. Even if one corrects for measurement error, reduced form investment regressions only explain about half of the variation in investment. In the cases of employment, firm-level data on average wages are unavailable in our data source (Compustat); so any employment demand equation that will be seriously misspecified. In terms of the other variables we consider – cash, equity issuance, short term debt issuance, long-term debt issuance, inventories, and shareholder distributions – it is highly likely that any of these variables and the funding gap respond to unobserved demand or technology shocks. This problem renders it even more difficult to specify an appropriate regression.

We tackle the uncertainty surrounding the correct specification of (1.4) via simulation of an economic model to determine if estimating (1.4) in a large sample produces erroneous results.

A Model of Pension Funding

We consider a discrete-time, infinite-horizon, partial-equilibrium model of a firm. First we describe technology and financing. Then we move on to a description of the model calibration and the simulation results.

Technology and Financing

A risk-neutral firm uses capital, k, and a variable factor of production, l, to produce output, and it faces a productivity shock, z. The firm's per period production function is given by $\pi(k, l, z)$. It is continuous, with $\pi(0, 0, z) = 0$, $\pi_z(k, l, z) > 0$, $\pi_k(k, l, z) > 0$, and $\pi_l(k, l, z) > 0$. Also, the Hessian with respect to k and l is negative definite and the usual Inada conditions hold. The shock z is observed by the producer before he makes his current period decisions. It takes values in $[\underline{z}, \bar{z}]$ and follows a first-order Markov process with transition probability $g(z', z)$, in which a prime indicates a variable in the next period; $g(z', z)$ has the Feller property. The firm is imperfectly competitive and its output price, x, is therefore a function of its output: $x \equiv x(\pi(k, l, z))$. We assume that this demand function is isoelastic with elasticity η. Labor is paid a real wage of w each period, and profits are taxed at a rate τ_c.

Without loss of generality, l and k lie in a compact set. Each period the firm sets an optimal level of l so that $\pi_l(k, l, z) = w$. The Inada conditions ensures that any optimal level of l lies in a compact set with a maximum of $\bar{l}$. As in Gomes (2001), define $\bar{k}$ as

$$(1 - \tau_c)\pi(\bar{k}, \bar{l}, \bar{z}) - d\bar{k} \equiv 0, \tag{1.5}$$

in which d is the capital depreciation rate, $0 < d < 1$. Concavity of $\pi(k, l, z)$ and the Inada conditions ensure that $\bar{k}$ is well-defined. Because $k > \bar{k}$ is not economically profitable, k lies in the interval $[0, \bar{k}]$. Compactness of the state space and continuity of $\pi(k, l, z)$ ensure that $\pi(k, l, z)$ is bounded.

Investment, I, is defined as

$$I \equiv k' - (1 - d)k. \tag{1.6}$$

The firm purchases and sells capital at a price of 1 and incurs adjustment costs that are given by

$$A(k, k') = ck\Phi_i. \tag{1.7}$$

For simplicity, $A(k, k')$ contains only a fixed component, $ck\Phi_i$, in which c is a constant, and Φ_i equals 1 if investment is nonzero, and 0 otherwise. The fixed cost is proportional to the capital stock so that the firm has no incentive to grow out of the fixed cost.[1] We omit a smooth adjustment cost because curvature of the

[1] Replacing ck with a fixed number, F, changes the analysis little because the capital stock is bounded.

profit function acts to smooth investment over time in the same way that quadratic adjustment costs do.

The firm inherits a pension liability, b, and must hold an asset, p, to counter the liability. This asset earns a stochastic rate of return, r, that follows a first order Markov process with transition probability $f(r', r)$. These returns are also taxed at a rate τ_c. For simplicity, we assume a full tax loss offset in the case of negative profits.

If $p(1 + r)$ falls below b, then the firm must make a contribution to p equal to $(b - p(1 + r))$. This provision restricts the choice set for p. The firm must also pay a lump-sum excise tax of τ. To make the choice set compact, we assume an arbitrarily high upper bound on assets, $\bar{p}$. This upper bound is imposed without loss of generality because our taxation assumption ensures bounded saving.

For simplicity all external finance takes the form of equity. To preserve tractability, we do not model costs of external equity as the outcome of an asymmetric information problem. Instead, we capture adverse selection costs and underwriting fees in a reduced-form fashion. Accordingly, we define equity issuance/distributions as

$$\begin{aligned} e(k, k', p, p', l, z, r) &\equiv e \\ &= x(\pi(k, l, z))\pi(k, l, z) - wl - (k' - (1 - d)k) - A(k, k') \\ &\quad + p(1 + r) - p' - \tau\Phi_b, \end{aligned} \tag{1.8}$$

in which Φ_b equals one if $p(1+r) - b < 0$. If $e > 0$, the firm is making distributions to shareholders, and if $e < 0$, the firm is issuing equity. For simplicity, the external equity-cost function is linear

$$\begin{aligned} \phi(e) &\equiv \Phi_e \lambda e \\ \lambda &\geq 0 \end{aligned}$$

in which Φ_e equals 1 if $e < 0$, and 0 otherwise.

The firm chooses (k', p', l) each period to maximize the value of expected future cash flows, discounting at the risk-free interest rate, δ. The Bellman equation for the problem is

$$\begin{aligned} V(k, p, z, r) = \max_{k', p', l} \Big\{ & e(k, k', p, p', l, z, r) + \phi(e) \\ & + \frac{1}{1 + \delta} \int\int V(k', p', z', r') \mathrm{d}g(z', z) \mathrm{d}f(r', r) \Big\} \end{aligned} \tag{1.9}$$

The first two terms represent the excess of cash inflows over cash outflows (net of issuance costs) and the last term represents the continuation value of the firm. The model satisfies the conditions for Theorem 9.6 in Stokey and Lucas (1989), which guarantees a solution for (1.9). Theorem 9.8 in Stokey and Lucas (1989) ensures a unique optimal policy function, $\{k', p', l\} = h(k, p, z, r)$, because the functional form chosen for $\phi(e)$ ensures that $e + \phi(e)$ is weakly concave in its first two arguments.

Simulations

We solve the model numerically and investigate its implications for reduced-form regressions via simulation. We first describe the parameterization of our baseline simulation and explain the properties of optimal firm behavior. We then explain the experiments we perform on the model and the results of these experiments.

Model Calibration

The production function is given by $\pi(k,z) = zk^{\theta}l^{1-\theta}$, in which we set θ to 0.3. We set the demand elasticity, η, so that the markup of price over marginal cost is 1.33. These two settings correspond to the estimates of labor's share and mark-ups from Rotemberg and Woodford (1992; 1999). We set the risk-free interest rate, δ, equal to 4%, which lies between the values chosen by Hennessy and Whited (2007) and Gomes (2001). We set the wage equal to 1.

To specify a stochastic process for the shock z, we follow Gomes (2001) and assume that z follows an $AR(1)$ in logs,

$$\ln(z') = \rho_z \ln(z) + v'_z, \tag{1.10}$$

in which $v' \sim N(0, \sigma_v^2)$. Our baseline parameter choices for $\rho = 0.66$ and $\sigma_v = 0.121$ are the averages of the estimates of these two parameters in Hennessy and Whited (2007). The stochastic return on pension assets is assumed to be $i.i.d.$ with a mean of 4% and a standard deviation of 20%. In this risk-neutral setting the mean of the shock equals the risk-free rate, and the standard deviation is set approximately equal to the standard deviation of the S&P500 index.

We follow Hennessy and Whited (2005) to parameterize the financing function, setting $\lambda_1 = 0.059$. To set the size of the pension liabilities, b, we first compute the steady-state labor force from a version of this model with no pension fund, and then compute the pension liability as this steady-state labor force times the following quantity: one third of the real wage in perpetuity, discounted at the risk-free rate, starting in 20 time periods.

To find values for the adjustment cost parameter, c, we turn to Cooper and Haltiwanger (2006), who estimate $c = 0.039$. We set the depreciation rate equal to 0.15, a figure approximately equal to the average in our data of the ratio of depreciation to the net capital stock.

Finally, to find a numerical solution we need to specify a finite state space for the four state variables. We let the capital stock lie on the points

$$\left[\bar{k}(1-d)^{40}, \ldots, \bar{k}(1-d)^{1/2}, \bar{k}\right].$$

We let the productivity shock, z, have 10 points of support, and we let the return on pension assets, r, have 5 points of support. We transform (1.10) and the i.i.d. process for r into discrete-state Markov chains using the method in Tauchen (1986). We let p have 20 equally spaced points in the interval $[0, \overline{p}]$, in which $\overline{p}$ is set to $\overline{k}/2$. The optimal choice of p never hits this upper bound.

We solve the model via iteration on the Bellman equation, which produces the value function $V(k, p, z, r)$ and the policy function $\{k', p', l\} = h(k, p, z, r)$. In the subsequent model simulation, the spaces for z and r are expanded to include 100 points, with interpolation used to find corresponding values of V, k, l, and p. The model simulation proceeds by taking a random draw from distribution of (z', r') (conditional on z and r), and then computing $V(k, p, z, r)$ and $h(k, p, z, r)$. We use these computations to generate an artificial panel of firms by simulating the model for 10,000 identical firms over 200 time periods, keeping only the last 20 observations for each firm.

Simulation Results

Knowledge of h and V also allows us to compute interesting quantities such as cash flow, Tobin's q, mandatory contributions, and distributions. Specifically, we define our variables to mimic the sorts of variables used in the literature.

Ratio of investment to the "book value" of assets	$(k' - (1 - d)k)/k$
Ratio of cash flow to the book value of assets	$(\pi(k, l, z) - wl)/k$
Tobin's q	$(V(k, p, z, r) + p - b)/k$
Ratio of equity issuance to the book value of assets	$-\min(0, e)/k$
Ratio of mandatory contributions to the book value of assets	$-\min(0, p(1 + r) - b)/k$
Ratio of the optimal funding gap to the book value of assets	$(p - b)/k$
Ratio of the realized funding gap to the book value of assets	$(p(1 + r) - b)/k$

As discussed by Erickson and Whited (2000), computation of average q using real-world data sets involves numerous judgment calls and imputations. Of course, these problems produce measurement error. In contrast, there is no measurement error when average q is computed from a structural model. Because it is impossible to remove measurement error from the real-world data, for some of our simulations we put the model on equal footing by adding a pseudo-normal error term, denoted u, to model-generated q. We set $\sigma_u = 2.4$. The implied R^2 from the regression of $(V + p - b)/k + u$ on $(V + p - b)/k$ is approximately 0.4 – a figure in line with the estimates in Erickson and Whited (2000).

Figure 1.1 depicts a histogram of the optimal ratios of $(p-b)/k$ for our simulated panel. This figure represents the gap between pension assets and pension liabilities *before* the firms are hit with the shocks r. The most striking feature of this figure is the tiny fraction of firm/year observations in which the firm finds it optimal to have a small funding surplus. Clearly firms anticipate the possibility that they will have to make mandatory contributions, and they therefore build a cushion to insure against

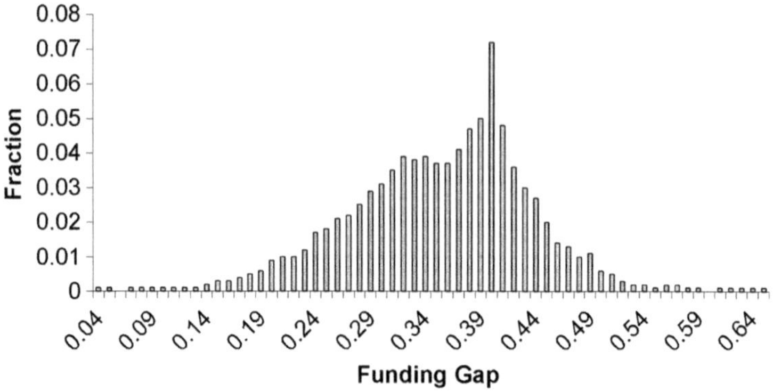

Fig. 1.1 Optimal simulated funding surpluses

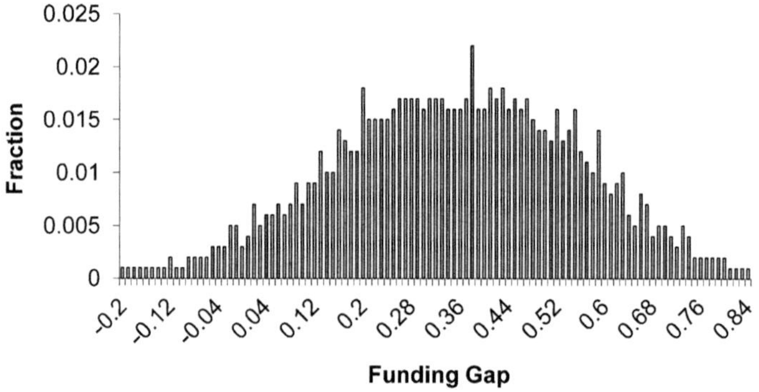

Fig. 1.2 Realized simulated funding surpluses and deficits

this possibility. This cushion is usually sizable, with most firms holding assets whose value is between 20 and 35% of the capital stock. When they do choose to have a small funding surplus, it happens when they have had a series of high positive productivity shocks. This figure depicts a histogram of optimal funding surpluses, as a fraction of the capital stock, chosen by the baseline simulated firms.

Figure 1.2 depicts a similar histogram of the realized ratios $(p(1+r)-b)/k$ for our simulated panel after the firms are hit with the shocks r. Approximately 4% of the firm-year observations end up with a negative funding gap, and some of these gaps are quite sizable, amounting to as much as 20% of the capital stock.

This figure depicts a histogram of realized funding surpluses and deficits, as a fraction of the capital stock, after the baseline simulated firms are hit with a shock.

Figure 1.3 portrays the coefficient α_2 in the following regression, which is from Rauh.

$$\frac{k'-(1-d)k}{k} = \alpha_0 + \beta\frac{V(k,p,z,r)+p-b}{k} + \alpha_1\frac{\pi(k,l,z)-wl}{k} + \alpha_2\frac{-\min(0,p(1+r)-b)}{k} + \alpha_3\frac{p-b}{k} + u. \quad (1.11)$$

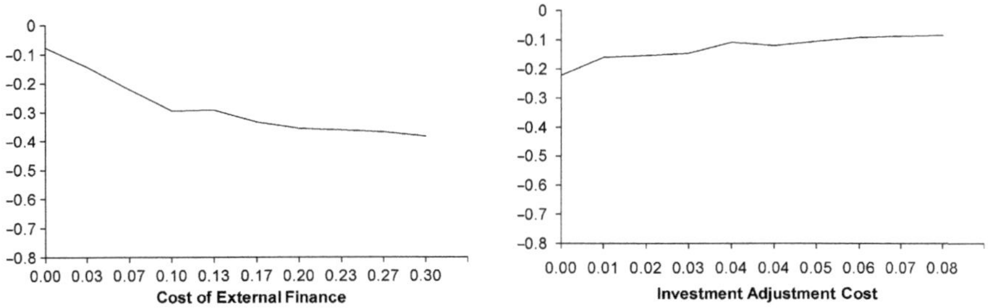

(a) Panel A: Investment Regression

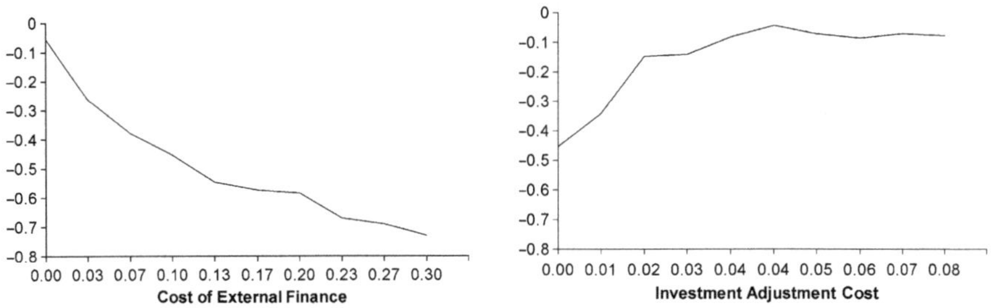

(b) Panel B: Labor Change Regressions

Fig. 1.3 Factor sensitivity to mandatory contributions. This figure depicts the coefficient α_2 in the regression

$$\frac{X}{k} = \alpha_0 + \beta\frac{V(k,p,z,r)+p-b}{k} + \alpha_1\frac{\pi(k,l,z)-wl}{k} + \alpha_2\frac{-\min(0,p(1+r)-b)}{k} + \alpha_3\frac{p-b}{k} + u.$$

In Panel A $X \equiv k' - (1-d)k$, and in Panel B $X \equiv l' - l$

The left side variable is the rate of investment. The regressors are Tobin's q, cash flow, mandatory contributions, and the funding gap. Recall that Rauh claims that this coefficient on mandatory contributions measures the response of investment to an exogenous resource shortfall.[2] Panel A of Fig. 1.3 plots the coefficient, α_2 as a function of the parameter describing the cost of external finance, λ, and the parameter describing the cost of adjusting the capital stock, c. Each graph is constructed by running 10 simulations, each with a different value for the parameter of interest, and then by interpolating between the points. In support of the basic empirical results in Rauh, the response of investment to mandatory contributions is negative. Further, this negative response becomes more negative with the cost of external finance, and it becomes less negative with the cost of adjusting the capital stock. The economic interpretation of these results, however, is complex, especially in light of our

[2] We have also tried subtracting optional pension contributions $(p' - p)$ from the cash flow term. We find very similar results.

next result that investment responds to mandatory contributions even when external finance is costless. This surprising result, however, occurs because (1.11) is an arbitrary regression specification that only approximates the highly nonlinear first order conditions for optimal investment. Therefore, the term corresponding to mandatory contributions picks up the effect of fundamental investment opportunities in addition to the effect of the cost of external finance.

Panel B examines the coefficient on mandatory contributions in a regression exactly analogous to (1.11), except that the left hand side variable is $(l' - l)/k$. The response of the change in employment to mandatory contributions closely resembles the response of investment. It become more negative as the cost of external finance increases and less negative as the cost of adjusting the capital stock increases. However, the interesting pattern here is the markedly higher coefficient on mandatory contributions for any configuration of financial and adjustment costs. This result makes sense because in this model labor is costless to adjust. In light of this costless adjustment, it is at first counter intuitive that labor becomes less responsive to mandatory contributions as the cost of adjusting the capital stock rises. However, the firm's technology constrains the range of the optimal mix of capital and labor. Therefore, although labor always adjusts more than the capital stock, it also inherits some of the sluggishness of the capital stock when adjustment costs rise.

The two main take-away points from this figure can be summarized as follows. First, the regression (1.11), although informative about the cost of external finance, is not perfectly specified, and can allow the inference of costly external finance even when external finance is costless. Second, the firm adjusts on the least costly margin.

We have also studied two other margins on which the firm adjusts: whether it ever uses external finance and whether it over-funds its pension assets after an adverse shock. The answer to both questions is a resounding yes. If we replace the left-hand-side variable in (1.11) with e/k, we find large negative coefficients on mandatory contributions that are about twice as large in absolute value as the coefficients depicted in Panel B. Although this response decreases slightly when the cost of external finance rises, it always remains stronger than the response of either labor or capital. Why does the firm adjust more on a financial margin than on a real margin? If a firm alters its factor inputs, its productivity and revenues change over a long horizon. In contrast, if the firm has to tap external finance, it pays a one-time fee that has a much smaller impact on its long-run value.

To examine the over-funding question, we replace the left-hand-side variable in (1.11) with a variable that is zero if the firm is not making mandatory contributions and that is otherwise the difference between actual and mandatory contributions. In this case we find a large positive coefficient that rises with the cost of external finance. This result mirrors the histogram in Fig. 1.1. Firms anticipate having to make mandatory contributions and build cushions to protect themselves from this event.

The impact of inserting measurement error in $(V(k, p, z, r) + p - b)/k$ into these regressions is large. For all of these regressions and for all underlying parameter values, the coefficients on mandatory contributions rise by a factor of 3–5 in absolute value. This result makes sense because mandatory contributions and $(V(k, p, z, r) + p - b)/k$ are highly negatively correlated, and because the effect of measurement error in one variable impacts the coefficients on other variables via their covariances with the mismeasured regressor: $(V(k, p, z, r) + p - b)/k$. One important lesson can be gleaned from this result. If the underlying regression is poorly specified, then examining the impact of mandatory contributions on factor demand may result in misleadingly large estimated effects.

We next examine whether using regression discontinuity can do a better job of detecting real and financial frictions. To this end we isolate those simulated observations that have a funding gap or surplus that is less than one percent of the value of pension liabilities. Figure 1.4 depicts the local response of real decisions – labor and capital – to moving from a small funding surplus to a small funding deficit. First, for both labor and capital, there is no local response if external finance is costless. This result stands in contrast to results from examining the regression (1.11), and it indicates that looking at local responses can be a more accurate method for detecting costly external finance. Second, and not surprisingly, capital and labor decrease

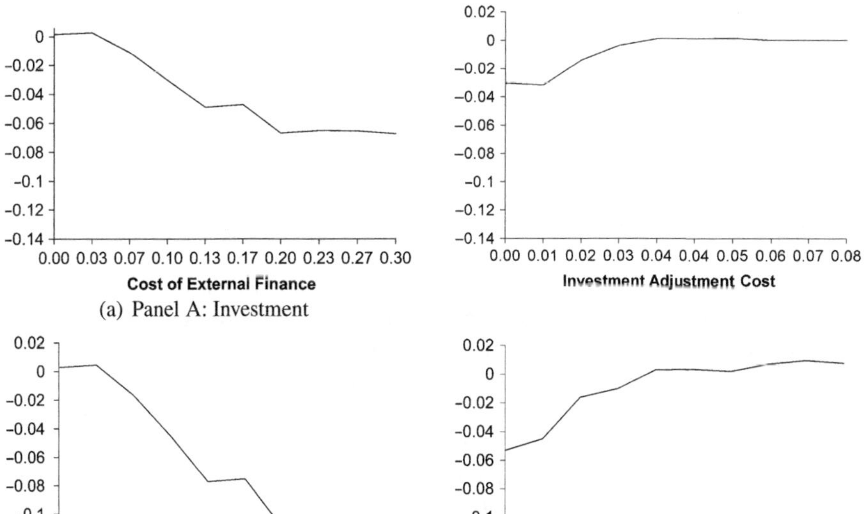

(a) Panel A: Investment

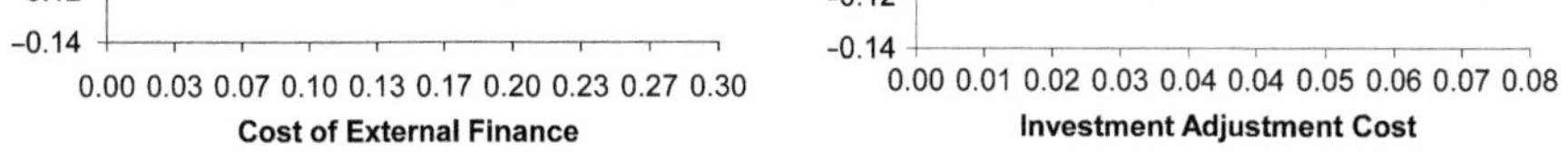

(b) Panel B: Labor Change

Fig. 1.4 Local response of real decisions to funding violations. This figure compares the average investment and average employment changes for firms that have funding surpluses no greater than one percent of liabilities to the same quantities for firms that have funding deficits no greater than one percent of liabilities

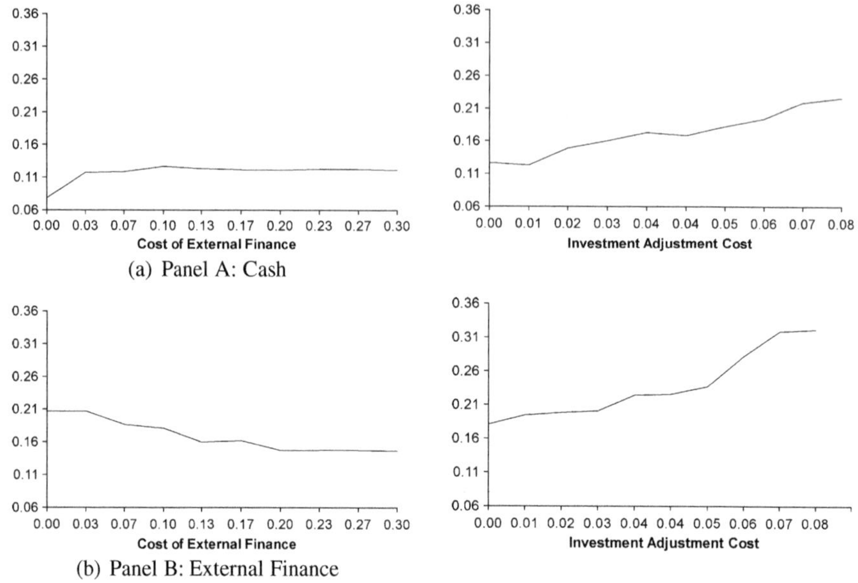

(a) Panel A: Cash

(b) Panel B: External Finance

Fig. 1.5 Local response of financial decisions to funding violations. This figure compares the average pension assets and average external financing for firms that have funding surpluses no greater than one percent of liabilities to the same quantities for firms that have funding deficits no greater than one percent of liabilities

less sharply as external finance becomes more costly and more sharply as investment adjustment costs rise. The monotonic relation between external finance and real adjustment also lends credence to examining local responses.

Figure 1.5 illustrates the local response of financial decisions – cash and external financing – to moving from a small surplus to a small funding deficit. First, if external finance is costless, the firm finances the entirety of the funding gap with external sources. The firm also uses some of the proceeds from this external financing to overfund the pension assets so as to avoid paying a lump sum deficit penalty in the future. As the cost of external finance rises, this behavior is attenuated but not erased. Even if the firm only gets to keep 70 cents of every dollar of external finance raised, it still uses this source of funds rather than cutting its factors of production.The intuition, again, is that this one-time equity issuance fee, although large, is not as large as the long-run cost of decreasing factors of production. Second, as the cost of adjusting the capital stock rises, the firm's financial responses to crossing the line from a surplus to a deficit rise. The firm is essentially substituting financial flexibility for the decrease in real flexibility.

Conclusion

This paper has sought to find out how firms react to exogenous cash shortfalls. On a purely theoretical basis, one would expect them to adjust on the margins that entail the fewest costs. Indeed, this intuition is confirmed in a model in which firms are subject to random cash shortfalls that arise because of the existence of an inherited pension plan that requires funding. We find that when financing costs are high, firms adjust on real margins and vice versa. This model also demonstrates that firms anticipate the probability of a shortfall by building a buffer stock of liquid assets to counteract the shock. Therefore, firms that do experience shortfalls do so after a particularly bad productivity shock. In sum, our model tells us that the relative magnitude of real versus financial adjustments is an empirical question and that one must be careful to account for the endogeneity of these shortfalls.

Acknowledgements I am grateful for helpful comments from Nathalie Moyen and from seminar participants at Columbia.

References

Bernanke BS, Gertler M (1988) Agency costs, net worth, and business fluctuations. Am Econ Rev 79:14–31

Blanchard OJ, Lopez-de-Silanes F, Shleifer A (1994) What do firms do with cash windfalls. J Financ Econ 36:337–360

Christiano LJ, EichenbaumM, Evans CL (2005) Nominal rigidities and the dynamic effects of a shock to monetary policy. J Polit Econ 113:1–45

Cooper R, Haltiwanger J (2006) On the nature of capital adjustment costs. Rev of Econ Stud 73:611–633

Erickson T, Whited TM (2000) Measurement error and the relationship between investment and q,. J Polit Econ 108:1027–57

Fazzari S, Hubbard GR, and Petersen B (1988) Financing constraints and corporate investment. Brookings Papers on Economic Activity 1:144–195

Gomes J (2001) Financing investment. Am Econ Rev 91:1263–1285

Gurley J, Shaw E (1955) Financial aspects of economic development. Am Econ Rev 45:515–538

Heckman JJ, and Robb R (1985) Alternative methods for evaluating the impact of interventions. Heckman J, Singer B (eds) Longitudinal Analysis of Labor Market Data, Cambridge: Cambridge University Press

Hennessy CA, Whited TM (2005) Debt dynamics. J Finance 60:1129–1165

Hennessy CA, Whited TM (2007) How costly is external financing? Evidence from a structural estimation. J Finance 62:1705–1745

Lamont O (1997) Cash flow and investment: evidence from internal capital markets. J Finance 52:83–109

Rauh J (2006) Investment and financing constraints: evidence from the funding of corporate pension plans. J Finance 61:33–71

Rotemberg JJ, Woodford M (1992) Oligopolistic pricing and the effects of aggregate demand on economic activity. J Polit Econ 100:1153–1207

Rotemberg JJ, and Woodford M (1999) The cyclical behavior of prices and costs. In: Taylor JB, Woodford M (Eds) Handbook of Macroeconomics, Vol. 1B. North Holland, Amsterdam, 1051–1135

Jeremy S (2003) Agency, information and corporate investment. Handbook of the Economics of Finance. G.M. Constantinides, Harris M, Stulz R (eds.) Elsevier Science, 109–163

Stokey NL, Lucas R E (1989) Recursive Methods in Economic Dynamics. Harvard University Press, Cambridge, Mass. and London

Tauchen G (1986) Finite state Markov-chain approximations to univariate and vector autoregressions. Econ Lett 20:177–181

Thistlethwaite D, Campbell D (1960) Regression-discontinuity analysis: An alternative to the ex post facto experiment, J Educ Psychol 51: 309–317

Van der Klaauw W (2002) Estimating the effect of financial aid offers on college enrollment: A regression-discontinuity approach. Int Econ Rev 43: 1249–1287

Chapter 2
Non-Tobin's q in Tests for Financial Constraints to Investment

Sílvio Rendon

Abstract Liquidity constrained firms may be under two very well identified investment regimes, constrained and unconstrained. In this paper I derive theoretical investment equations for both regimes and discuss the consequences of ignoring the specific form of the liquidity constrained regime. I also show that expressing the investment equation as a function of Tobin's q is by no means necessary in theory and in practice, in particular, it is not required to test for liquidity constraints.

Introduction

In this article I argue that so-called Tobin's q is not necessary at the theoretical nor at the empirical level to explain investment behavior. All possible questions of interest, such as tests for liquidity constraints, real effects of financial variables, and others, can be answered without relying on q as a concept. It is enough to solve a dynamic problem in which investment is the solution, a function of current and past state variables; this policy function can be directly estimated from the data.

The once prevailing Keynesian Tobin's q-theory explained investment as a function of a relative price q inside the IS-LM framework. In contrast, the neoclassical model of investment explained investment as a solution to a dynamic problem, that is, as a policy rule of investment as a function of current and past state variables. The prevailing Keynesian approach reacted to this challenge deriving q-theory from a choice- theoretic framework which explicitly takes account of adjustment costs associated with investment. In this assimilation, the definition of q was modified from Tobin's original formulation as a relative price to a variable that contained future investment opportunities. Instead of being a function of state variables, investment was now a function of q, the marginal value of capital over the price of capital.

S. Rendon
Department of Economics, Stony Brook University, Stony Brook, NY 11794, USA,
e-mail: srendon@ms.cc.sunysb.edu

G. Calcagnini and E. Saltari (eds.), *The Economics of Imperfect Markets*,
Contributions to Economics,
DOI: 10.1007/978-3-7908-2131-4_2, © Springer Physica-Verlag Berlin Heidelberg 2010

Moreover, to make this digression operational, the analysis focused on very special cases, so that "average q" coincided with "marginal q," a distinction that was absent in Tobin's original formulation. These special cases were elegantly derived, nevertheless they were restrictive and had several caveats that were immediately transmitted to the analysis of the data. The possible presence of financial constraints to firms' investment raised the issue of the measurement of q. The significance of cash flow in investment regressions on q suggested the existence of financial constraints only if q was well measured, otherwise it was just a result of measurement error in q and cash flow capturing what q was supposed to capture, future investment opportunities. Thus, the discussion on whether firms are liquidity constrained was the discussion on the measurement of q.

In this paper, I show that the investment problem can be solved directly as a function of state variables and estimated from the data. What I call "Non-Tobin's q," because it deviates strongly from Tobin's definition of q, is a concept that has done more harm than good to the investment literature, obscuring the solution to a straightforward dynamic problem and opening the doors to several unfruitful discussions on the measurability of q.

The paper is organized as follows. In the next section I explain how the modern concept of q differs from the concept of q proposed initially by Tobin. In Section Model, I set out a model, characterize the optimal policy rule for investment under an unconstrained and a liquidity constrained regime; investment is a function of capital and productivity, the state variables of the problem, not of q. In Section A Tractable Special Case, I analyze a special case, originally analyzed by Hayashi, when there is homegeneity of degree one in the production function. In Section Estimation, I discuss the estimation of the models developed in the previous sections. The main conclusions of this paper are presented in Section Concluding Remarks.

Background: q and Investment

The difficulty lies, not in the new ideas, but in escaping from the old ones, which ramify, for those brought up as most of us have been, into every corner of our minds. Keynes (1936)

Keynes's innovative ideas inspired much fruitful economic research that eventually became the mainstream way of economic thinking. Over time, as it normally happens, Keynes's ideas became old, so that, paradoxically, his statement applies now to his own ideas: it is difficult to escape from them. New ideas appeared, but they did not fully displace Keynesian concepts. That is what happened with the Keynesian q-theory of investment proposed by Tobin.

The neoclassical theory of investment was based on micro-foundations and agents' optimizing behavior. The investment function was the solution to a dynamic problem, thus, a choice variable as a function of state variables. However, the logic of the neoclassical approach never fully entered the subject of investment. The q-theory of investment was so influential that, under an alleged reconciliation, it managed to prevail over the neoclassical approach. Instead of inquiring directly on the determinants of investment, the question was transferred to finding investment's relationship with a derived, endogenous, unobservable object like q.

It will be instructive to review Tobin's q-theory of investment in its original formulation, to illustrate to what extent it differs from the neoclassical approach.

Tobin's q

Tobin's q theory states that a firm will invest until the ratio between the stock-market valuation of existing real capital assets and its current replacement cost, that is, q, equals one. In Keynes's (1936) terminology q can be seen as the ratio of the marginal efficiency of investment to the rate of interest. Formally, the wealth definition in Tobin (1969, p. 19) was

$$W = qK + M/p,$$

where W is wealth, K is capital, M is money and p is the price of the final good, also called by Tobin "the cost of producing capital." As it can be seen, q is basically a relative price: the price of capital in terms of the final good. Unlike Keynes, Tobin allowed the value of existing capital goods, or of titles to them, to diverge from their current reproduction cost. Accordingly, the real rate of return from holding capital r_K equals R/q, that is, the marginal efficiency of capital relative to the reproduction cost over the relative price q. As Tobin (1969, p. 20) states:

> "Suppose that the perpetual real return obtainable by purchasing a unit of capital at its cost of production p is R. If an investor must pay qp instead of p, then his rate of return ir R/q."

Thus, in Tobin's formulation the introduction of a relative price called q allows for a discrepancy between the interest rate and the rate of return on capital. Accordingly, he redefines the IS-LM space in terms of the rate of return on capital $r_K = R/q$ rather than on the interest rate R, as it can be seen in Fig. 2.1 (Fig. 3 in Tobin's article).

Only when $q = 1$ these two rates are equal and investment becomes zero. It is in this sense that we can understand Tobin's (1969, p. 21) statement:

> "The *rate* of investment – the speed at which investors wish to increase the capital stock – should be related, if to anything, to q, the value of capital relative to its replacement cost."

It is clear that investment will increase as a response to an increase in q, which is nothing else than the relative price of capital in terms of the final good, determined in an IS-LM equilibrium.

Non-Tobin's q

Unlike Tobin's and Keynes's investment theory, the neoclassical theory derived the investment function from the firm's optimizing behavior. Developed by Jorgenson

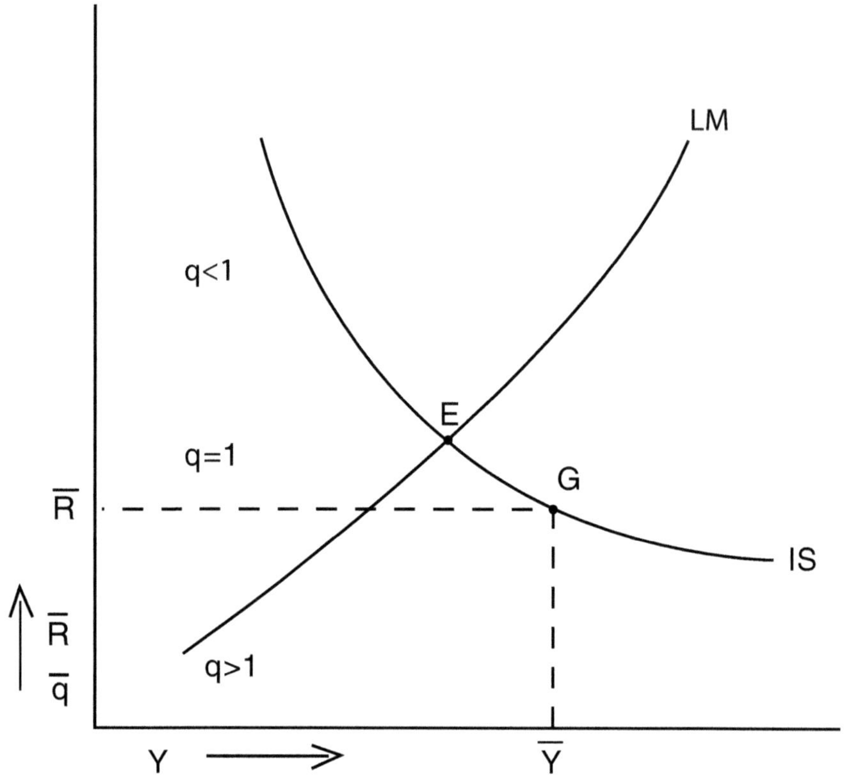

Fig. 2.1 Original Tobin's q in the IS-LM space Tobin (1969, p. 22)

(1963) it was extended to allow for adjustment costs to capital or an installation function by Lucas (1967a,b); Gould (1968). As noted by Lucas and Prescott (1971),

> "Explanatory variables in empirical studies of the demand for investment goods fall into three broad classes: variables measuring anticipated, future demand – sales, profits, stock prices indexes; variables measuring past decisions, the effects of which persist into the present – lagged capital stock and investment rates; and variables measuring current market opportunities - interest rates, factor prices, and, again, profits."

Investment theory at the time was concerned with the latter two classes of variables. They propose, by contrast,

> "an operational investment theory linking current investment to observable current and past explanatory variables, rather than to 'expected' future variables which must, in practice, be replaced by various 'proxy variables.' "

Their formulation was a rigorous analysis of the capital investment decision in the presence of convex costs of adjustment, as such an important progress over Tobin's prevailing q theory. To formulate a model the researcher has to set up an optimizing dynamic model and solve for the choice variables, expressing them as a function of the state variables, which are current and past variables.

It became clear that economic theory had to grow out from the optimizing behavior of the economic agents. The economic profession assimilated this methodological turn very rapidly, so that in the late seventies and early eighties several authors made efforts to reconcile the neoclassical approach with Tobin's and Keynes's approach. Under that line of research, Mussa (1977), Abel (1979, 1983), and Hayashi (1982) proposed dynamic models that allegedly showed that the neoclassical theory of investment was formally equivalent to Tobin's q theory of investment. They used models of the firm's present value maximization and obtained the optimal rate of investment as an increasing function of q. So, Abel (1985) defined q_t as the marginal valuation of capital divided by $w_{n+1,t}$ (the shock to the adjustment cost function): $q_t = V_{K,t}/w_{n+1,t}$. Hayashi (1982), on its turn, defined Tobin's *marginal* q as $q = \lambda/p_I$ and *average* q as $h = V/(p_I K)$, where λ is the present discounted value of additional future (after-tax) profits that are due to one additional unit of current investment. These definitions of q were totally different from Tobin's original formulation of q as a relative price.

Defined as the ratio between the marginal value and the price of capital, q was an object with "a remarkable information content" (Hayashi 1982):

> "All the information about the demand curve for the firm's output and the production function that are relevant to the investment decision is summarized by q. Expectations about future course of the rate of investment tax credits k are also incorporated in q and do not affect the form of the investment function."

The relevant investment equation, for instance (13) in Hayashi (1982), had the form:

$$\frac{I}{K} = \beta(\tilde{q}; t).$$

This reasoning, however, was at its heart against the logic of solving a dynamic programming (DP) problem, by determining the policy rules showing how control variables depend on state variables, which are current and past variables observed by the optimizing agent, as Lucas and Prescott (1982) were proposing for investment. A variable that summarizes information about the future, that is, future state or choice variables is an intermediate object, helpful in the process of solving the DP-problem, but cannot be an argument of the solution itself. One needs to go beyond this intermediate step and find a direct function between choice and state variables. Stating investment as a function of this q cannot be the solution to the firm's DP-problem. Interestingly, in Tobin's original formulation of q investment is a quantity expressed as a demand function of a relative price, a legitimate state variable.

Therefore, the Keynesian q theory of investment remained basically unchanged and just assimilated the formal optimizing tools used by the neoclassical approach. Moreover, in this assimilation the way to solve a firm's DP problem was changed by introducing an intermediate object in the policy rule. Thus, in investment theory the neoclassical work ended up being more a methodological than a conceptual contribution.

Once this intermediate object was introduced as a de facto argument in the investment equation, the focus of attention moved on to the issue of how operational the theory was and the observability of q. As q, now containing a derivative, was not observable anymore, in practice it had to be replaced by proxy variables. To bridge the gap between unobservable marginal q and its most likely proxy, observed average q, Hayashi (1982) introduced additional assumptions into the investment model: if the firm is a price-taker with constant returns to scale in both production and installation function, then marginal q and average q are the same.[1]

These steps were not at all necessary, as investment can be explained without any object like q. Moreover, pursuing this intermediate object has led researchers to make restrictive assumptions and lose focus in the analysis of investment. This has been the case with testing for financial constraints, where the investment function, in practice, was finally restricted to be an investment regression. In the next sections I set up a simple dynamic model of investment with a specific form of the financial constraint, and discuss its solution and the inconvenience, both in theory and in practice, of introducing an object of the kind of q in the investment equation.

Model

I start with the simplest model of investment without adjustment costs; then I incorporate convex adjustment costs to capital variations. Consider a firm that chooses investment to maximize the present discounted value of dividends:

$$E_0 \sum_{t=0}^{\infty} \frac{D_t}{(1+\rho)^t}.$$

The firm's output just depends on capital

$$Y = \theta K^{\alpha},$$

where the firm's productivity θ follows a Markov process $P(\theta'|\theta)$. Capital accumulation satisfies the law of motion:

$$K' = (1-\delta)K + p_K I,$$

where δ is the depreciation rate. The firm can issue equity up to a certain exogenous level which depends on the firm's productivity:

$$D \geq \overline{D}(\theta),$$

where $\overline{D}(\theta) \leq 0$. That is, the reward function D can become negative up to a certain level.

[1] In contrast, if the firm is a price-maker, then average q is higher than marginal q by what is legitimately called the monopoly rent.

Frictionless Capital Adjustment

In the simplest model with free adjustment to capital variations, dividends are defined as

$$D = \theta K^{\alpha} - p_K I,$$

the firm produces and invests. For this problem the Bellman Equation is

$$V(K,\theta) = \max_{K'} \left\{ \theta K^{\alpha} + p_K(1-\delta)K - p_K K' + \frac{1}{1+\rho} \int V\left(K',\theta'\right) \mathrm{d}P\left(\theta'|\theta\right) \right\}$$
$$\text{subject to } D \geq \overline{D}(\theta).$$

The corresponding Lagrange equation is then

$$\begin{aligned} L(K',\lambda) = \max_{K',\lambda} \Big\{ & \theta K^{\alpha} + p_K(1-\delta)K - p_K K' \\ & + \frac{1}{1+\rho} \int V(K',\theta')\mathrm{d}P\left(\theta'|\theta\right) \\ & + \lambda \left[\theta K^{\alpha} + p_K(1-\delta)K - p_K K' - \overline{D}(\theta) \right] \Big\} , \end{aligned} \tag{2.1}$$

so that the Euler Equation is

$$L_{K'} = -\left(1+\lambda\right) p_K + \frac{1}{1+\rho} E V_{K'} = 0.$$

Apparently, the solution to this problem is given by

$$\frac{E V_{K'}}{p_K} = (1+\lambda)\,(1+\rho)\,.$$

However, the object $\frac{EV_{K'}}{p_K}$ does not reveal anything. To really solve this problem we need to go further and take out the choice variables that are contained in the term $E V_{K'}$. Therefore, the solution to this problem is actually contained in the following condition:

$$\frac{E V_{K'}}{p_K} \equiv \frac{E\left[\theta'\left(1+\lambda'\right) \mid \theta\right]}{p_K} \alpha K'^{\alpha-1} + (1-\delta) = (1+\lambda)\,(1+\rho)\,,$$

that comes out from an application of the envelope theorem. That is, the expected marginal product of capital (MPK) in terms of capital goods, augmented by the depreciation rate, has to coincide with the interest rate, both adjusted by the shadow value of internal funds.

Consider the special case, when there are no liquidity constraints, $\lambda_t = 0, \forall t$. Then, the expected marginal product of capital net of depreciation simply equals the interest rate:

$$\frac{E\left[\theta'|\theta\right]}{p_K}\alpha K'^{\alpha-1}-\delta=\rho.$$

In this case, there is no need for further concern, as there is a straightforward explicit solution for capital next period and, therefore, investment:

$$K'(K,\theta)=\left[\frac{E\left[\theta'|\theta\right]\alpha}{p_K\left(\rho+\delta\right)}\right]^{\frac{1}{1-\alpha}},$$

$$I(K,\theta)=\left[\frac{E\left[\theta'|\theta\right]\alpha}{p_K\left(\rho+\delta\right)}\right]^{\frac{1}{1-\alpha}}-p_K(1-\delta)K.$$

Notice that capital next period does not depend on capital in the current period. Postulating an intermediate object like $q=\frac{EV_{K'}}{p_K}$ would be a needless complication in a straightforward solution to this problem.

Now, let us focus on the case with liquidity constraints. The constraint may or may not be currently binding:

$$\alpha\frac{E\left[\theta'\left(1+\lambda'\right)|\theta\right]}{p_K}K'^{\alpha-1}+(1-\delta)=\begin{cases}(1+\rho)\,,\text{ if }\lambda=0,\\(1+\rho)\left(1+\lambda\right),\text{ if }\lambda>0.\end{cases}$$

If the liquidity constraint binds, the solution for investment is simply given by $\theta K^{\alpha}-p_KI=\overline{D}(\theta)$:

$$I(K,\theta)=\frac{\theta K^{\alpha}-\overline{D}(\theta)}{p_K}.$$

These two regimes are selected according to a productivity-specific threshold $K^*(\theta)$ so that for $K\leq K^*(\theta)$ this constrained solution applies, and when $K>K^*(\theta)$ the interior solution regime shown above applies.

Hence, the solution for investment is given by two regimes that can be solved explicitly:

$$I=\min\left[\underbrace{\left[\frac{E\left[\theta'\left(1+\lambda'\right)|\theta\right]\alpha}{p_K\left(\rho+\delta\right)}\right]^{\frac{1}{1-\alpha}}-p_K(1-\delta)K}_{\text{currently unconstrained}},\underbrace{\frac{\theta K^{\alpha}-\overline{D}(\theta)}{p_K}}_{\text{constrained}}\right].$$

We learn the following from this exercise:

1. There is a threshold in capital that determines which regime applies. For a given productivity level, small amounts of capital are associated with binding liquidity constraints, while larger amounts with an interior solution
2. $EV_{K'}$ is basically expected MPK and, as such, an endogenous variable; it contains investment, the solution to the dynamic programming problem

3. We can determine whether a firm is currently financially constrained: it will invest all output plus allowed equity, $I = \frac{Y - \overline{D}(\theta)}{p_K}$, that is, the firm's financial position does affect investment, moreover, in a very particular way
4. It is, however, less obvious to determine whether the firm will be constrained in the future, as we do not know the future λs. The firm may be financially constrained in the future even if we reject that they are currently financially constrained.

In this simple model of investment with liquidity constraints we find some conclusions that will also apply to the specification with quadratic adjustment costs.

Costly Capital Adjustment

Now suppose that there are quadratic adjustment costs to capital, so that the reward function is:

$$D = \theta K^{\alpha} - p_K I - \frac{b}{2}\left(\frac{I}{K}\right)^2 K.$$

Then, the Bellman equation becomes

$$V(K,\theta) = \max_{K'}\left\{\theta K^{\alpha} + p_K I - \frac{b}{2}\left(\frac{I}{K}\right)^2 K + \frac{1}{1+\rho}\int V\left(K',\theta'\right) \mathrm{d}P\left(\theta'|\theta\right)\right\}$$
$$\text{subject to } D \geq \overline{D}(\theta),$$

which yields the following Euler equation

$$-\left[p_K + b\left(\frac{I}{K}\right)\right](1+\lambda) + \frac{1}{1+\rho} E V_{K'} = 0,$$

where $EV_{K'} = \alpha E\left[\theta'|\theta\right] K'^{\alpha-1} + p_K(1-\delta) + b(1-\delta)\frac{E[I'|\theta]}{K'} + \frac{bE\left[I'^2|\theta\right]}{2K'^2}$. Once again, this term is basically expected MPK augmented by the depreciation rate and the effect of adjustment costs. Notice that now investment appears in two terms: directly as $\frac{I}{K}$ and inside of $EV_{K'}$. The object $EV_{K'}$ is still endogenous. Unlike in the previous example, the Euler equation determines investment implicitly, not explicitly. We can express but not *explain* $\frac{I}{K}$ as a function of $EV_{K'}$.

This time there is no explicit solution even if there are no constraints at all: $\lambda_t = 0, \forall t$:

$$\frac{\alpha E\left[\theta'|\theta\right] K'^{\alpha-1} + p_K(1-\delta) + b(1-\delta)\frac{E[I'|\theta]}{K'} + \frac{bE\left[I'^2|\theta\right]}{2K'^2}}{p_K + b\left(\frac{I}{K}\right)} = 1+\rho.$$

In the numerator expected MPK is augmented by expected marginal capital adjustment costs, so that a recursive solution is needed, and the denominator includes current marginal adjustment costs, so that, unlike the case with no adjustment costs, capital next period does depend on capital in the current period.

Now, suppose there are liquidity constraints. Then the Euler equation becomes

$$\frac{E\left[(1+\lambda')\left(\alpha\theta' K'^{\alpha-1} + p_K(1-\delta) + b(1-\delta)\frac{I'}{K'} + \frac{bI'^2}{2K'^2}\right) \mid \theta\right]}{p_K + b\left(\frac{I}{K}\right)}$$

$$= \begin{cases} (1+\rho)\, p_K, \text{ if } \lambda = 0, \\ (1+\rho)\, p_K\,(1+\lambda), \text{ if } \lambda > 0. \end{cases}$$

Again, if liquidity constraints are not currently binding, $\lambda = 0$, we have an implicit and recursive solution. We only have an explicit solution for investment, if $\lambda > 0$. Indeed we have a quadratic equation that defines investment:

$$\theta K^{\alpha} - p_K I - \frac{b}{2}\left(\frac{I}{K}\right)^2 K - \overline{D}(\theta) = 0.$$

The solution for this equation is

$$I = -\frac{p_K}{b}K + \frac{1}{b}\sqrt{p_K^2 K^2 + 2bK\left[\theta K^{\alpha} - \overline{D}(\theta)\right]}. \tag{2.2}$$

Hence, there is only an explicit nonrecursive, static, solution when the liquidity constraint is binding.

This result does not basically change if we allow for short-term debt in the dividend definition,

$$D = \theta K^{\alpha} - p_K I - \frac{b}{2}\left(\frac{I}{K}\right)^2 - (1+r)B + B'.$$

Now the firm pays back $(1+r)B$ contracted in the previous period and decides on B' for next period. However, the Euler equation shown above does not change, that is, there is no term that captures debt in the investment Euler equation. The consequence of this extension is that when the dividend constraint is binding, $D = \overline{D}(\theta)$, the equation for investment is modified in the following way:[2]

$$I = \frac{1}{b}\sqrt{p_K^2 K^2 + 2bK\left[\theta K^{\alpha} - (1+r)B - \overline{D}(\theta)\right]} - \frac{p_K}{b}K.$$

And, if there are no adjustment costs it simply becomes

$$I = \theta K^{\alpha} - (1+r)B - \overline{D}(\theta).$$

[2] This is under the special case of no debt next period $B' = 0$. Generally speaking B' has to be solved from a system of two Euler equations, one equation for investment and another for debt.

Hitting the liquidity constraint means that the firm's financial position $D - \overline{D}(\theta)$ determines investment. Once again, there are two exclusive regimes, one in which financial constraints are not binding and the current financial position of the firm does not matter, and one in which financial constraints do matter and the financial position of the firm critically affects investment.

I conclude this section remarking that constrained and unconstrained solutions are exclusive: expected MPK determines investment only when the solution is unconstrained; the firm's financial position determines investment when the liquidity constraint is binding. That is, it is either the expected MPK or the financial position, not both at the same time. Notice also that this analysis is performed without constructing what has been called Tobin's q.

A Tractable Special Case

In the investment literature a very special version of this problem has been of particular interest, when both the production and the adjustment cost function exhibit homogeneity of degree one. In that case it has been stressed that the marginal and average value of the firm on capital, and thus, marginal and average q are the same. In the context of the simple model of investment with quadratic adjustment costs to capital, a similar result can be found:

Theorem 1 (Hayashi 1982). *For the case without liquidity constraints, $\lambda_t = 0, \forall t$, if $\alpha = 1$, then V is homogenous of degree one in capital, i.e., $V(K, \theta) = A(\theta)K$, where $A(\theta)$ is a function of θ. Proof: In Appendix.*

Corollary 1. *If $\alpha = 1$, then $\frac{V}{K} = V_K$.*

Corollary 2. *If $\alpha = 1$, then $\frac{I}{K} = -\frac{p_K}{b} + \frac{E[A(\theta')|\theta]}{b(1+\rho)}$.*

In that case, there is an AK-value function, so that $q = \frac{A(\theta)}{p_K}$, that is, q only depends on the stochastic process, not on capital, in the present or in the future, and on the structural parameters of the DP-problem. Thus, q is still an intermediate object, a transformation or sufficient statistic for current productivity.

This result does not only mean that marginal and average q are the same, but also that q is fully exogenous to capital. This result is important theoretically, as it is only current productivity that is informative about future investment opportunities, and empirically, as it implies that there is no endogeneity bias in an OLS regression of investment over q.

This tractable case has been analyzed for the interior but not typically for the liquidity constrained solution, which is as tractable as the unconstrained solution. From (2.2) we obtain

$$\frac{I}{K} = -\frac{p_K}{b} + \frac{p_K}{b}s, \tag{2.3}$$

where $s = \sqrt{1 + \frac{2b\theta K - \overline{D}(\theta)}{p_K^2 K}}$. This equation is linear and indeed not too different than the previous interior solution. Instead of having $q = \frac{A(\theta)}{p_K}$ here we have an s-term, a ratio between an explicit function of productivity, that comes from the adjustment cost function, and the user cost of capital. The q-term is informative about some expected value of the whole productivity process; the s-term is just informative about *current* productivity. The distinction is very subtle as both terms are in fact functions of current productivity, their difference being the specific forms that these functions assume.

Since this special case implies $Y = \theta K$, the s-term is observable and dependent on the value of output over the value of capital $\frac{Y}{p_K K}$. Thus, we have $s = \sqrt{1 + \frac{2b}{p_K} \frac{Y - \overline{D}(\theta)}{p_K K}}$, a quadratic transformation of an observable ratio.

As said above, the Euler equation for capital does not change if we extend the dividend definition allowing for, for instance, short-term debt. The s-term can be generally defined as $s = \sqrt{1 + \frac{2b}{p_K} \frac{CF}{p_K K}}$, where $CF = Y - (1 + r)B - \overline{D}(\theta)$; it is an non-linear increasing function of CF. This derivation will prove useful in the discussion about the estimation and testing for financial constraints.

Estimation

The estimation of investment under liquidity constraints has typically been made assuming convex adjustment costs. Hence, in the literature it is very common to derive the following equation from the Euler equation without any constraint:

$$\frac{I}{K} = -\frac{p_K}{b} + \frac{p_K}{b(1+\rho)} \frac{EV_{K'}}{p_K} \tag{2.4}$$

and then postulate the following linear investment equation

$$\frac{I_{it}}{K_{it}} = \beta_0 + \beta_1 q_{it} + u_{it}$$

where q stands for $\frac{EV_{K'}}{p_K}$, and the random term $u \sim N(0, \sigma^2)$ can be considered a measurement error in the investment-capital ratio. This equation accounts for investment in the absence of any friction other than capital adjustment costs.

The condition seen above, namely that $\alpha = 1$, solves two problems in estimating this investment equation: proxying for q by an observable and that q is an endogenous object. In that case, average and marginal q coincide, and one can safely proxy V_K, usually unobserved, by $\frac{V}{K}$, more easily observed. On the other hand, in general q contains the endogenous variable $\frac{I}{K}$, which could imply that even if this were the correct specification of the investment equation, an OLS estimation yields biased estimates of β_0 and β_1. However, the same condition that allows to proxy marginal by average q implies that q is fully exogenous and only depends on current productivity. Certainly, it is an empirical matter to test whether $\alpha = 1$ applies.

Following Fazzari et al. (1988) this benchmark equation is usually augmented by an extra term, forming thereby what has become the usual test for liquidity constraints:

$$\frac{I_{it}}{K_{it}} = \beta_0 + \beta_1 q_{it} + \beta_2 CF + u_{it}, \tag{2.5}$$

where CF stands for "cash flow." In the absence of financial constraints, it is argued, only q should matter:

$$H_0 : \beta_2 = 0$$

Thus, if this null hypothesis is rejected and cash flow turns out to significantly affect investment, it is argued that financial constraints are present. Most of the discussion around this approach has been centered in measuring q adequately and interpreting what a significant β_2 means. As established above, if the firm's financial position determines investment, then expected MPK does not. It cannot be that cash-flow and q determine investment together; it is either one or the other. If q 'explains' investment, cash-flow should not. If cash-flow explains investment, then q does not. Thus, the alleged test for liquidity constraints is not really based on the solution to the DP-problem, which rather suggests two different exclusive regimes.

These considerations notwithstanding, if the data contain currently constrained and currently unconstrained firms the estimation of (2.5) will yield mixed results. Liquidity constrained firms will make cash flow matter and diminish the importance of q, while liquidity unconstrained firms will make the q significant while undermining the importance of cash flow. To illustrate this point suppose that we estimate (2.5) with data in which there are π unconstrained firms and $1-\pi$ constrained firms. Now, we have a mixture of (2.4) and (2.3):

$$\frac{I}{K} = -\frac{p_K}{b} + \pi \frac{p_K}{b\,(1+\rho)} q + (1-\pi)\frac{p_K}{b} s, \tag{2.6}$$

where s was defined above as a nonlinear function of CF. Thus, (2.5) can be seen as an approximation to this expression. Even under the assumption that CF is a valid proxy for s, one can see that $\beta_2 = (1-\pi)\frac{p_K}{b}$, so that a significance test is basically informative about the proportion of constrained firms in the sample $(1-\pi)$.

To address this issue, the literature has divided firms into two groups, one which is a priori expected to be constrained, typically small firms, and the group which is expected to be unconstrained, larger firms. As seen above, there is a capital threshold $K^*(\theta)$ that indicates the regime that firms are facing. Certainly, the researcher does not know this productivity-specific capital threshold. Moreover, strictly speaking this threshold is endogenous, dependent on the model's parameters, and should be determined as part of the estimation procedure. This exercise, performed across several sample splits and for several countries, shows that firms that are a priori expected to be liquidity constrained exhibit greater sensitivity of investment to internal funds: $\beta_2^c > \beta_2^u$, where c stands for constrained and u stands for unconstrained.[3]

Thus, this estimation strategy addresses the issue of misclassification by conjecturing that coefficients of allegedly constrained firms may be just larger than those of allegedly unconstrained firms. It is an ex post validation of an a priori partition. However, notice that by the same token the investment-cash flow sensitivity has to be higher for constrained firms, it has to be true that $\beta_1^u > \beta_1^c$, that is, investment has to be more sensitive to q for unconstrained firms, if $\pi^u > \pi^c$. This issue has not been usually considered in the investment literature.

This estimation approach may be also problematic if the cash flow variable is correlated with investment, not because there are liquidity constraints but because q is mismeasured, so that it does not capture all investment opportunities. Then, cash flow might capture future investment opportunities not totally measured by q (Gomes 2001, Erickson and Whited 2000, Saltari and Travaglini 2003), or indicate other sources of misspecification in the investment model (Bond and Van Reenen 2007, Ejarque and Cooper 2004). Given this concern, Gilchrist and Himmelberg (1995) address the mismeasurement problem by proposing an alternative measure of q as following an AR(1) process. Then it is estimated using a VAR of firm fundamentals; nevertheless, cash flow enters significantly in the investment equation for constrained firms. On the other hand, interestingly, Gomes (2001) finds that even with liquidity constraints, standard investment regressions predict that cash flow is an important determinant of investment only if one ignores q. Conversely, he also obtains significant cash flow effects even in the absence of financial frictions. He suggests that cash-flow-augmented investment regressions work probably because of a combination of measurement error in q and identification problems. Alternatively, under the light of the derivations shown above, this result may just express that cash flow is strongly correlated with q, so that only one of these terms is significant both for the constrained and the unconstrained regime.

These measurement and estimation problems seem to arise from having q as the center of the theoretical concern as well as of the estimation strategy. An alternative approach has been to adopt estimation strategies that altogether do not require measuring q. In particular, in a General Method of Moments estimation the Euler condition for investment implied by a model of perfect capital markets typically strongly rejected for firms that are classified as constrained (Whited, 1994). Another alternative approach is to estimate the model's behavioral parameters using specific functions by the method explained by Rust (1994) and Eckstein and Wolpin

---

[3] Similar results are obtained when the sample is partitioned on the basis of bond ratings (Gilchrist and Himmelberg 1995), firm size (Gertler and Gilchrist, 1994), membership of an industrial keiretsu in Japan (Hoshi et al. 1991). A detailed review of this literature can be found in Hubbard (1998) and Bernanke et al. (1999). In contrast with these results Kaplan and Zingales (1997) find that the coefficient on cash flow does not increase monotonically across groups of firms as the degree of financial constraint increases. Actually, firms that seem less constrained according to several criteria have a higher coefficient on cash flow, as compared to more constrained firms. However, as shown by Pratap (2003), this result can be rationalized by the presence of liquidity constraints when capital adjustment costs are non-convex.

(1989). Liquidity constraints are then identified from the dynamics of a firm's evolution as formalized by the dynamic estimation process. Pratap and Rendon (2003) recover the underlying model's parameters by a Maximum Likelihood procedure and perform a likelihood ratio test on parameterized dividend constraints. Similarly, Hennessy and Whited (2007) recover the behavioral parameters of their theoretical model by Simulated Method of Moments estimation. They assume a specific equity cost function and test for statistical significance of bankruptcy and equity costs.[4]

These alternative estimation approaches show that financial constraints are significant and not an artificial result of an erroneous measurement of q. As such they are encouraging about the feasibility of estimating investment models and, moreover, answer all questions of interest without using q at all. Moreover, these approaches also allow researchers to analyze counterfactual simulations of alternative economic scenarios.

Concluding Remarks

In this paper I contend that Non-Tobin's q is a needless object both in the theoretical and practical analysis of investment.

Tobin's original formulation q is an observable relative price, the price of capital with respect to the price of a final good. In adapting his main ideas to fit into a micro-founded theory of investment, the definition of q was changed and became the marginal value of capital over the price of capital. The concept of q, however, is alien to the solution of a Dynamic Programming problem, in which choice variables, such as investment, have to be explained by current and past state variables. This modified or Non-Tobin's q was a derived, endogenous and unobservable object that brought more questions than answers to the investment literature.

To make the q-theory operational, restrictive assumptions, which were not usually empirically tested, were needed, so that q could be replaced in practice by proxy variables. Nevertheless, the issue of measuring q correctly never stopped being a concern and a possible source of biased and misleading results, especially in testing for financial constraints to firms. Cash flow variables, possibly capturing future investment opportunities that q should be capturing, were solidly significant across

[4] At the same time that the literature is moving toward more structural approaches one can also distinguish the trend to move in the opposite direction, toward performing "natural" experiments. This method consists of exploiting a policy change that affected the flow of credit to an identifiable subset of firms. Then the researcher computes "difference-in-differences," that is, a twofold comparison between observed variables of "control" and "treated" firms, observed "before" and "after" the policy change. For instance, Banerjee and Duflo (2004) exploit a 1998 reform in India that increased the maximum size below which a firm is eligible to receive priority sector lending. Control firms are those that were already in the "priority" sector. The result is that bank lending and firm revenues went up for the newly targeted firms in the year of the reform, so they conclude that there are severe credit constraints. Under this approach, measuring q is optional, as it is not needed to determine the treatment effect.

investment regressions. This result suggested the presence of important financial constraints or of severe measurement problems in q. This ambiguity was addressed by estimation strategies that did not require measuring q, finding that financial constraints were indeed important. Focusing on the measurement of q proved to be a big detour from the main topic of interest, explaining investment. In fact, the detour started long ago, when Non-Tobin's q was proposed as the main determinant of investment.

Acknowledgements I prepared this paper for the Conference: *The Economics of Imperfect Markets: Their Interaction and The Consequences for Economic Theory and Policy*, University of Rome, La Sapienza, Faculty of Economics, May 16 and 17 2008. I thank Giorgio Cacagnini, Germana Giombini and Enrico Saltari for their kind invitation to participate in this conference. I also thank them as well as several other participants for their useful comments. All errors and omission are only mine.

Appendix: Proof of Theorem 1

I proceed inductively; showing that $V'(K',\theta') = A'(\theta')\,K'$ implies $V(K,\theta) = A(\theta)K$.

Let $V'(K',\theta') = A'(\theta')\,K'$, then the Euler equation implies:

$$\frac{I}{K} = \frac{1}{b}\frac{1}{1+\rho}E\left[A'\left(\theta'\right)|\theta\right] - \frac{1}{b}p_K \equiv B(\theta).$$

Thus, the investment-capital ratio only depends on current productivity, not on capital, $\frac{I}{K}(K,\theta) = B(\theta)$. Or, in other words, investment is homogenous of degree one in capital.

Then, the firm's value is:

$$\begin{aligned} V(K,\theta) &= \theta K - p_K\left(\frac{I}{K}\right)K - \frac{b}{2}\left(\frac{I}{K}\right)^2 K + \frac{1}{1+\rho}E[A'(\theta')|\theta]K', \\ &= \left[\theta - p_K B(\theta) - \frac{b}{2}B^2(\theta) + \frac{1}{1+\rho}E[A'(\theta')|\theta]((1-\delta)+B(\theta))\right]K, \\ &= A(\theta)K. \end{aligned}$$

Thus, the value function is homogenous of degree one in capital.

References

Abel A (1979) Investment and the value of capital. Garland Publishing, New York
Abel A (1983) Optimal investment under uncertainty. Am Econ Rev 73:228–233
Abel A (1985) A stochastic model of investment, marginal q and the market value of the firm. Int Econ Rev 26:305–322

Banerjee A, Duflo E (2004) Do firms want to borrow more? Testing credit constraints using a directed lending program, CEPR Discussion Papers 4681, C.E.P.R. Discussion Papers
Bernanke B, Gertler M, Gilchrist S (1999) The financial accelerator in quantitative business cycle framework. In Taylor JB, Woodford M. Handbook of macroeconomics. Elsevier North Holland
Bond S, Van Reenen J (2007) Microeconometric models of investment and employment. In: Heckman J, Leamer E (eds) Handbook of econometrics, vol 6. Elsevier, Amsterdam, chapter 65
Ejarque J, Cooper R (2004) Financial frictions and investment: requiem in Q. Rev Econ Dynam 6:710–728
Eckstein Z, Wolpin K (1989) The specification and estimation of dynamic stochastic discrete choice models. J Hum Res 24:562–598
Erickson T, Whited TM (2000) Measurement error and the relationship between investment and q. J Polit Econ 108:1027–1057
Fazzari SM, Hubbard RG, Petersen BC (1988) Financing constraints and corporate investment. Brookings Papers Econ Activ 1:141–195
Gertler M, Gilchrist S (1994) Monetary policy, business cycles and the behavior of small manufacturing firms. Q J Econ 109:309–340
Gilchrist S, Himmelberg CP (1995) Evidence on the role of cash flow for investment. Journal of Monetary Economics 36:541–572
Gomes JF (2001) Financing investment. Am Econ Rev 91(5):1263–1285
Gould JP (1968) Adjustment costs in the theory of investment of the firm. Review of Economic Studies 35:47–55
Hayashi F (1982) Tobin's marginal Q and average Q: a neoclassical interpretation. Econometrica 50:215–224
Hennessy CA, Whited TM (2007) How costly is external financing? Evidence from a structural estimation. J Finance 62(4):1705–1745
Hoshi T, kashyap A, Scharfstein D (1991) Corporate structure, liquidity, and investment: evidence from Japanese industrial groups. Quarterly journal of Economics 106:33–60
Hubbard RG (1998) Capital-market imperfections and investment. J Econ Lit 36(1):193–225
Jorgenson DW (1963) Capital theory and investment behavior. Am Econ Rev 33:247–259
Kaplan SN, Zingales L (1997) Do investment-cash flow sensitivities provide useful measures of financial constraints? Q J Econ 112:169–216
Keynes JM (1936) The general theory of employment, interest and money. Macmillan (reprinted 2007), London
Lucas R (1967a) Adjustment costs and the theory of supply. J Polit Econ 75:321–334
Lucas R (1967b) Optimal investment policy and the flexible accelerator. Int Econ Rev 8:78–85
Lucas RE, Prescott EC (1971) Investment under uncertainty. Econometrica 39(5):659–681
Mussa M (1977) External and internal adjustment costs and the theory of aggregate and firm investment. Economica 47:163–178
Pratap S (2003) Do adjustment costs explain investment-cash flow insensitivity? J Econ Dynam Contr 27(11–12):1993–2006
Pratap S, Rendon S (2003) Firm investment in imperfect capital markets: A structural estimation. Rev Econ Dynam 6(3):513–545
Rust J (1994) Structural estimation of markov decision processes. In: Engle R, McFadden D (eds) Handbook of econometrics, vol IV. North Holland, Amsterdam
Saltari E, Travaglini G (2003) How do future constraints affect current investment? Top Macroecon 3(1):1101–1101
Tobin J (1969) A general equilibrium approach to monetary theory. J Money Credit Bank 1(1):15–29
Whited TM (1994) Debt, liquidity constraints and corporate investment: evidence from panel data. J Finance 47:1425–1459

Chapter 3
Cash Holdings, Firm Value and the Role of Market Imperfections. A Cross Country Analysis

Giorgio Calcagnini, Adam Gehr, and Germana Giombini

Abstract In this paper we evaluate the empirical importance of the contemporaneous presence of financial and labor market imperfections by studying cross-country differences in market valuations of listed companies and firms' cash holdings. Our results show that, as expected, financial market imperfections are positively correlated with firms' cash holdings and that the latter are larger wherever employment protection laws (EPL) are stricter. Moreover, stock markets value liquid companies less in economies with higher EPL levels.

Introduction

In this paper we empirically analyze the impact of labor and financial market imperfections on firm behavior by using two cross-country datasets of listed and unlisted firms. We focus on two aspects: first, we study firms' cash holdings in the presence of labor market imperfections. Secondly, we analyze how the market value of listed firms depends upon labor market imperfections and the joint impact of liquidity and labor market imperfections.

There are several reasons why the study of firm cash holdings is worth exploring. First, in a world of perfect financial markets and no contracting costs, firms do not demand (hold) cash because they can invest in all positive net present value (NPV) projects available to them and pay out the funds that they cannot invest in such

G. Calcagnini
Department of Economics and Quantitative Methods, Università di Urbino "Carlo Bo", Via Saffi 42, Italy,
e-mail: giorgio.calcagnini@uniurb.it

A. Gehr
Department of Finance, DePaul University, 1 E. Jackson, Chicago, IL, USA,
e-mail: agehr@mozart.depaul.edu

G. Giombini
Department of Economics and Quantitative Methods, Università di Urbino "Carlo Bo", Via Saffi 42, Italy,
e-mail: germana.giombini@uniurb.it

G. Calcagnini and E. Saltari (eds.), *The Economics of Imperfect Markets*, Contributions to Economics,
DOI: 10.1007/978-3-7908-2131-4_3,

projects to shareholders. However, in the presence of imperfect financialmarkets firms demand cash for different reasons. For example, when agency problems exist, i.e., when the interests of controlling shareholders are not aligned with those of outside investors, controlling shareholders prefer to keep funds in liquid assets that have a private benefit option attached to them that other assets do not have (Pinkowitz et al. 2006).

Second, as documented by Bates et al. (2008), the average cash-asset ratio held by companies in the US doubled from 10.48 to 24.03% between 1980 and 2004. This finding appears paradoxical because improvements in financial technology should reduce cash holdings. The authors explain the increase in the average cash ratio by citing a precautionary motive: the average cash ratio increases over the sample period because the cash flow risk for American firms has increased, inventories have fallen, and research and development expenditures have increased. In Bates et al. (2008), therefore, the cash ratio increased because of changes in firm characteristics.

Third, there is cross-country variability in the cash-assets ratio and the observed cross-country variability may reflect significant differences in institutional environments, in the degree of market imperfections and in the quality of domestic institutions, such as bankruptcy laws, the state of development of capital markets, and patterns of corporate governance (Ferreira and Vilela 2004).

Finally, the analysis of the role played by market imperfections and institutions in determining cash holdings provides a valuable background to the design of welfare-improving economic policies. The traditional models of financial management hold the institutional framework constant. We, however, are able to analyze the impact upon management of operating in a variety of environments in an international study. Indeed, strategies which might be optimal in a given institutional or legal environment are not necessarily optimal in another.

We are interested in looking at how the existence of financial and labor market imperfections affects firm value and, therefore, their growth. In our paper labor market imperfections are those created by the legal environment, as represented by employment protection laws (EPL): how much freedom does management have to change its labor force in response to changes in demand? If management is constrained from adjusting its labor expenses when demand changes, the firm essentially has a higher level of operating leverage and, in turn, a greater volatility of cash flows. Greater cash flow volatility, as Bates et al. (2008), have shown, changes the firm's optimal stock of cash. Operating leverage is the incurrence of a fixed operating cost. In the simplest case, with no labor market imperfections, we can regard labor as a variable cost. If, however, legislation makes it difficult or expensive to adjust the quantity of labor purchased, labor becomes, at least in part, a fixed cost. Higher operating leverage transforms a given level of sales volatility into operating income volatility. This will, in turn, modify management's optimal strategies. In particular, management will need to hold a larger quantity of cash holdings as a buffer against the larger fluctuations of cash inflows and outflows. Therefore, we should expect that tighter EPL increases cash holdings.

The purpose of the analysis is twofold. First, we regress cash holdings on a set of explanatory variables that we reasonably assume are proxies for the economic determinants of firms' cash holdings. As theoretical cash demand models are often considered alternative, but not mutually exclusive, we take a general-modeling approach by estimating an equation with several variables the effects of which on cash holdings are consistent with different theoretical interpretations. Among these variables, we focus our attention on the role played by labor market imperfections and study how firms' cash holdings vary with EPL over time and across countries. Second, for the sample of listed companies, we follow the Fama and French (1998) approach to regress firms' market value on their characteristics, such as: earnings and earning variations, net asset variations, research and development expenditure levels and variations, interest expenditure levels and variations, dividend levels and variations, change in liquidity, plus a country-level measure of labor market regulations (EPL). We estimate whether the accumulation of liquid assets is more highly valued in countries with financial and labor market imperfections.

Our results show that firms' cash holdings are higher whenever market imperfections are larger. Overall, the sign of the estimated coefficients is more consistent with the pecking order theory than with the trade off and the agency cost theories. Firms mainly hold cash because funding investment by means of internal funds is less expensive than by external funds. Further, due to the presence of imperfections, we show that financial markets attach a positive value to firms' cash holding changes, but that the contemporaneous presence of labor market imperfections decreases this value. In other words, financial markets recognize, and consistently price, that stricter employment protection laws determine less internal funding of investment and higher cash flow volatility. Another interpretation of this result is that the impact of changes in EPL on market values is the greatest for those companies with the highest cash holding accumulation.

The paper is organized as follows. Section Demand for Cash and Near-Cash Assets briefly discusses some recent empirical findings on the determinants of cash holdings and reviews the main theories. Then, in Section Empirical Specification, we describe our empirical specification, and in Section Data and Estimation Results, data and the estimation results. Section Firm Value and Labor Regulations, analyzes the impact of EPL on firm value and how EPL interacts with liquid assets. Section Concluding Remarks concludes.

The Demand for Cash and Near-Cash Assets

Studies on cash holdings date back to the 60s and the works of Selden (1961), Meltzer (1963), and Frazer (1964). More recently, interest in firm cash holdings has been revived by developments in the economics of imperfect markets (Ferreira and Vilela 2004), and by the observed increase in corporate cash holdings (Bates et al. 2008). As Opler et al. (1999) point out, many firms hold enough cash to pay off all of their outstanding debt, and firms seem to not be, in a sense, leveraged at all. The authors show that the demand for cash depends on the size of the firm, but there seem to be economies of scale in cash balances. Among others, Almeida et al. (2004), Kim et al. (1998) and Pinkowitz et al. (2006) find that the demand for cash is lower as a percentage of assets in large firms than in small firms. Risk also plays a role in the demand for cash, and Lins et al. (2008) find that, while managers prefer to obtain lines of credit to have liquidity for strategic investment opportunities, they hold cash to buffer against possible future cash shortfalls. Kim et al. (1998) find that the demand for cash increases along with variations in future cash flows. Almeida et al. (2004) find that firms' propensity to put aside cash from their cash flows depends on the existence of financial constraints. There is a general agreement that the demand for cash varies across industries, reflecting the financing patterns and the liquidity of their assets and liabilities. Pinkowitz et al. (2006) and Ferreira and Vilela (2004) carry out cross-country studies of corporate cash demand. Ferreira and Vilela (2004) find that firms in countries with superior investment protection hold more cash, and Pinkowitz et al. (2006) examine agency theoretical models of the demand for cash and find a strong link between cash and firm value in countries with strong investor protection. Foley et al. (2007), on the contrary, find that some of the large cash balances held by firms in reality belong to subsidiaries of US multinationals who wish to avoid the tax burden they would incur if these funds were returned to the parent firm as dividends.

More recently, Himmelberg et al. (2008) showed that firms demand cash because a fraction of labor and material inputs must be purchased out of cash holdings chosen one period in advance. Because cash has transaction value, it competes with fixed capital for the scarce resources of the firm. In the absence of adjustment costs, the optimal allocation between cash and non-cash assets equates their expected marginal returns. By using a sample of European companies, the authors find that (1) firms with production technologies that are relatively material and/or labor intensive will tend to maintain higher cash-to-asset ratios; (2) the optimal cash-asset ratio of the firm depends upon capital depreciation rates and interest rates; (3) cash has option value because cash gives the firm the option to produce in good states of the world. Thus, the model predicts firms facing more volatile demand or productivity shocks will allocate a higher fraction of their assets to cash.

There are three theories that can explain why firms demand cash, which have been derived from the corresponding theories of firm capital structure. These theories are departures from the Modigliani and Miller (1958) model according to which the market value of firms is independent of their capital structure in the presence of frictionless financial markets.[1] In Modigliani and Miller (1958) cash is considered as a zero net present value investment because there are no benefits from holding

[1] Modigliani and Miller (1963) analyze the impact of financial structure on firm value in the presence of corporate income taxes. Because interest payments on debt are tax deductible, whereas dividends are not, the introduction of corporate taxation implies that the invariance proposition does not hold anymore and affects the firm's choice of bond vs. equity financing. Indeed, the use of financial leverage adds to firm value via the present value of the interest tax savings on debt financing, with the result that the optimal capital structure of the firm would be 99% debt.

cash in a world of perfect capital markets lacking information asymmetries, transaction costs or taxes. Firms undertake all positive NPV projects regardless of their level of liquidity. Indeed, once we assume no transaction costs, no information costs, brokerage fees, or other costs associated with the purchase or sale of securities or other assets, internal and external funds are perfect substitutes. In contrast, the theories briefly discussed below can be derived from costly transaction theories in which the Modigliani and Miller assumptions are removed and, consequently, internal and external finance are not perfect substitutes, due to transaction costs, tax advantages, asymmetric information, financial distress costs, or agency problems.

Trade Off Theory

According to the trade off model firms demand cash for precautionary and transaction motives up to the point where marginal benefits of holding cash are equal to marginal costs (Baumol 1952; Tobin 1956; Miller and Orr 1966). In the presence of imperfect capital markets, the benefit for firms of holding cash is the cost avoidance associated with the external-fund raising or the liquidation of existing assets to finance their growth opportunities. Cash holding costs are mainly the opportunity cost of cash, i.e., the lower return of liquid assets relative to other investments of the same level of risk. The result of the trade off theory is the determination of an optimal level of cash holdings. Consequently, firms raise external funds infrequently and use cash and liquid assets as a buffer.

Pecking Order Theory

According to the pecking order theory, firms find the issuing of new equities very costly because of information asymmetries. Thus, firms finance their investments primarily with internal funds, then with debt and finally with equities (Leland and Pyle 1977; Myers 1984; Myers and Majluf 1984; Greenwald et al. 1984).[2] According to this theory, cash holdings are simply the result of financing and investment decisions and, therefore, no optimal cash level exists. Cash holdings are used as a buffer between retained earnings and investment needs.

[2] Myers (1984) notes the following pecking order for financing decisions: firms prefer internal sources of funds; firms adapt their dividend payout policies to reflect their anticipated investment opportunities; dividends are sticky. Moreover it is possible to find unpredictable fluctuations in profitability and investment opportunities. These elements imply that an internally generated cash flow may higher or lower than investment outlays; if external financing is required, firms issue the safest security first and equity issues remain a last resource.

Agency Cost Theory

In finance, agency costs arise when there is a separation between ownership and control and, therefore, differences exist between managers' decisions (the principal) vs. shareholders' interests (the agent). Indeed, according to the managerial capitalism theory (Martin et al. 1988) managers avoid using external funds because doing so would subject them to the discipline of the marketplace. According to the agency cost theory, agency costs include the principal's monitoring expenditures, the agent's bonding expenditure, and the residual loss from imperfect monitoring (Barnea et al. 1981; Jensen and Meckling 1976).

The free cash flow theory of Jensen (1986), suggests that managers have an incentive to build up cash in order to increase the amount of assets under their control and to gain discretionary power over firm investment decisions. Cash holdings play the same role as free cash flows because they are used to finance investment projects that capital markets would not be willing to finance. The cost of external finance increases because capital markets do not know whether managers are asking for funds to increase firm value or to pursue their own interests. Therefore, debt financing is considered a means to alleviate the conflicts between shareholders and management, reducing the amount of free cash available for managers.

Empirical Specification

In summary, cash holdings may have different theoretical explanations, mainly based on the fact that internal and external finance are not perfect substitutes for one another. Indeed, internal finance may be less costly than external because of transaction costs, tax advantages, asymmetric information, and agency problems.[3]

The trade off, the pecking order and the agency cost theories are alternative, but not necessarily mutually exclusive models for explaining firms' cash holdings, given the differences existing within each economy in terms of firms' size and business entity typology, including the regulations governing them. Therefore, several variables may enter an empirical specification that encompasses results concerning cash holding demand derived from the three theories. In a list, though not exhaustive, of explanatory variables for firms' cash demand we include: the investment-to-total asset ratio, the market-to-book value, the company size, the debt issue over total assets, the cash-flow to total asset ratio, the cash-flow volatility, the debt maturity, the collection and credit periods, and, finally, some measure of labor market imperfections.

[3] Tax savings arise when earnings are retained rather than paid out because a tax dividend is replaced with a lower tax on capital gains.

The Investment-to-Total Asset and the Market-to-Book Value Ratios

According to the trade off theory, higher growth opportunities are positively correlated to firms' cash holdings. Indeed, firms with strong growth opportunities either would bear greater financial distress costs in the case of forced liquidation, or might be forced to forgo profitable investment opportunities. We capture growth opportunities with both current capital expenditures (INV/TA) and the market-to-book value ratio (*MKTBOOK*), a rough measure of the Tobin's q.[4] The estimated coefficients of these two explanatory variables should both be positive because cash holdings allow firms to avoid financial distress. Indeed, the cost associated with cash shortage is higher for firms with valuable investment opportunities. According to the pecking order theory, higher investment opportunities generate higher demand for cash because firms prefer to use internal funds to finance investment projects. Therefore, in this case, as well, the expected sign for the estimated coefficients of both (INV/TA) and (*MKTBOOK*) is positive. However, if investment is not a proxy for growth opportunities, the estimated coefficient of (INV/TA) may show a negative sign: to finance their investment projects, firms use primarily accumulated cash (Saddour 2006). Thus, it is expected that cash holdings will decrease with investment. In the case of the free cash flow theory, cash is held by firms whose managers want to increase their personal power. Therefore, according to this theory, firms with poorer investment opportunities should hold more cash so that managers do not need to provide information about the firms' investment plans to capital markets operators. Consequently the estimated coefficients of INV/TA and *MKTBOOK* should be negative, in this case.

Firm Size

According to the trade off theory, the expected sign of the estimated coefficient of (*SIZE*) is negative because larger firms should generate lower cash demand, due to the presence of economies of scale in cash management. In the case of the pecking order theory larger firms are expected to have high levels of cash flow and, then, a positive estimated coefficient for *SIZE* is expected. A positive estimated coefficient is also expected in the case of the agency cost theories, given that agency costs are usually positively correlated with firm size.

Debt Issue

The predicted relationship between firms' issue of debt ($DEBT/TA$) and cash holdings is not clearly determined under the trade off model. On one hand, an increasing leverage increases the probability of financial distress and bankruptcy. Then, higher

[4] Variable definitions will be provided below.

$(DEBT/TA)$ values are expected to generate higher cash holding demand. On the other, debt is interpreted as a cash substitute; therefore, larger debt issues may be associated with lower cash holdings, and a negative estimated coefficient of $(DEBT/TA)$.

Cash Flow

Cash flow (CF/TA) is a substitute for cash holdings. Then, for the trade off theory, cash flow should be negatively correlated to cash holdings and the sign of the estimated coefficient of (CF/TA) is expected to be negative. Diversely, for the pecking order theory the estimated coefficient of (CF/TA) is expected to be positive, because cash flow is used to finance new profitable projects, to repay debts, to pay dividends and, finally, to accumulate cash. Agency cost theories provide no clear predictions regarding the effect of cash flow on cash holdings.

Cash Flow Volatility

Cash flow uncertainty $(SIGMA)$ should be positively related to cash holdings because more volatile cash flows increase the probability of cash shortages. Only the trade off theory provides a clear prediction on the expected effect of cash-flow volatility on cash holdings.

Debt Maturity

According to the trade off theory the impact of debt maturity $(DEBTMT)$ on cash holdings is not well determined a priori. On one hand, shorter debt maturity increases the likelihood of financial distress and should be positively correlated to cash holdings. On the other, Barclay and Smith (1995) argue that firms with the highest credit ratings issue relatively larger amounts of short-term debt. These firms have better access to capital markets and hold consequently less cash. Short-term debt can be used to finance current expenses, and thus can be seen as a cash substitute. Therefore, firms showing shorter debt maturity are expected to hold less cash. In this case as well, neither the pecking order theory nor the agency cost theory provide predictions regarding the effect of debt maturity on cash holdings.

Collection and Credit Periods

The collection period is defined as the number of days, on average, that a firm requires for collecting a credit sale. The length of the collection period indicates the effectiveness with which a firm's management grants credit and collects from customers. Therefore, the longer the collection period $(COLLPRD)$ is, the lower cash holdings are.

The credit period is defined as the number of days, on average, between the purchase of inputs and the payment made for them. It measures the credit period enjoyed by the firm in paying creditors. Therefore, the longer the credit period (*CREDPRD*) is, the higher cash holdings are. Again, no predictions are made regarding cash holdings related to collection and credit periods by either the pecking order theory or the agency cost theory.

EPL

As for the impact of EPL on cash holdings, we expect that higher levels of EPL make it reasonable for firms to hold higher levels of cash holdings. This positive correlation between EPL and cash holdings is consistent with the trade off theory. Indeed, as pointed out by Calcagnini and Giombini (2008) and Calcagnini et al. (2009) regulation can increase the cost the firm faces when expanding its productive capacity, and limits its capacity to respond to changes in fundamentals. Therefore, by increasing the likelihood of financial distress, higher EPL levels make it profitable for firms to increase their cash holdings.

Table 3.1 summarizes the predicted impact of each variable of model (3.1) on cash holdings according to the three theories.

Our empirical strategy is to estimate, by means of different econometric methods, the following model (3.1) which includes the set of explanatory variables previously discussed:

$$\begin{aligned}(CASH/TA)_{i,t} = {} & \beta_0 + \beta_1(INV/TA)_{i,t} + \beta_2(MKTBOOK)_{i,t} + \beta_3(SIZE)_{i,t} \\ & + \beta_4(DEBT/TA)_{i,t} + \beta_5(CF/TA)_{i,t} + \beta_6(SIGMA)_{i,t} \\ & + \beta_7(DEBTMT)_{i,t} + \beta_8(COLLPRD)_{i,t} \\ & + \beta_9(CREDPRD)_{i,t} + \beta_{10}(EPL)_{i,t} + d_t + \eta_i + \phi_j + v_{i,j,t}\end{aligned} \tag{3.1}$$

Table 3.1 Cash holdings theories

Theory	Trade off theory	Pecking order theory	Agency cost theory
Variable			
β_1-INV/TA	+	+	−
β_2-MKTBOOK	+	+	−
β_3-SIZE	−	+	+
β_4-DEBT/TA	+/−	−	−
β_5-CF/TA	−	+	
β_6-SIGMA	+		
β_7-DEBTMT	+/−		
β_8- COLLPRD	−		
β_9-CREDPRD	+		
β_{10}-EPL	+		

where i refers to the firm, j to the country and t to the time period. Each variable is defined as follows:

- CASH/TA = Cash/total assets
- INV/TA = Investment/total assets
- MKTBOOK = Market to book value
- SIZE = Company size (log (total assets))
- DEBT/TA = Debt issue/total assets
- CF/TA = Cash flow/total assets
- SIGMA = Industry sigma (standard deviation of cash flow/total assets)
- DEBTMT = Debt maturity (long term debt/current+non-current liabilities)
- COLLPRD = Collection period (days/100): accounts receivable divided by average daily credit sales
- CREDPRD = Credit period (days/100): accounts payable divided by average daily credit sales
- EPL = Employment protection legislation index (OECD)

Moreover, in (3.1) we also add time dummies d_t, fixed effects η_i and country dummies ϕ_j. Finally, $v_{i,j,t}$ is an idiosyncratic error term.

Data and Estimation Results

We use annual firm-level observations over the period 1995–2003 for eight European Countries (Belgium, France, Germany, Great Britain, Italy, The Netherlands, Spain) taken from AMADEUS, a comprehensive, pan-European database containing financial information on public and private companies. It is produced by Bureau van Dijk whose local providers collect balance sheet information from the national Chambers of Commerce. To allow for comparability, BvD has developed a uniform format, composed of 23 balance sheet items, 25 profit and loss account items, and 26 standard ratios. Additional information, such as industry and activity codes, the incorporation year of the firm in the register, and the quoted/unquoted indicator, complete the dataset. Because of the huge number of observations (over 1,000,000), that made estimations extremely cumbersone, we extracted a 25% random sample from the original database. The random sample mantains the same country distribution as of the original database.

For the group of European countries in our sample we find that the (unweighted) average cash-total asset ratio increased from 8.6 to 14.6% between 1995 and 2003, and the median values increased from 4.5 to 8.1%. As stated above, the observed cross-country variability may reflect significant differences in the degree of market imperfections and in the quality of domestic institutions. In particular, we are interested in analyzing how employment protection legislation affects cash holdings. For this purpose, we use the time series of the OECD EPL Index for total workers, Version 1; this excludes regulations on collective dismissals. EPL for regular workers mainly concerns the cost for employers of firing workers with regular contracts, and it is measured according to the strictness of the regulations for regular procedural inconvenience, notice and severance pay for no-fault individual dismissals, and the relative difficulty of dismissals. The strictness of EPL for temporary workers mainly concerns hiring practices such as type of contracts considered acceptable or number of successive contracts or renewals. The index is measured both for fixed-term contracts and for temporary agency workers. The overall EPL index theoretically ranges from 0 to 6, according to increasing strictness of employment protection laws.

Descriptive statistics are shown in Table 3.2. The average cash holding-to-total asset ratio is 13.43, while the median value is 7.44. France is the country with the highest values, 18.43 and 13.10 respectively, while Germany and The Netherlands show the lowest values. No clear-cut univariate relationship emerges between cash holdings and the other variables shown in Table 3.2. The only exception is the negative relationship observed between cash holdings and firm size. A more precise analysis of the determinant of firm cash demand will require a multivariate analysis that we will carry out by means of model (3.1).

Table 3.3 shows estimates of the unbalanced panel data model (3.1). We estimate model (3.1) by using an instrumental variable approach, because some explanatory variables are endogenous and we need to instrument them to obtain consistent estimates.[5]

The explanatory variables display statistically significant coefficients, with the exception of the cash-flow volatility coefficient, while the estimated coefficients reflect the mixed predictions on cash holdings provided by the three theoretical theories. Comparing the sign of the estimated coefficients shown in the first two columns of Table 3.3 with the expected signs shown in Table 3.1, and limiting the analysis to the first five common variables, the results seem to favor the pecking order theory.[6] Indeed, four out of five estimated coefficients in the first two columns of Table 3.3, namely the coefficients of variables INV/TA, *MKTBOOK*, *SIZE* and CF/TA, have the expected sign according to the pecking order theory. However, the remaining variables, namely $DEBT/TA$, *DEBTMT*, *COLLPRD*, *CREDPRD* and *EPL*, show estimated coefficients consistent with the trade off theory. This latter result is no surprise, given the complexity of the economic environment and the differences in firms' size and business entity typologies within and across countries. However, crucial to this paper's purpose, we find that the estimated coefficient of EPL is positive and statistically significant; i.e., higher EPL levels are associated with higher cash holdings. This result implies that more rigid labor markets, by increasing the likelihood of financial distress, make it profitable for firms to accumulate cash holdings.

---

[5] Unlike Baum et al. (2006) our panel data model is static. We also estimated a dynamic panel data model, but we failed to reject the null hypothesis of the Arellano and Bond test for first order residual autocorrelation.

[6] Columns (1) and (2) differ for the type of instruments used: first differences in the first case and levels in the second case. Results for the endogenous variables (INV/TA and CF/TA) do not change significantly by using previous period levels of the same variables as instruments; but, according to the Hansen test, the instrument's power is lower than the case of first-differenced instruments.

Table 3.2 Firm cash holdings. Descriptive statistics: 1995–2003

Country	Statistics	CASH/TA	INV/TA	SIZE	SIGMA	CF/TA	DEBTMT	COLLPRD	CREDPRD	MKTBOOK	DEBT/TA	EPL
Belgium	Nr Obs	5,077	4,280	5,112	5,112	5,112	3,815	5,112	5,112	5,112	4,280	5,112
	Mean	9.58	0.42	9.29	0.33	9.59	21.19	0.71	0.53	81.96	−0.30	2.40
	Median	4.96	−0.48	9.08	0.18	9.11	17.64	0.67	0.48	88.44	−0.05	2.20
France	Nr Obs	104,495	89,433	107,829	107,829	107,829	22,822	107,829	107,829	107,829	89,433	107,829
	Mean	18.43	0.41	6.49	0.35	10.50	24.83	0.70	0.45	88.14	−0.17	3.00
	Median	13.10	−0.63	6.29	0.18	9.74	20.59	0.70	0.40	91.91	0.00	3.00
Germany	Nr Obs	557	425	567	567	567	313	567	567	567	425	567
	Mean	6.39	1.00	10.66	0.32	9.27	28.15	0.12	0.20	87.17	0.65	2.60
	Median	2.04	0.00	10.65	0.18	7.68	21.43	0.00	0.15	88.39	0.00	2.50
Italy	Nr Obs	50,174	42,730	51,240	51,240	51,240	2,702	51,240	51,240	51,240	42,730	51,240
	Mean	7.35	1.23	8.38	0.29	6.72	11.59	0.71	0.52	92.45	0.05	2.62
	Median	3.08	0.00	8.25	0.18	5.54	9.06	0.73	0.56	95.61	0.00	2.59
Netherlands	Nr Obs	348	294	353	353	353	103	353	353	353	294	353
	Mean	6.90	1.19	10.57	0.31	11.84	21.04	0.75	0.28	84.68	−0.36	2.34
	Median	3.06	−0.16	10.24	0.18	11.48	22.22	0.65	0.24	94.16	0.00	2.10
Spain	Nr Obs	63,205	52,530	64,709	64,709	64,709	54,480	64,709	64,709	64,709	52,530	64,709
	Mean	11.20	2.33	6.98	0.33	9.01	23.12	0.87	0.10	89.41	0.31	3.01
	Median	6.48	0.19	6.83	0.18	8.10	18.88	0.83	0.00	93.85	−0.33	3.10
UK	Nr Obs	12,835	10,789	13,252	13,252	13,252	9,532	13,252	13,252	13,252	10,789	13,252
	Mean	9.41	1.25	8.59	0.34	10.38	20.53	0.60	0.36	91.29	−0.03	0.64
	Median	3.58	0.22	8.51	0.18	10.01	14.97	0.61	0.33	98.67	0.00	0.60
Total	Nr Obs	236,691	200,481	243,062	243,062	243,062	93,767	243,062	243,062	243,062	200,481	243,062
	Mean	13.43	1.13	7.21	0.33	9.28	22.88	0.74	0.36	89.42	0.01	2.78
	Median	7.44	−0.26	7.13	0.18	8.33	18.43	0.73	0.31	93.41	0.00	3.00

Our calculations based on the AMADEUS – Bureau van Dijk database

Column (3) shows the estimated coefficients of a fixed effect model. In this case, we assumed that each explanatory variable is exogenous. The main difference between the results shown in columns (1) and (2) is the negative and significant estimated coefficients of the investment-to-total assets ratio INV/TA. However, the latter result is to be expected: the within-group estimator is inconsistent and downward biased in the presence of endogenous explanatory variables.

Finally, column (4) shows the estimated coefficients of model (3.1) obtained by using the Fama and MacBeth (1973) two step procedure estimator. This econometric

Table 3.3 Firm cash holdings: IV estimates. Amadeus 1995–2003

Explanatory variables	(1) Instruments: first-differenced	(2) Instruments: levels of vars	(3) Fixed-effects	(4) Fama and MacBeth (1973) two step procedure
INV/TA[a]	0.027***	0.027***	−0.104***	−0.115***
	[0.006]	[0.004]	[0.003]	[0.009]
MKTBOOK	0.021*	0.029***	0.023***	0.018**
	[0.011]	[0.009]	[0.004]	[0.005]
SIZE	6.408***	5.948***	3.227***	−1.935***
	[0.346]	[0.286]	[0.086]	[0.136]
DEBT/TA	0.025***	0.023***	0.113***	0.171***
	[0.007]	[0.006]	[0.004]	[0.013]
CF/TA[a]	0.079***	0.093***	0.207***	0.422***
	[0.013]	[0.010]	[0.003]	[0.020]
SIGMA	0.033	0.064	0.090	1.949**
	[0.079]	[0.070]	[0.058]	[0.814]
DEBTMT	−0.087***	−0.087***	−0.098***	−0.140***
	[0.007]	[0.006]	[0.002]	[0.008]
COLLPRD	−10.620***	−10.596***	−8.666***	−2.601***
	[0.228]	[0.194]	[0.080]	[0.129]
CREDPRD	2.811***	3.222***	2.772***	−0.806**
	[0.241]	[0.199]	[0.119]	[0.254]
EPL	0.536**	0.539***	0.839***	1.619***
	[0.228]	[0.188]	[0.090]	[0.316]
Year dummy	Yes	Yes	Yes	Yes
Constant			−10.194***	20.474***
			[0.641]	[0.975]
Observations	61,162	89,758	195,508	195,508
Number of clusters	24,054	29,494	34,184	
R^2	0.127	0.127	0.116	0.156
F test (p-value)	0.000	0.000	0.000	0.000
Hansen test (p-value)	0.343	0.187		

Robust standard errors in brackets; $^{*}p < 0.1$, $^{**}p < 0.05$, $^{***}p < 0.01$; [a] instrumented variables procedure is as follows. In the first step, a cross-sectional regression is performed for each time period. Regressions are estimated independently for each subsample, allowing coefficients on control variables to vary across subsamples. Then, in the second step, the final coefficient estimates are obtained as the average of the first step coefficient estimates. The estimator permits testing for the significance of coefficient combinations, as in ordinary linear regressions. R-squared is computed as the average value of the R-squares from the cross-sectional regressions in the first step of the Fama–MacBeth procedure. The main differences concern the coefficients of the investment-to-total assets ratio INV/TA, of firm dimension *SIZE*, and of the credit period *CREDPRD*, which are all negative and statistically significant, as opposed to those shown in columns (1) and (2). Again, these estimates might be affected by endogeneity problems that cannot be controlled by this estimation procedure.

Firm Value and Labor Regulations

In the previous section we showed that, in the presence of market imperfections, firms' cash holdings are not just an accounting balance, but they seem to be linked to other important characteristics of firms and the economic environment in which they operate. To confirm this result, in this section we analyze how firms' market values change with cash holding accumulation and, contemporaneously, with labor market regulations (as measured by EPL). Specifically, for a sample of listed companies we estimate whether liquid assets are valued less in countries with capital and labor market imperfections. To do so we use the Fama and French (1998) and Pinkowitz et al. (2006) approach. Fama and French (1998) developed a valuation regression that relates firm value to firm characteristics. Even if this valuation regression does not specify a functional form resulting directly from a theoretical model, it does a good job in explaining the cross-section variation in firm values.

The starting equation of the Fama and French (1998) model is as follows:

$$
\begin{aligned}
(V/TA)_{i,t} = {} & \beta_0 + \beta_1(E/TA)_{i,t} + \beta_2(dE/TA)_{i,t} + \beta_3(dE/TA)_{i,t+1} \\
& + \beta_4(dTA/TA)_{i,t} + \beta_5(dTA/TA)_{i,t+1} + \beta_6(RD/TA)_{i,t} \\
& + \beta_7(dRD/TA)_{i,t} + \beta_8(dRD/TA)_{i,t+1} + \beta_9(I/TA)_{i,t} \\
& + \beta_{10}(dI/TA)_{i,t} + \beta_{11}(dI/TA)_{i,t+1} + \beta_{12}(D/TA)_{i,t} \\
& + \beta_{13}(dD/TA)_{i,t} + \beta_{14}(dD/TA)_{i,t+1} + \beta_{15}(dV/TA)_{i,t+1} + \varepsilon_{i,t}
\end{aligned}
$$

where:

- V/TA = (Market value of equities + Book value of debt)/total assets
- E/TA = (Income before income tax + Net items – Appropriation to untaxed reserves – Income tax – Minority interests + Interests and related expense)/total assets
- TA = Total assets

- RD/TA = Research and development expense/total assets
- I/TA = Interest expense/total assets
- D/TA = Total dividend/total assets
- L/TA = (Cash + Short term investment)/total assets
- $d(X/TA)_t = ((X_t - X_{t-1})/A_t$ and $d(X/TA)_{t+1} = ((X_{t+1} - X_t)/A_t$.

The authors control for profitability, i.e., expected cash flow, with the current, past and future earning variables (E/TA). The past and future change in total assets (dTA/TA) are meant to proxy for the net investment component of the expected net cash flow. In the Fama and French (1998) model, next period variables are introduced to control for the change in expectations.

Pinkowitz et al. (2006), analyze the agency cost theory in the framework of the investor protection offered by a country's laws, i.e., to what extent does the law protect the owners of a firm from exploitation by the firm's management and protect outside shareholders from the predations by insiders? In the presence of agency problems, investing in cash can negatively affect firm value, by enabling managers to avoid the discipline of the marketplace.

The aforesaid authors use the Fama and French (1998) valuation approach to estimate the relationship between market value and cash holdings by splitting the change in assets into its cash (L) and noncash (NA) components. The idea is that managers can turn liquid assets into private benefits at a lower cost than with other assets. Liquid assets therefore represent a promising opportunity to investigate the implications of agency theory. Pinkowitz et al. (2006) find that the relationship between cash holdings and firm value is much weaker in countries with poor investor protection than in other countries, supporting the implications of the agency theory. Indeed, agency theory predicts that the value of corporate cash holdings is lower in countries with poor investor protection, because of the greater ability of controlling shareholders to extract private benefits from cash holdings in such countries.

Besides capital market imperfections, we analyze the impact of labor market regulations on firms' market value. As we described in previous sections, labor market imperfections lower firms' value. On one hand, they reduce the freedom management has to change the labor force in response to changes in demand and, consequently, increase cash flow volatility and the likelihood of financial distress.[7] On the other, there may be an indirect effect of EPL on firms' value: firm values are deemed to be lower in the presence of EPL because, *ceteris paribus*, it increases the amount of cash they must hold in the face of adverse demand shocks.

The regression equation (Model 3.2) is a modified version of the Pinkowitz et al. (2006) (2) to which we added the *EPL* variable and the interaction term $EPL * dL$, where dL stands for changes in cash holdings. We expect both estimated coefficients of *EPL* and $EPL * dL$ to be negative.

[7] Calcagnini et al. (2009) showed that EPL reduces firm investment by increasing firm adjustment costs. Smaller growth opportunities, due to less investment, may result in lower market values.

$$\begin{aligned}(V/TA)_{i,t} = {} & \beta_0 + \beta_1(E/TA)_{i,t} + \beta_2(dE/TA)_{i,t} + \beta_3(dE/TA)_{i,t+1} \\ & + \beta_4(dNA)_{i,t} + \beta_5(dNA)_{i,t+1} + \beta_6(RD/TA)_{i,t} + \beta_7(dRD/TA)_{i,t} \\ & + \beta_8(dRD/TA)_{i,t+1} + \beta_9(I/TA)_{i,t} + \beta_{10}(dI/TA)_{i,t} \\ & + \beta_{11}(dI/TA)_{i,t+1} + \beta_{12}(D/TA)_{i,t} + \beta_{13}(dD/TA)_{i,t} \\ & + \beta_{14}(dD/TA)_{i,t+1} + \beta_{15}(dV/TA)_{i,t+1} + \beta_{16}(dL/TA)_{i,t} \\ & + \beta_{17}(dL/TA)_{i,t+1} + \beta_{18}(EPL)_{i,t} \\ & + \beta_{19}(EPL)_{i,t} * (dL/TA)_{i,t} + \varepsilon_{i,t} \end{aligned} \tag{3.2}$$

where:

- NA = Total assets − Cash and short term investment
- L/TA = (Cash + Short term investment)/total assets

Data and Estimation Results

Our data are obtained from Compustat Global. The Compustat Global database provides authoritative financial and market data on publicly traded companies. We selected companies located in 10 countries which had as their fiscal year end December 31 and for which we had information on share closing prices and the number of shares outstanding. The initial sample was composed of 6,834 companies for a total of 67,063 observations. To reduce the effects of outliers, we trimmed our sample at the 1% level by dropping 0.5% observations on the tail of each variable. We ended up with an unbalanced panel data that contains 6,758 companies, for a total of 6,1391 observations for the time period 1988–2006. Table 3.4 shows descriptive statistics for our sample.

Model (3.2) estimates are shown in Table 3.5. Column (1) shows our estimates of the standard Fama and French (1998) model in which the cash contribution to firms' market value is split into its cash and noncash component as in Pinkowitz et al. (2006). The estimated coefficients show the contribution to firms' market value of levels and changes of the following variables: earnings, research and development expenditures, interest expenditures, and dividends. The results show that both current and future changes in net assets ($(dNA/TA)_{i,t}$ and $(dNA/TA)_{i,t+1}$, respectively) have positive and statistically significant estimated coefficients, as does the change in current and future cash component of cash holdings ($(dL/TA)_{i,t}$ and $(dL/TA)_{i,t+1}$, respectively). As expected, therefore, cash holdings increase the market value of the firm.

Column (2) shows results of the standard model with the addition of the EPL variable. As expected, the estimated coefficient of EPL is negative and statistically significant ($\hat{\beta}_{18} = -0.079$) – firms that operate in stricter labor markets are valued less than firms that operate in more flexible labor markets. Cash and noncash components of cash holdings continue to display positive and statistically significant estimated coefficients as in the standard model of column (1).

Table 3.4 Firm value and employment protection. Descriptive statistics: compustat 1988–2003

Country	Statistics	V/TA	E/TA	NA/TA	RD/TA	I/TA	D/TA	L/TA	EPL
Canada	Nr Obs	4,543	4,259	4,820	4,820	4,557	4,713	4,820	4,074
	Mean	1.66	0.02	0.89	0.01	0.02	0.01	0.11	0.78
	Median	1.30	0.05	0.97	0.00	0.02	0.00	0.03	0.78
France	Nr Obs	4,708	5,120	5,645	5,646	5,437	850	5,645	4,600
	Mean	1.43	0.04	0.86	0.01	0.02	0.02	0.14	2.99
	Median	1.16	0.05	0.91	0.00	0.01	0.01	0.09	2.98
Germany	Nr Obs	4,722	5,046	5,383	5,384	5,305	2,795	5,383	4,672
	Mean	1.50	0.01	0.87	0.01	0.02	0.02	0.13	2.61
	Median	1.22	0.04	0.93	0 .00	0.02	0.01	0.07	2.46
Italy	Nr Obs	1,124	1,277	1,319	1,319	1,315	671	1,319	840
	Mean	1.32	0.03	0.89	0.00	0.02	0.02	0.11	2.69
	Median	1.17	0.04	0.93	0.00	0.01	0.01	0.07	2.70
Japan	Nr Obs	3,563	3,876	4,510	4,510	4,411	3,578	4,510	3,667
	Mean	1.44	0.02	0.80	0.01	0.01	0.01	0.20	2.00
	Median	1.17	0.03	0.84	0.00	0.01	0.01	0.16	2.03
Netherlands	Nr Obs	1,612	1,694	1,755	1,755	1,719	1,329	1,755	1,474
	Mean	1.61	0.06	0.89	0.01	0.02	0.02	0.11	2.48
	Median	1.28	0.07	0.95	0.00	0.02	0.02	0.05	2.73
Portugal	Nr Obs	351	394	399	399	397	154	399	354
	Mean	1.20	0.04	0.94	0.00	0.02	0.02	0.06	3.70
	Median	1.08	0.05	0.96	0.00	0.02	0.01	0.04	3.67
Spain	Nr Obs	1,125	1,304	1,345	1,345	1,333	640	1,345	1,081
	Mean	1.34	0.05	0.92	0	0.02	0.02	0.08	3.19
	Median	1.19	0.06	0.96	0	0.02	0.02	0.04	3.05
UK	Nr Obs	5,844	6,131	6,435	6,445	6,336	4,589	6,435	5,046
	Mean	1.81	0.01	0.85	0.02	0.02	0.03	0.15	0.64
	Median	1.41	0.06	0.91	0.00	0.01	0.03	0.09	0.60
United States	Nr Obs	27,703	22,379	29,618	29,630	27,985	29,100	29,618	25,327
	Mean	1.92	0.02	0.85	0.04	0.02	0.01	0.15	0.21
	Median	1.44	0.06	0.94	0.00	0.02	0.00	0.06	0.21
Total	Nr Obs	55,295	51,480	61,229	61,253	58,795	48,419	61,229	51,135
	Mean	1.74	0.02	0.86	0.02	0.02	0.01	0.14	1.09
	Median	1.33	0.05	0.93	0.00	0.02	0.01	0.07	0.60

Our calculations based on Compustat

Finally, column (3) shows estimated coefficients of the equation that includes both EPL and the interaction term $(EPL)_{i,t} * (dL/TA)_{i,t}$. The estimated coefficients of both EPL and the interaction term are statistically significant ($\hat{\beta}_{18} = -0.078$ and $\hat{\beta}_{19} = -0.694$, respectively) and, as expected, negative.

Therefore, estimated coefficients confirm our hypotheses about the impact on firm value of labor market imperfections and the interaction between changes in firms' liquidity and labor market imperfections. First, firms' market value is directly and negatively affected by the existence of more rigid labor markets. Secondly, the interaction of labor market imperfections and liquidity accumulation is negative –

Table 3.5 The Change in the value of cash and employment protection. Fama and MacBeth (1973) estimates. Compustat 1988–2003

Explanatory variables	(1) Fama and French (1988) model	(2) Employment protection effect	(3) Employment protection and liquidity interaction
$(E/TA)_{i,t}$	0.709**	1.110	1.079
	[0.259]	[0.667]	[0.671]
$(dE/TA)_{i,t}$	0.320**	0.135	0.148
	[0.117]	[0.271]	[0.271]
$(dE/TA)_{i,t+1}$	1.056***	1.156***	1.166***
	[0.171]	[0.309]	[0.309]
$(dNA/TA)_{i,t}$	0.681***	0.479***	0.498***
	[0.074]	[0.152]	[0.154]
$(dNA/TA)_{i,t+1}$	0.736***	0.764***	0.763***
	[0.130]	[0.131]	[0.130]
$(RD/TA)_{i,t}$	6.934***	6.463***	6.452***
	[0.615]	[0.608]	[0.605]
$(dRD/TA)_{i,t}$	0.306	−0.091	−0.126
	[0.817]	[1.007]	[1.000]
$(dRD/TA)_{i,t+1}$	6.090***	5.977***	5.790***
	[0.770]	[0.797]	[0.760]
$(I/TA)_{i,t}$	−3.663***	−5.035***	−4.920***
	[0.638]	[0.784]	[0.798]
$(dI/TA)_{i,t}$	−5.750***	−3.070	−3.128
	[0.916]	[2.481]	[2.489]
$(dI/TA)_{i,t+1}$	−7.833***	−8.938***	−9.023***
	[1.288]	[1.467]	[1.445]
$(D/TA)_{i,t}$	6.996***	7.474***	7.569***
	[0.571]	[0.716]	[0.733]
$(dD/TA)_{i,t}$	−1.153*	−0.707	−0.461
	[0.633]	[0.918]	[0.877]
$(dD/TA)_{i,t+1}$	2.914**	3.417***	3.592***
	[1.067]	[1.104]	[1.073]
$(dL/TA)_{i,t}$	1.814***	1.611***	1.730***
	[0.151]	[0.197]	[0.491]
$(dL/TA)_{i,t+1}$	1.302***	1.285***	1.284***
	[0.244]	[0.245]	[0.246]
$(dV)_{i,t+1}$	−0.129*	−0.126	−0.125
	[0.068]	[0.072]	[0.072]
$(EPL)_{i,t}$		−0.079*	−0.078*
		[0.040]	[0.042]

(*continued*)

Table 3.5 (Continued)

Explanatory variables	(1) Fama and French (1988) model	(2) Employment protection effect	(3) Employment protection and liquidity interaction
$(EPL)_{i,t} * (dL/TA)_{i,t}$			−0.694**
			[0.264]
Constant	1.336***	1.354***	1.344***
	[0.027]	[0.095]	[0.099]
Observations	26,717	23,646	23,646
Number of time periods	17	16	16
R^2	0.343	0.381	0.384
F test (p-value)	0.00	0.00	0.00

Standard errors in brackets. $^{*}p < 0.1$, $^{**}p < 0.05$, $^{***}p < 0.01$

the market value of liquidity is lower in the presence of larger market imperfections. In other words, we find that financial markets recognize, and consistently price the reduced internal funding opportunities and higher cash flow volatility caused by stricter employment protection.

Concluding Remarks

The paper has analyzed the impact of imperfect financial and labor markets on firms' asset management and on their market value.

For firm cash holdings, we estimated an empirical cash holding equation by an instrumental variable approach. To interpret and sign the estimated coefficients of the explanatory variables, we made use of three well known theories, namely, the trade off, the pecking order, and the agency cost theories.

Overall, our findings are more in line with results from the pecking order theory according to which firms hold cash because internal funds are less expensive than the external ones when financing investment. Precautionary and transaction motives, associated with the trade off theory, come second.

As for the role of labor market regulations, our results show that, in the presence of imperfect markets, cash holdings are positively associated with EPL levels: higher EPL levels, by increasing the likelihood of financial distress, make it profitable for firms to increase their cash holdings.

The economic importance of cash holdings was also tested by the response of markets. Specifically, our results show that firms' market value is positively affected by the accumulation of cash holdings, but negatively affected by an economic environment characterized by strict labor market regulations. Moreover, the contemporaneous presence of financial and labor market imperfections reduces the market value of cash holdings, because stricter labor market regulations decrease internal funding for investment and increase higher cash flow volatility.

References

Almeida H, Campello M, Weisbach MS (2004) The Cash Flow Sensitivity of Cash. The Journal of Finance 59:1777–1804
Barclay MJ, Smith CW Jr (1995) The mature structure of corporate debt. J Finance 50:609–631
Barnea A, Haugen RA, Senbet LW (1981) Market imperfections, agency problems, and capital structure: a review. Financ Manag 10:7–22
Bates TW, Kahle KM, Stulz R (2008) Why do US firms hold so much more cash than they used to? Fisher College of Business Working Paper No. 2007-03-006. Available at SSRN: http://ssrn.com/abstract=927962
Baumol WS (1952) The transactions demand for cash: an inventory theoretic approach. Q J Econ 66:546–556
Calcagnini G, Giombini G (2008) Does employment protection legislation affect firm investment? The European Case, mimeo. University of Urbino Carlo Bo, Italy
Calcagnini G, Giombini G, Saltari E (2009) Financial and labor market imperfections and investment. Econ Lett 102:22–26
Fama EF, French KR (1998) Taxes, financing decisions, and firm value. J Finance 53:819–843
Fama EF, MacBeth JD (1973) Risk, return, and equilibrium: empirical tests. J Polit Econ 81:607–636
Ferreira MA, Vilela A (2004) Why do firms hold cash? evidence from EMU countries. Eur Financ Manag 10:295–319
Foley CF, Hartzell JC, Titman S, Twite G (2007) Why do firms hold so much cash? A tax-based explanation. J Financ Econ 87:579–607
Frazer WJ Jr (1964) The financial structure of manufacturing corporations and the demand for money: Some empirical findings. Journal of Political Economy 72:176–183
Greenwald B, Stiglitz J, Weiss A (1984) Information imperfections in the capital market and macroeconomic fluctuations. Am Econ Rev 74:194–199
Himmelberg CP, Love I, Sarria-Allende V (2008) A cash-in-advance model of the firm: theory and evidence, World Bank manuscript
Jensen M (1986) Agency costs of free cash flow, corporate finance and takeovers. Am Econ Rev 76:323–329
Jensen M, Meckling WH (1976) Theory of the firm: managerial behavior, agency costs and ownwrship structure. J Financ Econ 3:305–360
Kim CS, Mauer DC, Sherman AE (1998) The determinants of corporate liquidity: theory and evidence. J Financ Quant Anal 33:335–359
Leland H, Pyle D (1977) Information asymmetries, financial structure, and financial intermediation. J Finance 32:371–387
Lins KV, Servaes H, Tufano P (2008) What drives corporate liquidity? An International Survey of Strategic Cash and Lines of Credit. AFA 2008 New Orleans Meetings Paper. Available at SSRN: http://papers.ssrn.com/sol3/papers.cfm?abstract_id=971178
Martin JD, Cox SH, MacMinn RD (1988) The theory Of finance. Evidence and applications. The Dryden Press, New York
Meltzer AH (1963) The demand for money: Across-section study of business firms, Journal of Political Economy 71:219–246
Miller MH, Orr D (1966) A model of demand for money by firms. Q J Econ 80:413–435
Modigliani F, Miller MH (1958) The cost of capital, corporation finance and the theory of investment. Am Econ Rev 48:261–297
Modigliani F, Miller MH (1963) Corporate income taxes and the cost of capital: a correction. Am Econ Rev 53:433–443
Myers S (1984) The capital structure puzzle. J Finance 39:575–592
Myers S, Majluf N (1984) Corporate financing decisions when firms have investment informations that investors do not. J Financ Econ 13:187–220

Opler T, Pinkowitz L, Stulz R, Williamson R (1999) The determinants and implications of corporate cash holdings. J Financ Econ 52:3–46
Pinkowitz L, Stulz R, Williamson R (2006) Does the contribution of corporate cash holdings and dividends to firm value depend on governance? A cross-country analysis. J Finance 61:2725–2751
Saddour K (2006) Why do French Firms Hold Cash? Working Paper 068
Selden RT (1961) The postwar rise in the velocity of money: A sectoral analysis, Journal of Finance 16:483–545
Tobin J (1956) The interest-elasticity of transactions demand for cash. Rev Econ Stat 38:241–247

Chapter 4
Multiple Bank Relationships and the Main Bank System: Evidence from a Matched Sample of Japanese Small Firms and Main Banks

Kazuo Ogawa, Elmer Sterken, and Ichiro Tokutsu

Abstract Based on a matched sample of Japanese small firms and main banks we investigate the bank-firm relationships in the early 2000s. We obtain new findings. First, even small firms with a main bank relation have multiple bank relationships. Second, firms tied with a financially weak main bank increase the number of bank relations. Third, longer duration of a main bank relation increases the number of bank relations. Moreover we find that firms with fewer bank relations pledge personal guarantees to their main banks and are charged a higher interest rate. This suggests that firms take actions against the monopoly power of a main bank.

Introduction

Diamond (1984) demonstrates that the cost of information production of financial intermediation is minimized by delegating information production to a single bank rather than direct monitoring by individuals. Interpreting the delegated monitoring argument from the point of view of borrowers, it is optimal for the firm to borrow from one bank to avoid duplicating information production.

In Japan main banks have played the role of delegated monitors as well as the suppliers of loans to their affiliated firms. Information of affiliated firms is accumulated in main banks by way of long-term, multiple, transactions. Moreover, main

K. Ogawa
Institute of Social and Economic Research, Osaka University, 6-1 Mihogaoka, Ibaraki, Osaka 567-0047, Japan,
e-mail: ogawa@iser.osaka-u.ac.jp

E. Sterken
Department of Economics, University of Groningen, Groningen, Netherlands,
e-mail: e.Sterken@rug.nl

I. Tokutsu
Graduate School of Business Administration, Kobe University, Rokkodai 2-1, Nada, Kobe 657-8501, Japan,
e-mail: tokutsu@port.kobe-u.ac.jp

G. Calcagnini and E. Saltari (eds.), *The Economics of Imperfect Markets*, Contributions to Economics,
DOI: 10.1007/978-3-7908-2131-4_4,

banks have provided affiliated firms with a variety of services besides loans. Main banks are often delegated to collect bills as well as settlement of bills payable and give customers professional advices on financial affairs, production and investment plans. Main bank employees often hold managerial positions in, sometimes financially troubled, client firms for purpose of direct monitoring.[1]

However, there are also costs of a single bank relation. In the course of single lending borrower's information is exclusively accumulated into this single bank, which leads to an informational monopoly. An information monopoly enables banks to extract rents from borrowers. For example, main banks sometimes charge a higher loan interest rate. In fact Weinstein and Yafeh (1998) obtain the evidence that the cost of capital for firms with a close bank relation is higher than that for their peers. The information lock-in effect also makes it difficult for firms to switch lenders.[2] This is well-known as the hold-up problem. One solution to solve this problem is to engage in multiple bank relationships.

There is another factor that prompts firms to establish multiple bank relations. Massive bad loans and subsequent shortage of equity capital in the late 90s to the early 2000s plunged a number of Japanese financial institutions into financial difficulties. Faced with poor main bank health, the affiliated firms had incentives to diversify loan transactions with other banks in order to reduce liquidity risk. Therefore it is interesting to see how bank-firm relations in Japan changed in the midst of financial turmoil of the late 90s to the early 2000s. This study is an empirical attempt along this line and examines whether Japanese small and medium-sized firms (SMEs hereafter) with main bank relations relied upon these multiple bank relations and if so why.[3]

Our study has several features. First, we use a unique micro data set of small and medium-sized firms called Survey of the Corporate Financial Environment (abbreviated as SCFE). The survey has been conducted by the Small and Medium Enterprise Agency of Japan since 2001. The questionnaire contains a number of interesting issues on bank-firm relations such as the number of bank relations, the name of the main bank the firm is affiliated with and the duration of a main bank relationship. This enables us to construct a matched sample of main banks and client firms. Based on this matched sample, we investigate how a main bank health affects the number of bank relations of the affiliated firms.

Secondly, we investigate how serious the hold-up problem is for the firm tied with its main bank. The SCFE has qualitative information on the strength of main bank relations such as whether firms disclose their information to the main bank or

---

[1] Hoshi et al. (1991), using firm-level data, obtain the evidence that the firms affiliated with a main bank enjoy a lower external finance premium than independent firms.

[2] See Sharpe (1990) and Rajan (1992) for a theoretical analysis of the association of banking relation with an information monopoly.

[3] Ogawa et al. (2007) examine the determinants of multiple bank relationships for large listed firms. Uchida et al. (2006) examine the effect of bank size on the strength of the bank-firm relationships which among other things is measured by the number of bank relations. They use the same data set as ours, but only the 2002 survey.

whether firms pledge for collateral or a personal guarantee. This information is useful in measuring the extent to which the main bank exploits its client as information monopolist.[4]

Let us summarize our main findings. We find that firms with longer relations with their main banks also have more relations with other banks. A firm, whose main bank has a low capital ratio, increases the number of relations with other banks. It is more likely that firms pledge personal guarantees when firms have longer relations with their main banks, disclose information to their main banks and the number of banks with which the firms have relations at all is smaller. Our evidence suggests that even the SMEs indeed diversified liquidity risk in the period of financial turbulence in the late 90s to the early 2000s by increasing transactions with other banks. We also confirm that there is dark side of the main bank system or a hold-up problem for SMEs.

This paper is organized as follows. Section Data Characteristics and Descriptive Statistics of Bank-Firm Relationships, explains the characteristics of the data set we use and shows a variety of descriptive statistics on bank-firm relations. Section Determinants of Multiple Bank Relations and the Impact of Main Bank Relations on Loan Contracts sets up an empirical model to determine the multiple bank relationships and examines the impact of main bank relations on loan contracts. Section Estimation Results and Their Implications to Main Bank Relationship presents the estimation results and an interpretation of the results. Section Concluding Remarks summarizes and concludes the paper.

Data Characteristics and Descriptive Statistics of Bank-Firm Relationships

The SCFE, conducted by the Small and Medium Enterprise Agency of Japan, is the first Japanese micro survey to ask small and medium-sized firms a number of questions regarding bank-firm relations. In each wave of the survey, a questionnaire is sent to about 15,000 firms, mainly SMEs, of which about 7,000–9,000 firms respond.

Since our interest lies in multiple bank relations in case a firm has contact with a main bank, we show some descriptive statistics on this issue. The sample period covers the years 2001–2003. First, we can compute the fraction of firms that have a main bank relation. In the survey a main bank is defined as the financial institution which the firm perceives to be the main bank, irrespective of the loan shares.[5] Table 4.1 shows the fraction of firms with a main bank relation and illustrates that more than 90% of the firms have a link with a main bank. Table 4.2 shows the

[4] Ono and Uesugi (2005) also examine the role of collateral and personal guarantees in bank-firm relationships using the SCFE. Their study relies on cross sectional data of the 2002 survey but ours are a panel data of 2001–2003.

[5] The firms are asked to choose only one bank as their main bank, so that there are no multiple main banks by the design of the survey.

Table 4.1 Reply to the question: Do you have your "Main Bank"?

		(Percentages) 2001	2002	2003
(1)	Yes	95.6	94.4	92.6
(2)	No	4.4	5.6	7.4

Source: Small and medium enterprises agency, *Survey of the corporate financial environment*, 2001, 2002, 2003

Table 4.2 Main bank by type of financial institutions

		(Percentages) 2001	2002	2003
(1)	City banks, long-term credit banks (LTCB) and trust banks	34.9	33.7	28.9
(2)	Regional banks including second-tier regional banks	49.6	51.6	53.5
(3)	Shinkin banks and credit cooperatives	12.4	11.7	15.2
(4)	Public financial institutions	2.3	2.1	1.8
(5)	Others	0.8	0.8	0.6
(6)	Total	100.0	100.0	100.0

Source: Small and medium enterprises agency, *Survey of the corporate financial environment*, 2001, 2002, 2003

type of main banks. About half of the main banks are regional banks and one-third is in the class of large banks, such as city banks, long-term credit banks and trust banks. The fraction of shinkin banks or credit cooperatives as a main bank is only 12–15%.

The average length of a main bank relation of firms in 2002 is 26.4 years, which indicates that SMEs have longstanding close ties with their main banks. But SMEs have multiple bank relationships, too. Table 4.3 shows the descriptive statistics of the number of bank relationships. The average number of bank relationships is 3.47 in 2003 to 5.12 in 2002 and the median number is 3 in 2001 and 2003 to 4 in 2002 for firms with a main bank relation and this number is as large as that for the firms without a main bank. Firms have multiple relationships with both large banks and regional banks. It should be noted that the median is rather low, compared to Japanese large listed firms. In fact Ogawa et al. (2007) report that the median number of bank relations is 6–7 for Japanese listed firms for the period of 1981–1999.

Three variables on the terms of loan contracts with main banks are available in the SCFE. The first is whether a firm pledges collateral to its main bank and the second one is whether a firm pledges personal guarantees.[6] Table 4.4 shows that the fraction of firms that pledge collateral or personal guarantees to their main banks is more than 70 irrespective of the sample year. The third variable is the short-term interest rate of borrowings from a main bank. Figure 4.1 shows the histogram of

[6] A personal guarantee is defined as a contractual obligation of the firm owner or other parties to repay the principal in case of default.

Table 4.3 Mean and median numbers of bank relationship

	2001			2002			2003		
	Firms with main bank	Firms without main bank	Total	Firms with main bank	Firms without main bank	Total	Firms with main bank	Firms without main bank	Total
(1) City banks, LTCB and trust banks	1.36 (1)	1.64 (0)	1.38 (1)	1.44 (0)	1.52 (0)	1.44 (0)	0.88 (0)	0.90 (0)	0.89 (0)
(2) Regional banks	1.48 (1)	1.28 (1)	1.47 (1)	1.74 (1)	1.59 (1)	1.73 (1)	1.22 (1)	0.84 (0)	1.19 (1)
(3) Shinkin banks and credit cooperatives	0.50 (0)	0.48 (0)	0.50 (0)	0.55 (0)	0.45 (0)	0.54 (0)	0.43 (0)	0.32 (0)	0.42 (0)
(4) Public financial institutions	0.54 (0)	0.42 (0)	0.54 (0)	0.65 (0)	0.37 (0)	0.63 (0)	0.48 (0)	0.31 (0)	0.46 (0)
(5) Others	0.50 (0)	0.81 (0)	0.51 (0)	0.75 (0)	1.45 (0)	0.79 (0)	0.46 (0)	0.65 (0)	0.48 (0)
(6) (1)+(2)+(3)	3.34 (3)	3.40 (2)	3.35 (3)	3.72 (3)	3.56 (2)	3.72 (3)	2.53 (2)	2.07 (1)	2.50 (2)
(7) (1)+(2)+(3)+(5)	3.72 (3)	4.11 (3)	3.74 (3)	4.47 (3)	5.01 (3)	4.50 (3)	2.99 (2)	2.72 (2)	2.97 (2)
(8) (1)+(2)+(3)+(4)+(5)	4.39 (3)	4.63 (3)	4.40 (3)	5.12 (4)	5.38 (3)	5.13 (4)	3.47 (3)	3.03 (2)	3.44 (3)
(9) Number of observations	7,204	330	7,534	7,570	450	8,020	6,821	549	7,370

Source: Small and medium enterprises agency, *Survey of the corporate financial environment*, 2001, 2002, 2003
Notes: The values in parenthesis are median observations

Table 4.4 Fraction of firms that pledge collateral and / or personal guarantees to their main banks

	(Percentages)		
	2001	2002	2003
(1) Pledge collateral	75.8	71.3	–
(2) Pledge personal guarantees	70.0	71.7	73.7

Source: Small and medium enterprises agency, *Survey of the corporate financial environment*, 2001, 2002, 2003

this short-term interest rate in 2002. It should be noted that the distribution of the short-term interest rate is skewed to the right and thus high interest rate relative to its mean is charged on some firms reflecting a loan risk premium.

In the subsequent analysis we pick the firms in the SCFE with information on bank-firm relations available for the entire period of 2001–2003. This sample consists of 2,138 firms in total. We further choose the firms that satisfy the following conditions. First, we select firms with a main bank that is a private bank, defined as a city bank, long-term credit bank, regional bank, shinkin bank or credit cooperative. Second, the firm has a bank-firm relation with the main bank in 2002 for

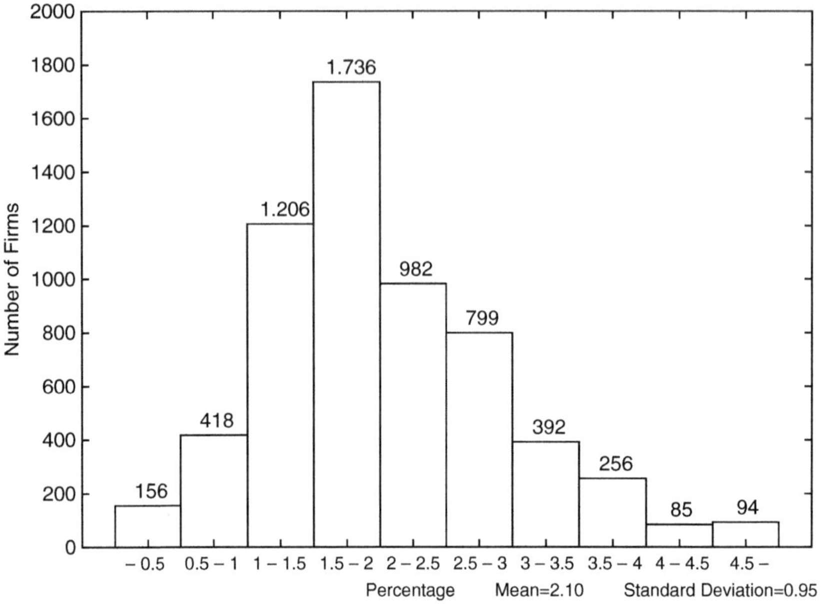

Fig. 4.1 Frequency distribution of the short-term interest rate of borrowing from a main bank: 2002 Survey

2 years or more.[7] So our panel data is unbalanced and the final number of firm-year observations is 5,166. Table 4.5 shows descriptive statistics of the major variables. For all variables but the debt-asset ratio, the mean value is larger than the median, indicating that the frequency distribution is skewed to the right. The large standard deviations also imply that the frequency distributions have a wide dispersion.

For our sampled firms, the information on the bank-firm relations in the SCFE is combined with the balance sheet information as well as the profit-loss statements of the TSR (Tokyo Shoko Research) database. Moreover, we can make use of the financial statements of the main bank itself as well, so we now have a matched sample of borrowers and main banks.

Determinants of Multiple Bank Relations and the Impact of Main Bank Relations on Loan Contracts

In this section we discuss the determinants of the number of bank relations of small Japanese firms. We also relate the terms of loan contracts, like the pledge of personal guarantees and the contract interest rate, that gauge the effects of main bank relations on the design of loan contracts.

---

[7] We can identify the main bank of the sampled firms in the SCFE only in 2002, so that the firms of which the length of the main bank relation is less than two years are excluded since we cannot identify their main banks in 2001 or 2003.

Table 4.5 Descriptive statistics of major variables in our panel data set

Variables		Mean	Median	Standard deviation
(1)	Tangible assets excluding land and construction in progress / total assets	0.1814	0.1391	0.1652
(2)	Inventories / total assets	0.1004	0.0696	0.1071
(3)	Loans payable / total assets	0.3694	0.3509	0.2655
(4)	Accounts receivable-trade / total assets	0.2590	0.2337	0.1766
(5)	Accounts payable-trade / total assets	0.2146	0.1754	0.1789
(6)	Debt-asset ratio	0.7036	0.7472	0.2517
(7)	Total assets	4,050.4	1,364.7	8,024.8
(8)	Sales	4,027.3	1,618.6	7,271.2
(9)	Number of employees	141.6	44.0	644.5

Units: one million yen for total assets and sales and person for number of employees
Source: Small and medium enterprises agency, *Survey of the corporate financial environment* 2001, 2002, 2003

Determinants of Multiple Bank Relations Under the Main Bank System

Why does a firm, closely tied with its main bank, have multiple bank relations? To find a clue to this question, it is important to understand why main bank financing is so prevalent in Japan. A main bank holds a large share of loans of affiliated firms, which gives a strong incentive to collect information about firms' prospects and to monitor the firms. It helps to mitigate problems due to asymmetric information that lead to adverse selection and/or moral hazard. The studies of Kaplan and Minton (1994), Sheard (1994a), Kang and Shivdasani (1995, 1997), Miyajima (1998), and Morck and Nakamura (1999) provide evidence that main banks closely monitor their client firms and dispatch directors to them in the event of financial distress. Close monitoring also helps to identify the types of distress their clients face and thus reduce the cost of this distress (Hoshi et al. (1990) and Sheard (1994b)). However, it should be noted that concentration of information about client firms by a main bank is a double-edged sword and creates monopoly exploitation, the hold-up problem.

Thus one important determinant of a multiple bank relation is the extent to which the hold-up problem is severe for the firm. If a main bank relation is not affected by heavy competition, a main bank might consider using the acquired private corporate information to extract rents, thus distorting entrepreneurial incentives and causing inefficient investment choices. The firm affiliated with the main bank might increase the number of bank relationships in order to act against this exploitation. Thus it is natural to include a variable to measure the degree of the hold-up problem in explaining the number of bank relations. We choose the length of a main bank relation, measured by the number of years since the inception (*MYEAR*). It should be noted that this variable plays another role in explaining the number of bank relations. Since the information of the client firm is accumulated in the main bank in the course of making loans, the news that the main bank has a long and stable relation with the client firm signals that the firm is a good one in terms of profitability, sales growth, and financial conditions, and so on. Other banks might judge the quality of the firm from the news and start business with the firm without investing much in gathering information about the firm.

This is quite similar to the case where a firm's stock price rises when good news about the relation with its main bank is revealed to the market.[8] It is also similar to a sequential complementarity between bank loans and public debt financing. It is only after borrowers are exposed to strict monitoring by banks that firms can raise funds in the capital market. In our context the firm earns good reputation after long and strict monitoring by the main bank, which attracts outside banks granting new loans to the firm.[9]

Another incentive for the firm with a main bank to have multiple bank relations is insurance against lack of liquidity. Suppose that a firm has a long-term profitable project. When that project is liquidated prematurely at the refinancing stage, the firm will incur a tremendous loss. This might happen if the main bank cannot roll over its initial loan and the firm in liquidity need has to apply for loans from non-relation banks (arm's – length financiers). These banks probably think that the applying firms have lemon projects. To avoid this disastrous situation, the firm might have multiple bank relations and diversify its liquidity risk. Detragiache et al. (2000) present a theoretical model in which multiple bank contacts can reduce liquidity risk. In the early stage of financing a project, a main bank acquires private information about the continuation value of the project. At the refinancing stage the firm might need to borrow from non-main banks due to unexpected liquidity shocks that makes it difficult to roll over initial loans. In the worst case, where the firm faces a severe adverse selection problem, the firm is unable to refinance the project by getting loans from other banks. Thus it will be profitable for the firm to establish multiple relations, because it reduces the probability of early liquidation. This model is applicable to the late 90s to the early 2000s in Japan when banks suffered from massive non-performing loans and the banks' balance sheets deteriorated severely. To test this conjecture, we include the banks' balance sheet variables as explanatory variables in explaining the number of bank relations. We choose two variables: the ratio of non-performing loans to total loans (*BADLOAN*) and the equity capital ratio of the bank. The Basel Accord states that banks, engaged in international business, should keep the capital ratio above 8% and domestic banks should maintain 4% capital base at minimum. Therefore we construct two capital ratio variables. The *CAPITAL1* variable stands for the capital ratio of the main bank engaged in international business, while the *CAPITAL2* variable stands for the capital ratio of a domestic main bank.

Lastly we incorporate the type of main bank to give additional information on the bank-firm relation. In order to estimate the effects of bank type on the number of

---

[8] For the announcement effect of bank loans on stock prices there are numerous event studies. For example, see James (1987), Billett et al. (1995), and Shockley and Thakor (1998).

[9] For complementarity between bank loans and public debt, see Diamond (1991), Hoshi et al. (1993), and Chemmanur and Fulghieri (1994).

bank relations, we include two dummy variables for the type of main bank: *DCITY* for city, long-term credit, and trust banks and *DREGION* for regional banks.

We also include conventional explanatory variables to determine the number of bank relations.[10] These are the debt-asset ratio (*DEBTR*), the ratio of operating profits to sales (*PROFITSL*), the ratio of liquid assets (cash, deposits and securities) to total assets (*LIQAST*), the ratio of land asset to total assets (*LNDAST*), and the logarithm of total assets (*LASSET*). The debt-asset ratio measures the effect of a firm's capital structure on the number of bank relations. A large debt-asset ratio may increase the probability of multiple bank relations, because the probability of default is likely to be higher for more leveraged firms and the adverse selection problem is more severe. Profitability of the firm, measured by the *PROFITSL* variable, will have a positive effect on the number of bank relations and the liquidity-rich firm does not need additional bank loans, thus leading to a lower number of bank relations. The ratio of land to total assets, proxy of the collateral size, has a positive effect on the number of bank relations, because having abundant collateral assets will attract non-relation banks. The effect of firm size on the number of bank relations is measured by the logarithm of total assets of the firm. The industry dummies (*DIND*1-*DIND*26) as well as year dummies (*YEAR*1, *YEAR*2) are also included.[11,12] The equation to determine the number of bank relationships of small firms is given by:

$$\begin{aligned} NBANK_{it} = {} & a_0 + a_1 MYEAR_{it} + a_2 BADLOAN_{it} + a_3 \frac{1}{CAPITAL1_{it} - 0.08} \\ & + a_4 \frac{1}{CAPITAL2_{it} - 0.04} + a_5 DEBTR_{it} + a_6 PROFITSL_{it} \\ & + a_7 LIQAST_{it} + a_8 LNDAST_{it} + a_9 LASSET_{it} + a_{10} DCITY_{it} \\ & + a_{11} DREGION_{it} + \sum_{J=1}^{26} b_J DINDJ_{it} + c_1 DYEAR1_{it} \\ & + c_2 DYEAR2_{it} + \varepsilon_{it} \end{aligned} \tag{4.1}$$

where $NBANK_{it}$: number of bank relationships for the i-th firm in period t.

In (4.1), where ε_{it} denotes a white-noise residual, we take account of nonlinear effects of the capital ratio on the number of bank relations. As the capital ratio of a main bank approaches the lower bound of the capital requirement, the affiliated firm may accelerate transactions with other banks in fear that its main bank might stop providing loans.

[10] There are numerous empirical studies on the number of bank relationships. For example, see Ongena and Smith (2000a,b) and Volpin (2000) for international evidence on multiple bank relationship. Horiuchi (1993, 1994) present a descriptive analysis of multiple bank relations of Japanese firms.

[11] The SCFE records industry code to which each sample firm belongs.

[12] The subscripts i and t refer to firm and period, respectively.

Impact of a Main Bank Relationship on the Loan Contract Terms

When a firm's main bank is the sole supplier of loans, the main bank accumulates proprietary information of the firm and might take advantage of its information monopoly. The terms of loan contracts are written so that they are favorable to the main bank. For example, the main bank might charge a higher loan interest rate or demand personal guarantees to secure monopoly rents. However, as the number of bank relations increases, the borrower gains more bargaining power and the terms of loan contracts become more favorable to the borrower. In other words, severity of the hold-up problem will be reflected in the terms of the loan contract.

To test this hypothesis, we estimate the following equations that associate the terms of a loan contract with main bank relation variables. The terms of the loan contract are measured by two variables: a binary variable whether a borrower pledges personal guarantees to its main bank (*GUARANT* equals 1 if borrower pledges personal guarantees, and 0 otherwise) and the short-term interest rate charged by its main bank (*INTRATE*).[13] We include three explanatory variables that represent a main bank relation. First, the bargaining power of the borrower is measured by the number of bank relations (*NBANK*) examined above. More bank relations increase the bargaining power of the borrower, which decreases the probability that the borrower pledges personal guarantees. The borrower will also face a lower interest rate. Second, the extent to which a borrower is informationally exploited is measured by the length of a main bank relation measured in years (*MYEAR*). The longer the main bank relation is, the more likely a borrower pledges personal guarantees and the borrower will face a higher interest rate. The third description is a binary variable whether the firm discloses information about the firm's balance sheet, profit-loss statement and other situations surrounding the firm to its main bank (*DINFORM* equals 1 if a main bank is informed, and 0 otherwise).

We also include the variables of firm attributes as well as main bank attributes. As for the firm and main bank attributes, we use the same explanatory variables of (4.1) to determine the number of bank relations. We include two additional variables to represent lending attitudes of the main bank towards the firm. One is a dummy variable (*DINCREASE*) that takes 1 if the firm is asked to borrow more than applied, and 0 otherwise. The other is a dummy variable (*DREJECT*) that takes 1 if the loan application by the firm is rejected or reduced by its main bank.[14]

The equation to be estimated is as follows:

$$\begin{aligned} GUARANT_{it} = {} & a_0 + a_1 NBANK_{it} + a_2 MYEAR_{it} + a_3 DINFORM_{it} \\ & + a_4 BADLOAN_{it} + a_5 \frac{1}{CAPITAL1_{it} - 0.08} \end{aligned}$$

[13] Pledging collateral to a main bank is also useful information to gauge the impact of information monopoly on the terms of loan contract. However, information of collateral is not available in the 2003 SCFE.

[14] 26 Industry dummy variables (*DINDJ*) as well as year dummies (*DYEAR*) are also included as explanatory variables.

$$+a_6\frac{1}{CAPITAL2_{it}-0.04}+a_7DEBTR_{it}+a_8PROFITSL_{it}$$
$$+a_9LIQAST_{it}+a_{10}LNDAST_{it}+a_{11}LASSET_{it}+a_{12}DCITY_{it}$$
$$+a_{13}DREGION_{it}+a_{14}DINCREASE_{it}+a_{15}DREJECT_{it}$$
$$+\sum_{J=1}^{26}b_JDINDJ_{it}+c_1DYEAR1_{it}+c_2DYEAR2_{it}+u_{it} \quad (4.2)$$

where u_{it}: a white noise error term.

The short-term interest rate equation is similar to (4.2) except that we substitute *GUARANT* by *INTRATE* and add the *GUARANT* variable to the explanatory variables to estimate the effects of personal guarantees on the short-term interest rate.

Estimation Results and Their Implications to Main Bank Relationship

Determinants of Multiple Bank Relationship under Main Bank System

The number of bank relationships takes positive integers, so we apply two estimation models for count data: a Poisson random-effects model where a gamma distribution is assumed for random firm-specific effects and a negative binomial random-effects model wherein it is assumed that the dispersion parameter is a random variable with a beta distribution.[15] We measure the number of bank relations in two different ways. One is the total number of bank relationships (*NBANK*1) including borrowings from non-banks, insurance companies and public financial institutions. The other is the one that excludes public financial institutions (*NBANK*2). Estimation of the number of bank relations including and excluding public financial institutions may yield different results because public financial institutions for SMEs may have business with firms led by different motives.

We first show the estimation results with *NBANK*1 as the number of bank relations. The first column of Table 4.6 shows the results of the Poisson model and the second column shows the results obtained with the negative binomial model. The length of the main bank relation (*MYEAR*) has a positive effect on the number of bank relations and it is significant at the 10% level in the Poisson model. This result can be interpreted in two different ways. In one interpretation the length of a main bank relation is taken as the extent to which the hold-up problem is severe.

[15] See Hausman et al. (1984) and Cameron and Trivedin (1998) for details on the estimation of a count data model in a panel data setting.

Table 4.6 Determinants of multiple bank relationships: estimation results of the poisson random effects model and the negative binomial random effects model

Dependent variable: *NBANK*1		
	Poisson	Negative binomial
Bank-firm relationship variable		
(1) *MYEAR*	0.000075 (1.65)	0.000065 (1.36)
Bank-related variables		
(2) *BADLOAN*	−0.1208 (−0.43)	−0.0970 (−0.33)
(3) $\frac{1}{CAPITAL1 - 0.08}$	0.0021 (3.17)[a]	0.0018 (2.55)[b]
(4) $\frac{1}{CAPITAL2 - 0.04}$	−0.0003 (−0.59)	−0.0002 (−0.41)
(5) *DCITY*	0.2026 (4.42)[a]	0.1729 (3.72)[a]
(6) *DREGION*	0.0184 (0.44)	0.0044 (0.10)
Firm-related variables		
(7) *DEBTR*	0.6136 (10.2)[a]	0.5836 (9.74)[a]
(8) *PROFITSL*	−0.0025 (−0.20)	−0.0032 (−0.25)
(9) *LIQAST*	−0.5744 (−5.34)[a]	−0.5190 (−4.74)[a]
(10) *LNDAST*	−0.0646 (−0.60)	−0.0335 (−0.31)
(11) *LASSET*	0.0869 (9.93)[a]	0.0987 (10.8)[a]
(12) *ALPHA*	0.2503 (24.1)[a]	
(13) *R*		55.6299 (6.31)[a]
(14) *S*		4.5797 (20.7)[a]
(15) Log likelihood	−11,104.96	−11,082.16
(16) Number of observations	4,917	4,917

Notes: *ALPHA* is the variance estimate of the gamma distribution of the exponential random effects. *R* and *S* are the parameters of the beta distribution. The coefficient estimates of constant, year dummies and industry dummies are suppressed. The values in parentheses are t-ratios
[a], [b]: significant at the 1% and 5% level, respectively

The longer the main bank relation is, the more severe the hold-up problem is, so that the main bank extracts a monopoly rent from the affiliated firm. To prevent informational exploitation, the firm increases the number of bank relations. The other interpretation takes the length of a main bank relationship as an indicator of reputation of the firm gained through close monitoring by the main bank. It reveals that the affiliated firm has a good record of business which makes other banks think the firm worth lending to. For the time being we do not have evidence to distinguish between the two interpretations, but we will come back to this point later.

As for the effects of the main bank health on the number of bank relations, the capital ratio of the main bank has a significantly negative effect on the number of bank relations of the affiliated firms, irrespective of the estimation model. It implies that the firm whose main bank has a low capital ratio increases the number of bank relations and that the effect gets larger as the capital ratio approaches to the minimum level. In the late 90s to the early 2000s the capital ratio of Japanese banks deteriorated rapidly and it induced the affiliated firms to diversify liquidity risk by increasing transactions with other banks.

We also have significantly positive effects of the city bank dummy on the number of bank relations. The news that a firm has a tie with a city bank as its main bank sends a signal that the main bank is large enough to bail out the affiliated firm in financial distress backed up by the policy authority, which in turn induces other banks to lend to the firm.

The other variables have an anticipated effect on the number of bank relations. The firm size, measured by the logarithm of total assets, and the debt-asset ratio have significantly positive effects on the number of bank relations, while the ratio of liquid assets to total assets has a significantly negative effects on the number of bank relations.

As for the case with *NBANK*2 as the number of bank relations, the estimation results, which is not shown in the text, remain essentially unaltered. The length of a main bank relation has a positive effect on the number of bank relations and main bank health has a negative effect on the number of bank relations as before.

Impact of Main Bank Relationship on Loan Contracts

To examine the effect of a main bank relation on the terms of loan contracts, we estimate the following two equations. The first relates the main bank relation to the *GUARANT* variable that takes 1 if borrower pledges personal guarantees to its main bank. We apply the probit random-effects model to estimate (4.2).[16] The estimation results of (4.2) are shown in Table 4.7. The first column corresponds to the estimation result with the total number of bank relationships measured by *NBANK*1. All the variables of a main bank relation (*NBANK*, *NYEAR*, *DINFORM*) exert a significant effect on whether firms pledge personal guarantees to their main banks. The firms with longer relations with their main banks and fewer number of bank relations are more likely to pledge personal guarantees. Moreover, the firms disclosing information to their main banks are more likely to pledge personal guarantees. This indicates that a main bank can take a strong stand on the terms of loan contract by making its affiliated firm pledge personal guarantees when the main bank has accumulated information on the client firm in the course of a long relationship and the client firm has fewer banks to rely on. In other words, a main bank extracts monopoly rents from its affiliated firms.

We also obtain interesting findings on the effects of other explanatory variables on whether firms pledge personal guarantees to their main banks. It is more likely that smaller firms with a higher debt-asset ratio pledge personal guarantees to their

[16] For the probit random-effects model, the likelihood is expressed as an integral which is computed using a Gauss–Hermite quadrature.

Table 4.7 Determinants of personal guarantees pledge: estimation results of the probit random effects model

		*NBANK*1	*NBANK*2
Bank-firm relationship variables			
(1)	*MYEAR*	0.00087 (4.90)[a]	0.00085 (4.80)[a]
(2)	*NBANK*1 or *NBANK*2	−0.0183 (−2.11)[b]	−0.0359 (−3.93)[a]
(3)	*DINFORM*	1.3668 (6.83)[a]	1.4310 (6.94)[a]
Bank-related variables			
(4)	*BADLOAN*	−2.7377 (−2.45)[b]	−2.4523 (−2.19)[b]
(5)	$\dfrac{1}{CAPITAL1 - 0.08}$	−0.0025 (−0.94)	−0.0025 (−0.95)
(6)	$\dfrac{1}{CAPITAL2 - 0.04}$	0.0012 (0.88)	0.0011 (0.80)
(7)	*DCITY*	−1.2893 (−6.88)[a]	−1.2409 (−6.66)[a]
(8)	*DREGION*	−0.4656 (−2.75)[a]	−0.4497 (−2.68)[a]
Firm-related variables			
(9)	*DEBTR*	1.9062 (8.72)[a]	1.9292 (8.83)[a]
(10)	*PROFITSL*	0.0529 (0.88)	0.0529 (0.91)
(11)	*LIQAST*	1.5664 (4.04)[a]	1.5429 (3.99)[a]
(12)	*LNDAST*	2.7176 (6.75)[a]	2.6954 (6.71)[a]
(13)	*LASSET*	−0.2126 (−6.02)[a]	−0.2104 (−6.03)[a]
(14)	*DINCREASE*	0.2164 (2.74)[a]	0.2256 (2.85)[a]
(13)	*DREJECT*	0.3671 (2.35)[b]	0.3277 (2.10)[b]
(14)	σ_{u_i}	1.5086 (18.9)[a]	1.4853 (18.7)[a]
(15)	Number of observations	4,888	4,841

Notes: σ_{u_i} is the standard deviation of firm-specific error component. See the notes in Table 4.6 for the other notations

main bank. Smaller banks, such as shinkin banks and credit cooperatives, are more likely to demand personal guarantees to their client firms in loan contracts. The estimation results are essentially unaltered when the total number of bank relationships is measured by *NBANK*2 (the second column of Table 4.7). Note that the coefficient estimate of the total number of bank relations is almost doubled in absolute value. It implies that the firms with fewer numbers of private bank relations are more likely to pledge personal guarantees, which appears consistent with the informational position monopoly by the main bank.

The other equation relates the main bank relation including the *GUARANT* variable to the short-term interest rate charged by the main bank (*INTRATE*). The estimation results are shown in Table 4.8.[17] The first column of Table 4.8 corresponds to the estimation results with the total number of bank relations measured

[17] We apply the random-effects GLS model to the short-term interest rate equation so that it is consistent with the personal guarantee equation.

Table 4.8 Determinants of the short-term interest rate: estimation results of GLS random effects model

	*NBANK*1	*NBANK*2
Bank-firm relationship variables		
(1) *MYEAR*	0.0720 (1.06)	0.0777 (1.13)
(2) *NBANK*1 or *NBANK*2	−4.2441 (−1.36)	−6.9002 (−2.06)[b]
(3) *DINFORM*	176.7622 (1.86)	194.2020 (2.02)[b]
(4) *GUARANT*	165.0629 (5.28)[a]	165.0432 (5.25)[a]
Bank-related variables		
(5) *BADLOAN*	945.0657 (2.40)[b]	937.7299 (2.37)[b]
(6) $\frac{1}{CAPITAL1 - 0.08}$	−1.7653 (−1.86)	−1.7245 (−1.81)
(7) $\frac{1}{CAPITAL2 - 0.04}$	0.1875 (0.40)	0.1884 (0.40)
(8) *DCITY*	−466.1888 (−7.75)[a]	−463.5448 (−7.70)[a]
(9) *DREGION*	−256.6120 (−4.87)[a]	−257.4379 (−4.88)[a]
Firm-related variables		
(10) *DEBTR*	930.7149 (11.7)[a]	928.9016 (11.6)[a]
(11) *PROFITSL*	31.8776 (1.86)	31.7974 (1.85)
(12) *LIQAST*	−119.7744 (−0.84)	−128.4952 (−0.90)
(13) *LNDAST*	222.0394 (1.61)	215.7634 (1.57)
(14) *LASSET*	−153.2928 (−12.0)[a]	−152.2786 (−12.0)[a]
(15) *DINCREASE*	−156.0833 (−5.78)[a]	−159.3143 (−5.86)[a]
(16) *DREJECT*	406.0307 (8.47)[a]	410.0320 (8.51)[a]
(17) σ_{u_i}	585.2917	583.3151
(18) $\sigma_{e_{it}}$	572.4374	574.2528
(19) Number of observations	4,159	4,139

Notes: σ_{u_i} is the standard deviation of firm-specific error component, while $\sigma_{e_{it}}$ is the standard deviation of idiosyncratic error component. See the notes in Table 4.6 for the other notations.

by *NBANK*1. Here we also find that the main bank extracts rents from its affiliated firms in a relatively weak position. That is to say, a main bank charges a higher short-term interest rate on the client firms that disclose their information and pledge personal guarantees to their main bank. The effects of the *DINFORMT* and *GUARANT* variables on the short-term interest rate are also significantly positive when the total number of bank relationships is measured by *NBANK*2, which is shown in the second column of Table 4.8. However the effect of the number of bank relations on the short-term interest rate differs between the two cases. When the number of bank relations is confined to private financial institutions, it has a significantly negative effect on the short-term interest rate. However, once the public financial institutions are taken into consideration, it is no longer significant. This evidence lends further support to our findings that firms face the hold-up problem. It is because public financial institutions are less likely to offer a high interest rate in order to extract monopoly rents, and thus inclusion of public financial institutions in the number of bank relations makes the association of the short-term interest rate with informational monopoly less clear.

Lastly note that the level of the short-term interest rate is also dependent on the firm characteristics as well as bank characteristics. A higher short-term interest rate is charged on a smaller firm with a high debt-asset ratio and high profitability. Smaller banks with a high bad loan ratio tend to charge higher short-term interest rate on their client firms.

Concluding Remarks

In this study we constructed a matched sample of firms and their main banks by combining a unique micro survey of SMEs collected by the Small and Medium Enterprise Agency of Japan with financial statements of firms and banks. Based on the matched sample, we investigated the bank-firm relations of SMEs in the presence of a main bank as dominant lender in the early 2000s when Japanese banks were burdened with massive non-performing loans. We obtain new findings on a bank-firm relation of SMEs. After confirming that SMEs have multiple bank relations even when the firms had their main bank, we examined the determinants of multiple bank relations. Among others, we found that the firms tied with a financially weak main bank increased the number of bank relationships to diversify liquidity risk. We also found that the length of a main bank relationship had positive effects on the number of bank relations. This is interpreted as either the influence of a reputation effect of client firms or firms' counterbalance actions against the monopoly power of main bank. To go further into this issue, we examined the determinants of personal guarantees pledge in loan contracts and the short-term interest rate charged by the main bank. It was found that firms with fewer bank relations that disclosed their private information to their main banks were more likely to pledge personal guarantees to their main bank and were charged a higher short-term interest rate. Our evidence lends support for the prevalence of the hold-up problem and thus we may conclude that main bank extracts rents from their client firms.

It is often argued that relationship banking is important for SMEs. It is true that relationship banking can mitigate asymmetry of information between a main bank and client firms that leads to inefficient loan allocation due to adverse selection and the lemon problem, but we also have to bear in mind that too much concentration of information in one bank creates another hold-up problem and monopoly rents earned by main bank also distorts firms' resource allocation.

Acknowledgements An earlier version of this paper was presented at the seminar of the Research Project on Change in Financial and Industrial Structure of the Research Institute of Economy, Trade and Industry (RIETI), the workshop on Banking of the Centre for Research in Banking, Insurance and Finance (CIBIF) of the University of Groningen, and the Monetary Economics Workshop (MEW). We are grateful to Jan P.A.M. Jacobs and the participants of the seminar and workshop for helpful comments and suggestions. This research was partially supported by Grant-in-Aid for Scientific Research (16330038) from the Japanese Ministry of Education, Culture, Sports, Science and Technology from 2004 to 2006. Any remaining errors are the sole responsibility of the authors.

References

Billett MT, Flannery MJ, Garfinkel JA (1995) The effects of lender identity on a borrowing firmfs equity return. J Finance 50:699–718

Cameron CA, Trivedin PK (1998) Regression analysis of count data. Cambridge University Press, New York

Chemmanur TJ, Fulghieri P (1994) Reputation, renegotiation and the choice between bank loans and publicly traded debt. Rev Financ Stud 7:475–506

Detragiache E, Garella P, Guiso L (2000) Multiple vs. single banking relationships: theory and evidence. J Finance 55:1133–1161

Diamond DW (1984) Financial intermediation and delegated monitoring. Rev Econ Stud 51:393–314

Diamond DW (1991) Monitoring and reputation: the choice between bank loans and privately placed debt. J Polit Econ 99:699–721

Hausman J, Hall BH, Griliches Z (1984) Econometric models for count data with an application to the patents-R&D relationship. Econometrica 52:909–938

Horiuchi A (1993) An empirical overview of the Japanese main bank relationship in relation to firm size Rivista Internationale di Scienze Economiche e Commerciale 40:997–1018

Horiuchi T (1994) The effect of firm status on banking relationships and loan syndication. In: Aoki M, Patrick H (eds) The Japanese main bank system. Oxford University Press, Oxford, pp 258–294

Hoshi T, Kashyap AK, Scharfstein D (1990) The role of banks in reducing the costs of financial distress in Japan. J Financ Econ 27:67–88

Hoshi T, Kashyap AK, Scharfstein D (1991) Corporate structure, liquidity, and investment: evidence from Japanese industrial groups. Q J Econ 106:33–60

Hoshi T, Kashyap AK, Scharfstein D (1993) The choice between public and private debt: an analysis of post-deregulation corporate financing in Japan. NBER Working Paper, 4421

James C (1987) Some evidence on the uniqueness of bank loans. J Financ Econ 19:217–235

Kang J-K, Shivdasani A (1995) Firm performance, corporate governance and top executive turnover in Japan. J Financ Econ 38:29–58

Kang J-K, Shivdasani A (1997) Corporate restructuring during performance declines in Japan. J Financ Econ 46:29–65

Kaplan SN, Minton BA (1994) Appointments of outsiders to Japanese corporate boards: determinants and implications for managers. J Financ Econ 36:225–258

Miyajima H (1998) Sengo Nippon Kigyo niokeru Jyotai Izonteki Governance no Shinka to Henyo – Logit Model niyoru Keieisha Kotai Bunseki karano Approach – (The evolution and change of contingent governance structure in the J-firm system – An approach to presidential turnover and firm performance). Keizai Kenkyu 49:97–112 (in Japanese)

Morck R, Nakamura M (1999) Banks and corporate control in Japan. J Finance 54:319–339

Ogawa K, Sterken E, Tokutsu I (2007) Why do Japanese firms prefer multiple bank relationship? some evidence from firm-level data. Econ Syst 31:49–70

Ongena S, Smith DC (2000a) What determines the number of bank relationships? cross country evidence. J Financ Intermediation 9:26–56

Ongena S, Smith DC (2000b) Bank relationships: a review. In: Harker PT, Zenios SA (eds) Performance of financial institutions: efficiency, innovation, regulation. Cambridge University Press, Cambridge, pp 221–258

Ono A, Uesugi I (2005) The role of collateral and personal guarantees in relationship lending: evidence from Japan's small business loan market. RIETI Discussion Paper Series 05-E-027

Rajan RG (1992) Insiders and outsiders: the choice between informed and arm's length debt. J Finance 47:1367–1400

Sharpe SA (1990) Asymmetric information, bank lending, and implicit contracts: a stylized model of customer relationships. J Finance 45:1069–1087

Sheard P (1994a) Bank executives on Japanese corporate boards. Bank Jpn Monetary Econ Stud 12:85–121

Sheard P (1994b) Main banks and the governance of financial distress. In: Aoki M, Patrick H (eds) The Japanese main bank system. Oxford University Press, Oxford, pp 188–230

Shockley RL, Thakor AV (1998) Bank loan commitment contracts: data, theory, and test. J Money Credit Bank 29:517–534

Uchida H, Udell GF, Watanabe W (2006) Bank size and lending relationships in Japan. RIETI Discussion Paper Series 06-E-029

Volpin PF (2000) Ownership structure, banks, and private benefits of control. IFA Working Paper, London Business School

Weinstein DE, Yafeh Y (1998) On the cost of a bank-centered financial system: evidence from the changing main bank relations in Japan. J Finance 53:635–672

Chapter 5
The Role of Fixed Assets in Reducing Asymmetric Information

Antonio Affuso

Abstract The paper presents a model where fixed assets play a role in reducing credit rationing. The basic idea is that when loans are collateralized and firms are credit constrained, the amount borrowed is generated by the value of the collateral. I use a classical credit rationing model to explain the link between firms' debt capacities and asset value in the case of distress. As we shall see, the price of fixed assets depends on whether there are firms that repurchase them. In fact, it depends on the number of *bad* firms in the economy as well as on the liquidity of *good* firms. In this model, a separating equilibrium can only occur if there exist a number of *bad* firms that go bankrupt and if there exist *good* firms with sufficient liquidity. Each firm derives positive externalities from the existence of other firms. Indeed, the optimal leverage of firms depends on the possibility of repurchasing the distressed assets.

Introduction

In recent years a large and growing number of theories have been proposed to explain credit rationing. Many economists have linked the latter to problems of imperfect information, and my paper thus investigates the role of real assets in reducing asymmetric information.

When loans are collateralized and firms are credit constrained, the amount borrowed is determined by the value of collateral.

I combine a credit rationing model with the idea that firms' debt capacity and investments are linked to the value of assets in the case of distress. In my model the extent of credit rationing is linked to the value of distressed assets, and is thus mitigated by the existence of *bad* firms.

My main contribution is to show how each *good* firm derives positive externalities from the existence of *bad* firms. This is because the optimal leverage of firms depends on the possibility of repurchasing the assets. The liquidated assets may or may not be under-priced, and this depends on the quantity of *bad* firms.

A. Affuso
University of Parma, via Kennedy, 6, 43100-Parma, Italy,
e-mail: antonio.affuso@unimi.it

G. Calcagnini and E. Saltari (eds.), *The Economics of Imperfect Markets*,
Contributions to Economics,
DOI: 10.1007/978-3-7908-2131-4_5,

In my analysis, I endogenize the price of assets, which depends on whether there are firms to repurchase them. It is linked to the number of *bad* firms in the economy as well as to the liquidity of good firms. This implies that a separating equilibrium can only occur in the model if there exist a number of *bad* firms that go bankrupt and if there exist a number of *good* firms with sufficient liquidity.

My model differs from others put forward in the literature and discussed in the next section, because debt overhang originates from the absence of initial cash and not from an agency problem. I investigate what happens if a small firm has to invest without initial cash. The debt overhang here is a consequence of investment and does not depend on decisions by investors who want to prevent the firm from undertaking a negative net present value project.

I consider only projects with a positive net present value, and I assume that assets have value only for other firms in the industry.

Finally, my model also includes financial intermediaries acting as sellers of the assets of failed firms.

The paper is organized as follows: Section Related Literature presents a brief review of the literature, Section Model describes the model, and the last section concludes.

Related Literature

The two seminal works on this subject are those by Jaffee and Russell (1976), who demonstrate how credit rationing arises as a means of market response to adverse selection, and by Stiglitz and Weiss (1981), who show that credit rationing can be an equilibrium phenomenon if either the lender is imperfectly informed about the borrowers, or the lender is unable directly to control the borrowers' behavior. In fact, when the interest rate affects the nature of the transaction, it may not clear the market. Stiglitz and Weiss show that higher interest rates induce firms to undertake projects with lower probabilities of success but higher payoffs when successful.

Hence higher interest rates do not necessarily lead to higher profits when banks have an excess demand for credit. But the interest rate is not the only term in debt contracts. Bester (1985, 1987) shows that no credit rationing will occur in equilibrium if banks compete by choosing collateral requirements and the rate of interest to screen investors' riskiness. Banks may use contracts with different collateral requirements as a self-selection mechanism.

Other authors have developed a theory of collateral linked to the value of assets. There are two main studies in this regard. The first is by Williamson (1988) in which he shows that redeployable assets also have high liquidation value because they are good candidates for debt finance. When assets are managed improperly, the manager will be unable to pay the debt, and creditors will take the assets away from him and redeploy them.

Williamson demonstrates that redeployability is an important determinant of liquidation value and debt capacity. He also shows that if asset specificity becomes high, then asset redeployability becomes low. Williamson does not address the problem of specialized assets. The second main paper is by Shleifer and Vishny (1992), who analyze the price of non-redeployable assets in liquidation relative to their value in best use. They show that a firm in financial distress tends to sell its assets at prices below value in best use. Shleifer and Vishny call this difference between price and value in best use "asset illiquidity." The main reason for asset illiquidity is the general equilibrium aspect of asset sales.

When firms cannot repay the debt and sell assets, the highest-valuation potential buyers are likely to be other firms in the industry. But where these firms are in difficulties themselves, they are unlikely to be able to raise sufficient funds to buy the distressed assets. When industry buyers cannot buy the assets and industry outsiders face significant costs in acquiring and managing the assets, assets in liquidation fetch prices below their value in best use.

In Kiyotaki and Moore (1995), durable assets also serve as collateral for loans. Kiyotaki and Moore show that borrowers' credit limits are affected by the prices of the collateralized assets, and that these prices are affected by the size of the credit limits in turn. The idea is that bad times for the economy are times when the liquidation value of collateral is low, since the potential buyers of these assets are constrained. This leads to low debt capacity, which further reinforces the bad times, causing collateral values to fall, and so on. Kiyotaki and Moore describe this as a collateral amplification mechanism.

Araujo and Minetti (2003) propose a theory in which financial intermediaries operate as an internal market for corporate assets. But intermediaries can perform their role as internal markets for assets only if they have written debt contracts that enable them to repossess assets if a firm defaults. Debt, however, has a cost in capital reallocation, because distressed firms are the best users of assets.

Model

The model has three periods, 0, 1, and 2. There are banks and firms. Each firm is one of two types, *good* or *bad*, which are represented in the economy in proportions q and $(1-q)$.

There are two possible states of the world – prosperity p with probability $0 < s < 1$ and depression d with probability $(1\text{-}s)$ – and uncertainty about the state is resolved in period 1.

At initial date 0, firms want to invest a fixed amount I in a project that generates future cash flow y in each of the two subsequent periods. No firm has liquid funds, but each firm owns an amount A of collateralizable wealth, where A cannot be used to finance investment directly because it consists of illiquid assets. Hence, the firm must borrow the entire amount I by issuing debt in period 0. This generates the *debt overhang* for firms in period 1.

The cash flows from the investment are y_{tj}^{i}, where $t = 1, 2; i = p, d; j = G, B$. The subscripts t and j indicate the period and the type of firm (*Good* or *Bad*), the superscript i indicates the state of the world, p (prosperity), and d (depression). I assume that the cash flow is constant across periods:

$$y_{1j}^{i} = y_{2j}^{i} \tag{5.1}$$

and that

$$y_{tG}^{d} = y_{tG}^{p} = y_{tB}^{p} = y > y_{1B}^{d} = 0 \tag{5.2}$$

which means that *good* firms are always able to generate y from the investment, whereas *bad* firms can do this only in prosperity.

All firms have access to the same technology. The only difference between the two types is that they have different levels of "capability" to generate revenue in depression.

I assume that the Net Present Value of the project is positive even for bad firms:

$$sy - I \geq 0 \tag{5.3}$$

The financial sector consists of many intermediaries in competition, like firms. Lenders decide the contract terms at date 0. Entrepreneurs borrow I at date 0 and promise to repay R at date 1.

In period 1 each firm has to repay its debt, which is a necessary condition to reach period 2. R can be seen as a cost that the entrepreneur pays to move into period 2.

I assume that in prosperity all firms can pay R, whereas in depression only *good* firms can. All firms are the same size but they have different levels of "capability." In the model, q are *bad* firms because they do not repay debt in depression:

$$y_{1B}^{d} = 0 \tag{5.4}$$

and $(1 - q)$ are *good* firms and have a positive cash flow even in depression:

$$y > 0 \tag{5.5}$$

The ability to pay debt is a signal for banks, because although they have no opportunity to observe capabilities, they can observe which firms fail. They can thus decide whether or not assets have to be liquidated. The liquidated assets are resold on the market and are bought by firms with sufficient liquidity.

Good firms expect an additional cash flow $y_j = y_{tj}^{i} = y$ if they purchase the distressed assets. So, if the asset value is pA, the condition for firms to be willing to purchase assets is:

$$y - pA \geq 0 \tag{5.6}$$

from which we obtain the equilibrium price of assets if there is competition between firms:

$$p^c = \frac{y}{A} \tag{5.7}$$

For lenders, the return on the loan depends on different firms' capabilities. Their expected return is:

$$E(b) = s[qR + (1-q)R] + (1-s)(1-q)R \tag{5.8}$$

if $R \leq y$.

Indeed, in prosperity, banks will obtain the payment of the debt from all firms:

$$[qR + (1-q)R] = R \tag{5.9}$$

In depression, the amount will depend on the distribution of abilities, so that only *good* firms repay debt:

$$(1-q)R \tag{5.10}$$

The assets of failed firms are resold on the market. The value of these assets depends on whether there are other firms in the industry standing by to repurchase the assets in case of distress. In my model I consider industry-wide shocks, but some firms are hit harder than others and this depends on capabilities. Hence the asset value depends on liquidity of *good* firms in period 1.

Following Shleifer and Vishny (1992), I do not allow renegotiation of the firm's debt contract once the state of the world has been revealed and the purchase opportunity has become available. This assumption implies that good firms cannot obtain new loans in period 1 to buy distressed assets.

Debt overhang precludes the firm from raising capital, so that the necessary condition in order for firms to be able to purchase the distressed assets is:

$$y - R \geq pA \tag{5.11}$$

The price above which there is no market is thus:

$$\bar{p} = \frac{y-R}{A} \tag{5.12}$$

Remark. If there is a perfectly efficient market, $pA = y$ and 5.11 is never satisfied.

The overall liquidity surplus will be:

$$(1-q)(y-R) \tag{5.13}$$

hence, the quantity of demanded assets will be:

$$A^D = \begin{cases} \frac{(1-q)(y-R)}{p} & \text{if } p \le \frac{y-R}{A} \\ 0 & \text{if } p > \frac{y-R}{A} \end{cases}$$

and the quantity of sold assets will be:

$$A^S = qA \tag{5.14}$$

which depends not on price, but on the number of failed firms. Consequently, in equilibrium we have:

$$\frac{(1-q)(y-R)}{p} = qA \tag{5.15}$$

from which:

$$\hat{p} = \frac{(1-q)(y-R)}{qA} \tag{5.16}$$

If $\hat{p} > \bar{p}$, *good* firms do not buy distressed assets because the cost is too high. Thus we have a market if and only if:

$$y - R \ge \hat{p}A \tag{5.17}$$

From which we can obtain $q*$, the proportion of *bad* firms under which there is no assets market:

$$q* = \frac{1}{2} \tag{5.18}$$

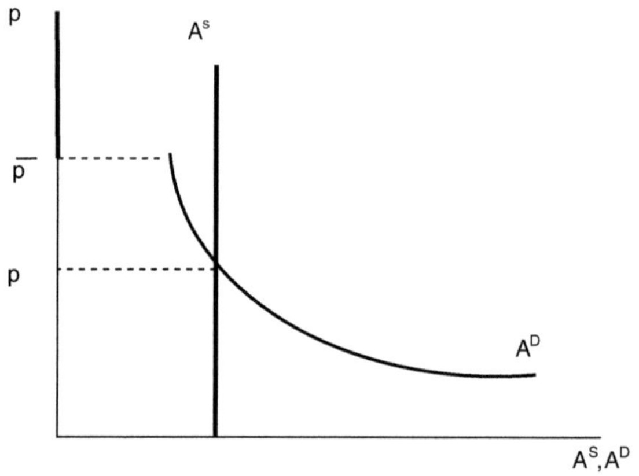

Fig. 5.1 The equilibrium

Graphically (Fig. 5.1): At the level $\hat{p}$ the quantity of demanded assets is:

$$A^D = (1 - q)A \tag{5.19}$$

When $q < \frac{1}{2}$ there is no equilibrium in the market because $A^D > A^S$

Without Collateral

This section discusses the benchmark case where contracts do not require collateral.

The firm will pay *R* if the investment return is positive, *0* otherwise.

If the bank knows the type of firm, it can ask for two different levels of *R*, the amount of debt if the investment is successful. These different levels result from the number of firms of the different types and from the probability of depression. For *bad* firms, because the probability that *R* will be paid is lower and this depends on the probability of prosperity, we have:

$$R_B = \frac{I}{s} \tag{5.20}$$

For *good* firms, *R* will be:

$$R_G = I \tag{5.21}$$

So, $R_G \leq R_B$.

But lenders cannot distinguish the type of firm that benefit from loan. They only know that there are $(1 - q)$ solvent firms and q insolvent firms. Consequently they offer only one contract that provides a single *R*, and they decide whether to finance all or nothing. They will finance all firms if:

$$[sq + s(1 - q) + (1 - s)(1 - q)]R \geq I \tag{5.22}$$

But perfect competition in the loans market drives the interest rate down, so that condition 5.22 holds with equality in equilibrium:

$$[sq + s(1 - q) + (1 - s)(1 - q)]R = I \tag{5.23}$$

from which we can calculate R^{NC}, (no collateral):

$$R^{NC} = \frac{I}{[s + (1 - s)(1 - q)]} \tag{5.24}$$

With Collateral

In this section I assume that banks require some type of collateral on loans. The aim is to induce the *good* firms to signal their quality. The lender may request initial assets as collateral, and if a firm does not repay R, the bank can resell those assets on the market. The collateral thus consists of the assets of the firm at date 0, when it applies for a loan. The firm loses A when it goes bankrupt and offers collateral to the bank but if it does not sign the contract with collateral requirement, it can sell its assets on the market, although it incurs a private cost $0 \leq \delta < 1$. The idea is that if *bad* firms resell their assets on the market directly, they do not obtain the entire value, because they sustain costs. The smaller δ is, the greater costs are.

Good firms will supply collateral, because their failure probability is 0. The bank's expected payoff from financing a *good* firm is the same as without collateral:

$$sR + (1 - s)R \tag{5.25}$$

The expected payoff of *good* firms is not the same as without collateral because they can now buy distressed assets either directly from failed firms or from banks. I assume that the acquiring firm is indifferent between buying assets directly or from the bank. *Bad* firms have an incentive to obtain a contract aimed at *good* firms in cases where the payoff for bad firms is greater, even though they have to provide collateral. I suppose that banks offer two distinct contracts, (R_G, pA) and $(R_B, 0)$, in an attempt to separate the types. This pair of contracts must satisfy these incentive compatibility and individual rationality constraints:

$(IC.G)$
$$s(Y - R_G) + (1 - s)(Y - R_G + y - pA) \geq s(Y - R_B) + (1 - s)(Y - R_B + y - pA)$$

$(IR.G)$
$$sR_G + (1 - s)R_G \geq I$$

$(IC.B)$
$$s(Y - R_G) - (1 - s)pA \leq s(Y - R_B) + (1 - s)\delta pA$$

$(IR.B)$ $\quad sR_B \geq I$ s *IR.G* and *IR.B* are satisfied with equality on the hypothesis of perfect competition in the credit market. *IC.B* is also satisfied with equality. But assume thet *IC.B* is not satisfied with equality. The bank can obviously increase returns to *good* firms by reducing R_G. The original situation was thus not profit maximizing.

This system has solutions:

$$R_G = I \tag{5.26}$$

$$R_B = \frac{I}{s} \tag{5.27}$$

$$pA = \frac{I}{(1 + \delta)} \tag{5.28}$$

pA is the minimum value of the collateral in order for it to be effective. But because it is determined endogenously, we must calculate the minimum price under which the collateral does not work. This price is:

$$p* = \frac{I}{(1+\delta)A} \tag{5.29}$$

The higher the ratio I/A, the greater $p*$ becomes because the ratio I/A shows the risk for the lender. Moreover, $p*$ depends on the private cost that firms incur in selling assets. If δ rises, the *bad* firms have more opportunity to pretend to be good. $p*$ is the lower bound of the separating equilibrium area. If:

$$\hat{p} < p* = \frac{I}{(1+\delta)A} \tag{5.30}$$

this means that the price in the assets market is below the lower bound, so that the collateral requirement is not sufficient to separate the types and *bad* firms have an incentive to pretend. Under all the same conditions, the price $\hat{p}$ will decrease if the number of *bad* firms increase. Consequently, the greater q is, the greater the probability that *bad* firms will pretend.

Proposition 1. *If the asset price is too low, no separating equilibrium exists.*

Proof. Suppose that this is the case. Hence the lender offers two contracts, $C_1 = (R_G, \hat{p}A)$ and $C_2 = (R_B, 0)$, but because $\hat{p} < p*$, *bad* firms also want C_1. In this case, *IC.B* is not satisfied and all firms sign C_1.

If the value of the assets is so low that it does not offset the advantage of pretending, the requirement for collateral is not sufficient to have a separating equilibrium.

It is not possible to have the separating equilibrium even if:

$$p > \bar{p} = \frac{y-R}{A} \tag{5.31}$$

In fact, because $\bar{p}$ is the upper bound of the separating equilibrium area, if $p > \bar{p}$, $A^D(p) = 0$. So the requirement of collateral is not sufficient to produce a separating equilibrium.

Proposition 2. *If the asset price is too high, the separating equilibrium exists only for* $pA = \bar{p}A$

Proof. If the lender offers two contracts, $C_1 = (R_G, pA)$ and $C_2 = (R_B, 0)$, because $p > \bar{p}$, the assets market does not exist and $C_1 = C_2$.

But because at $p = \bar{p}$ we have $A^D > A^S$, the lender can always sell the assets at $\bar{p}$. It consequently offers two contracts $C_1 = (R_G, \bar{p}A)$ and $C_2 = (R_B, 0)$

The necessary condition for the separating equilibrium to come about is that $p* < p \leq \bar{p}$. See also Fig. 5.2

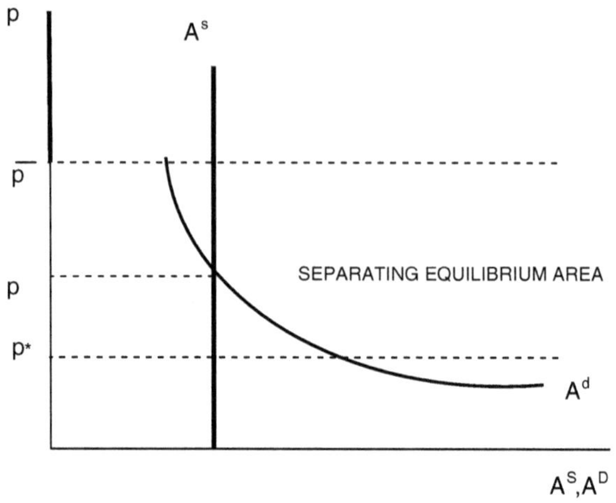

Fig. 5.2 Separating equilibrium with collateral

When the collateral is not sufficient to achieve the separating equilibrium, banks offer only one contract without collateral, such that:

$$sR + (1 - s)(1 - q)R = I \tag{5.32}$$

from which:

$$R = R^{NC} = \frac{I}{[s + (1 - s)(1 - q)]} \tag{5.33}$$

Good firms pay more with this contract if:

$$R > R_G \tag{5.34}$$

that is:

$$\frac{I}{[s + (1 - s)(1 - q)]} > I \tag{5.35}$$

which is $\forall q > 0$. This shows that *good* firms always pay more if banks do not separate. But with this contract, *bad* firms pay less and *good* firms pay more than when there are two different contracts. As in the original Jaffee and Russell (1976), and Stiglitz and Weiss (1981) papers, *good* firms subsidize *bad* firms.

If the number of *bad* firms compared to the number of *good* firms increases, this reduces the liquidity of the system and increases the supply of assets. The combination of these two effects reduces the asset price. If $\hat{p}$ is less than $\bar{p}$, the existence of a market for distressed assets is guaranteed, but there is no guarantee that the demand for collateral is effective. In fact, if q increases to the extent that the price falls below $p*$, the collateral is useless (Fig. 5.3).

In order for a separating equilibrium to exist, there must be a number of *bad* firms in the system. The existence of inefficient firms has positive externalities because it helps to create the assets market and to create a more efficient equilibrium.

If δ decreases, the cost that *bad* firms must pay in order to resell their assets if they go bankrupt increases. So *bad* firms have a greater incentive to demand the same contract as *good* firms. If $\hat{p}$ is smaller than $p*$, the price is not sufficient to compensate *bad* firms for choosing their contract. If private costs are high, it is more likely that the separating equilibrium does not exist (Fig. 5.4).

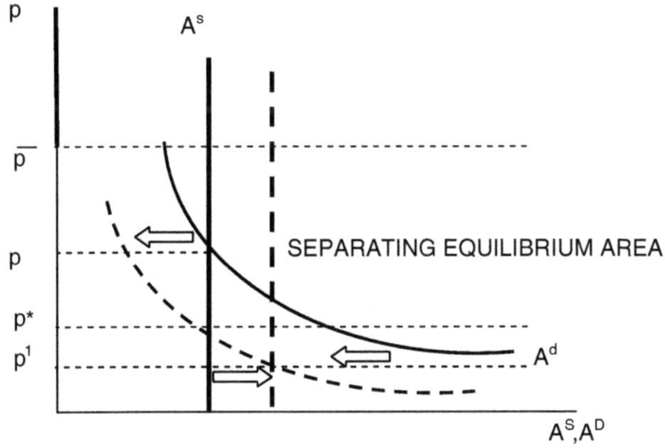

Fig. 5.3 Effectiveness of collateral

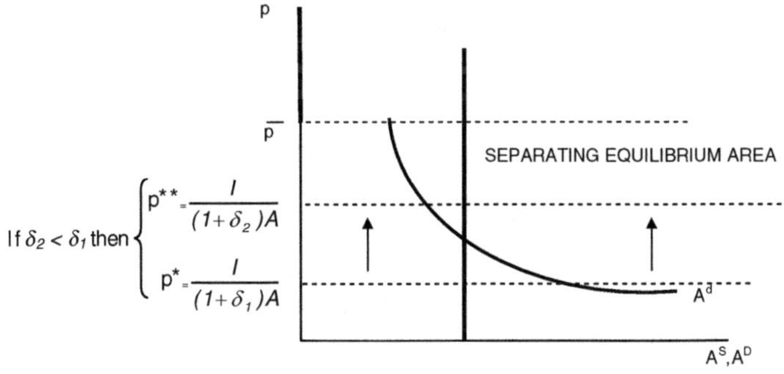

Fig. 5.4 Effectiveness of collateral and reselling costs

Conclusion

I have developed a credit rationing model with adverse selection in which optimal debt levels depend on asset price determined on the second hand market. In the model, the assets can be redeployable (Williamson 1988) or not; their second hand value in fact depends on the number of other firms. In particular, assets are bought exclusively by firms in the industry and not by outsiders. Firms are divided into two groups: *good* firms which are able to earn sufficient cash flow to repay the debt and to invest in distressed assets, even in bad times; and *bad* firms, which fail if there is a depression. This is a model in which financial intermediaries act as internal markets for assets. In fact, if a *bad* firm signs a contract with collateral requirement, when it fails, it leaves its assets to the bank and the bank resells the assets on the market. Using this model, I have shown that the existence of the separating equilibrium depends on the asset price. If the asset price is too low on the market, the only possible equilibrium is a pooling equilibrium. I have shown that *good* firms can enjoy positive externalities from the existence of *bad* firms, because for a certain number of *bad* firms it is possible for a more efficient equilibrium to come about. Nevertheless, if the number of *bad* firms increases over a certain threshold, no separating equilibrium is possible. In this model, when firms go bankrupt, if they have not offered guarantees to the bank, they can resell their assets on the market. But they cannot obtain the entire value of their assets, because they must pay some costs. I have shown that if these costs increase, the incentive to bad firms to pretend to be *good* also increases. Hence, it is more probable that there is no separating equilibrium.

References

Araujo L, Minetti R (2003) Banks as markets for firm assets, vol 25. Michigan State University, Working Paper

Bester H (1985) Screening vs. rationing in credit markets with imperfect information. Am Econ Rev 75(4):850–855

Bester H (1987) The role of collateral in credit market with imperfect information. Eur Econ Rev 31(4):887–889

Jaffee DM, Russell T (1976) Imperfect information, uncertainty, and credit rationing. Q J Econ 90(4):651–666

Kiyotaki N, Moore J (1995) Credit cycle. NBER, Working Paper 5083

Shleifer A, Vishny RW (1992) Liquidation value and debt capacity: a market equilibrium approach. J Finance 47(4):1343–1366

Stiglitz JE, Weiss A (1981) Credit rationing in markets with imperfect information. Am Econ Rev 70(3):393–410

Williamson OE (1988) Corporate finance and corporate governance. J Finance 43(3):567–591

Chapter 6
Financial Development and Long-Run Growth: Cross-Sectional Evidence Revised

Corrado Andini

Abstract In a seminal article, Levine et al. (2000) provide cross-sectional evidence showing that financial development has positive average impact on long-run growth, using a sample of 71 countries. We argue that the evidence is sensitive to the presence of outliers.

Introduction

The effect of financial development on long-run GDP growth is a long-memory controversial issue in economics. As noted by Levine (2003), the issue seems to divide economists in two groups. On the one side, there are those who argue, following Schumpeter (1912), that financial development accelerates growth. On the other side, there are those who maintain, following Robinson (1952), that financial development simply follows growth. The same type of disagreement seems to divide the opinions of two recent Nobel laureates. Indeed, while Miller (1998) considers that "financial markets contribute to economic growth in a proportion that is almost too obvious for serious discussion", Lucas (1988) points out that "the importance of financial matters is very badly over-stressed".

This brief introduction helps to show that the topic of the link between finance and growth is mainly an empirical issue related to the estimation of the causal impact of financial development on real growth. In this manuscript, we focus on the cross-sectional evidence provided by Levine et al. (2000).

Using indicator-variables on the legal origin of the countries in their sample as reported by La Porta et al. (1998), Levine et al. (2000) measure the causal impact of financial development on the mean of the conditional growth distribution, finding evidence of positive impact. Although the authors perform an outliers' sensitivity analysis and argue in favour of the robustness of their results, Levine et al. (2000) do not use a median-regression technique to identify potential outliers. We do exactly the latter and find that the mean-based results provided by Levine et al. (2000) are not entirely robust to the presence of outliers.

C. Andini
Universidade da Madeira, Portugal CEEAplA, Portugal, IZA, Germany
e-mail: andini@uma.pt

G. Calcagnini and E. Saltari (eds.), *The Economics of Imperfect Markets*, Contributions to Economics,
DOI: 10.1007/978-3-7908-2131-4_6,

Empirical strategy

The data-set explored in this paper can be downloaded from the website of Ross Levine, at: http://www.econ.brown.edu/fac/Ross_Levine/IndexLevine.htm. The sample descriptive statistics are reported by Levine et al. (2000, p. 68)[1]. The sample has a cross-sectional dimension and contains detailed information on 71 countries over the 1960–1995 period.

Levine et al. (2000, henceforth LLB) use three indicators of financial development: PRIVATE CREDIT, i.e. credit by deposit money banks and other financial institutions to private sector divided by GDP; COMMERCIAL-CENTRAL BANK, i.e. assets of deposit money banks divided by assets of deposit money banks plus central bank assets; and finally LIQUID LIABILITIES, i.e. liquid liabilities of the financial system (currency plus demand and interest-bearing liabilities of banks and non-banks financial intermediaries) divided by GDP.

LLB distinguish among three types of conditioning sets: the simple conditioning set, including the average number of schooling years in 1960 and the level of GDP in 1960; the policy conditioning set, which extends the simple conditioning set by considering measures of government size, inflation, black market premium, openness of trade; and the full conditioning set which, in turn, extends the policy conditioning set by adding indicators of revolutions and coups, political assassinations, and ethnic diversity.

Using the generalized method of moments (GMM), LLB estimate an empirical model of the following type:

$$G_i = \beta_0 + \beta_1 F_{ji} + \beta_2 X_{hi} + e_i \tag{6.1}$$

where G represents the average growth rate of real GDP per-capita in country $i = 1, \ldots, 71$ from 1960 to 1995, F is an indicator of financial development of type j (one of the three previously described indicators), X is a conditioning set of type h (one of the three previously described conditioning sets), and β_1 is the main parameter of interest.

The first-stage regression results are based on a regression model of the following type:

$$F_{ji} = \alpha_0 + \alpha_1 Z_i + \alpha_2 X_{hi} + u_i \tag{6.2}$$

where Z is a set of legal-origin dummies playing the role of instrumental variables for financial development (the Scandinavian origin is the excluded category).

To re-evaluate the empirical findings by LLB, we first try to replicate their results using a two-step efficient GMM estimator. Afterwards, we look for potential outliers by using a median-regression technique. Specifically, we keep the issue of the endogeneity of F into account by implementing the procedure suggested by Arias et al. (2001), which is an instrumental-variable technique for quantile regression (IVQR) and consists of two stages. In the first stage, we run an ordinary-least-squares

[1] We perfectly replicate the sample descriptive statistics.

estimation of model (2) and obtain predicted values of F which are used for replacing actual values of F in model (1). In the second stage, we run a quantile-regression estimation of model (1), using the quantile-regression estimator of Koenker and Bassett (1978). Since our interest is the median impact, we focus on the fifth decile (IVQR5).

Note that the quantile-regression estimator of Koenker and Bassett (1978) is highly robust to the presence of extreme values of the dependent variable (Buchinsky, 1994, p. 411). As we will see in the next section, this feature turns out to be useful for the identification of potential outliers. Further, note that, by running (in the second stage) a simple ordinary-least-squares estimation of model (1) rather than a quantile regression, one obtains a standard two-stage-least-squares (2SLS) estimate of β_1, measuring the mean impact of F on G. We present both IVQR5 and 2SLS estimates.

Estimation Results

First of all, it is worth stressing that we are able to perfectly replicate the findings of LLB on p. 43, related to model (2).

Table 6.1 presents our main estimation results, related to model (1). The first four columns compare the GMM estimates provided by LLB, and reported in Column 1, with our GMM (replication exercise), 2SLS and IVQR5 estimates. The last four columns focus on the outliers' sensitivity analysis, performed using the GMM estimator.

Column 2 vs. Column 1

Unlike model (2), we are not able to perfectly replicate the GMM results[2] reported by LLB on p. 46. However, the only relevant difference concerns with the coefficient of the variable COMMERCIAL-CENTRAL BANK (say CCB), in the group of results that are related to the policy conditioning set. Specifically, LLB claim that the coefficient of CCB is statistically significant at 5% level while we find that this coefficient is not statistically significant (p-value 0.160). Nevertheless, as one can see by comparing Column 1 and Column 2, our replication exercise confirms the results presented by LLB.

---

[2] As already mentioned, we use a two-step efficient GMM estimator, selected (among the existing types of GMM estimators) for being the one that, after repeated replication attempts, provides the closest estimates to those presented by LLB. It is worth stressing that LLB do not clearly report which type of GMM estimator is used in their cross-sectional analysis.

Table 6.1 The impact of financial development on growth

	(1) GMM LLB	(2) GMM Replication	(3) 2SLS	(4) IVQR5	(5) GMM without Korea, Malta and Taiwan	(6) GMM without Zaire and Niger	(7) GMM without Korea	(8) GMM without Korea and Malta
Simple conditioning set								
PRIVATE CREDIT	2.515 (0.003)	2.515 (0.004)	2.472 (0.007)	2.576 (0.001)	1.023 (0.118)	2.478 (0.003)	2.088 (0.027)	2.070 (0.034)
COMMERCIAL–CENTRAL BANK	10.861 (0.001)	9.954 (0.003)	8.446 (0.011)	7.986 (0.021)	4.785 (0.097)	9.818 (0.004)	7.552 (0.014)	7.436 (0.020)
LIQUID LIABILITIES	1.723 (0.045)	1.844 (0.041)	2.507 (0.014)	1.973 (0.101)	1.046 (0.127)	1.394 (0.110)	1.633 (0.046)	1.608 (0.067)
Policy conditioning set								
PRIVATE CREDIT	3.222 (0.012)	3.364 (0.037)	3.400 (0.040)	2.871 (0.074)	1.168 (0.439)	3.274 (0.028)	3.011 (0.139)	2.943 (0.164)
COMMERCIAL–CENTRAL BANK	9.641 (0.021)	10.627 (0.160)	12.906 (0.040)	11.180 (0.401)	3.542 (0.483)	12.792 (0.054)	5.135 (0.382)	4.397 (0.461)
LIQUID LIABILITIES	2.173 (0.020)	1.934 (0.063)	2.869 (0.029)	2.290 (0.369)	1.120 (0.251)	1.718 (0.101)	1.817 (0.070)	1.820 (0.088)
Full conditioning set								
PRIVATE CREDIT	3.356 (0.005)	3.462 (0.020)	3.386 (0.013)	1.934 (0.139)	1.492 (0.265)	3.140 (0.024)	3.390 (0.076)	3.329 (0.094)
COMMERCIAL–CENTRAL BANK	11.289 (0.001)	12.971 (0.057)	14.878 (0.009)	8.673 (0.320)	8.581 (0.363)	11.132 (0.026)	12.964 (0.168)	12.427 (0.192)
LIQUID LIABILITIES	2.788 (0.003)	2.648 (0.010)	3.232 (0.006)	2.812 (0.024)	1.404 (0.124)	2.155 (0.033)	2.319 (0.016)	2.337 (0.027)

P-values of t-statistics in parentheses

Column 3 vs. Column 1

Interestingly, we find that the 2SLS estimates, focusing on the impact of F on the conditional mean of G (likewise the GMM estimator), are consistent with the GMM findings obtained by LLB, even for the above-referred case of the CCB coefficient.

Column 4 vs. Column 1

In contrast to the GMM and 2SLS findings, the IVQR5 estimation provides a different picture of the causal nexus between financial development and growth. Particularly, six out of the nine estimated coefficients are not statistically significant at 5% level[3], thus suggesting that the median impact of financial development on growth is doubtful.

In addition, the results on the median impact seem to be at odds with the evidence on the mean impact provided by LLB (and confirmed by our replication analysis). Particularly, since our median-based estimator is not sensitive to the presence of extreme values of the dependent variable, the natural step onwards consists of checking whether the mean-based results by LLB are driven by the existence of countries with extreme values of growth.

Column 5 vs. Column 1

We test the extreme-values' hypothesis by running a two-step efficient GMM estimation of model (1) and using a sample that excludes those countries whose growth rates are higher than 6%, as suggested by the box-plot in Fig. 6.1. These countries are Korea, Malta and Taiwan (the box-plot seems to indicate that there are only two very high-growth countries, but they are actually three because two points are overlapping; see Table 6.2). Specifically, the fifth column in Table 6.1 reports that none out of the nine estimated coefficients is statistically significant at 5% level, with only one being significant at 10% level. All the coefficients have the expected positive sign but their magnitude is lower than suggested by LLB. Therefore, the cross-sectional evidence on the average positive impact of financial development on real GDP growth disappears if three very high-growth countries are removed from the LLB sample.

Column 6 vs. Column 1

Since Fig. 6.1 also indicates the existence of two (overlapping) extremely-low values of growth (see Table 6.2), we perform a further GMM estimation by excluding

[3] The standard errors are bootstrapped.

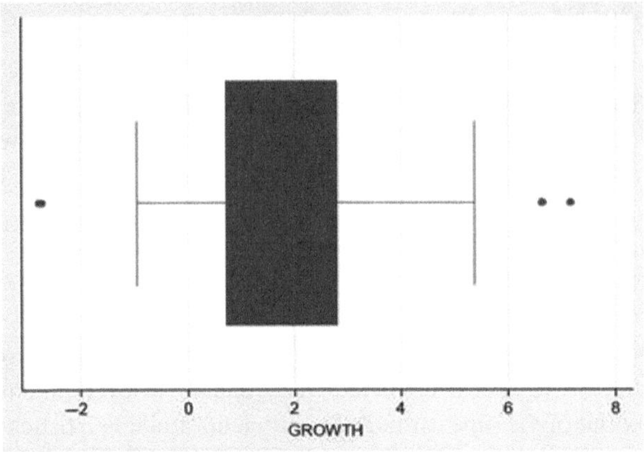

Fig. 6.1 Box-plot of the growth distribution

those countries whose growth rates are lower than −2%, i.e. Zaire and Niger. In this case, however, the estimation results, presented in the sixth column of Table 6.1, are roughly consistent with those proposed by LLB.

Column 7 vs. Column 1

As an additional robustness check, to deeper inspect the results presented in Column 5, we run a GMM estimation using a sample that excludes the country with the highest growth rate, i.e. Korea. The seventh column in Table 6.1 shows that the cross-sectional evidence on the causality between finance and growth becomes mixed. On the one hand, the results based on the simple conditioning set are in line with those provided by LLB. On the other hand, if the conditioning set is extended (see policy and full conditioning), the results point against a causal positive average impact of financial development on growth because only one out of six coefficients is significant at 5% level.

Column 8 vs. Column 1

As a final check, we perform a further GMM estimation using a sample that excludes the two countries with the highest growth rates, i.e. Korea and Malta. Again, the results point against the LLB findings because only three out of nine coefficients are found to be significant at 5% level. The results are very similar to those obtained when just Korea is removed from the sample (Column 7).

Table 6.2 Average growth rate of real GDP per capita, 1960–1995

Korea (Republic of)	7.16	Mexico	1.97
Malta	6.65	Kenya	1.96
Taiwan (China)	6.62	United Kingdom	1.96
Cyprus	5.38	India	1.92
Thailand	4.88	Sweden	1.89
Japan	4.30	Fiji	1.85
Malaysia	4.11	United States	1.71
Portugal	3.65	Costa Rica	1.61
Ireland	3.25	Chile	1.45
Greece	3.22	Switzerland	1.42
Norway	3.18	Philippines	1.16
Mauritius	3.02	New Zealand	1.12
Iceland	3.01	Trinidad and Tobago	1.12
Italy	2.93	Papua New Guinea	1.12
Brazil	2.93	Uruguay	1.03
Austria	2.89	Guatemala	0.93
Spain	2.88	Zimbabwe	0.84
Israel	2.81	Nepal	0.77
Finland	2.80	Bangladesh	0.71
Sri Lanka	2.70	Argentina	0.62
Pakistan	2.70	Honduras	0.60
Barbados	2.65	Togo	0.46
Belgium	2.65	Jamaica	0.42
Syrian Arab Republic	2.51	South Africa	0.39
Dominican Republic	2.50	Bolivia	0.36
Germany	2.45	Peru	0.06
France	2.43	Guyana	−0.28
Ecuador	2.39	Sierra Leone	−0.34
Canada	2.39	Senegal	−0.44
Paraguay	2.38	Liberia	−0.47
Colombia	2.23	El Salvador	−0.61
Netherlands	2.20	Haiti	−0.66
Denmark	2.18	Venezuela	−0.88
Panama	2.03	Ghana	−0.96
Australia	1.98	Niger	−2.75
		Zaire	−2.81

Conclusions

This paper provides four main results. First, the cross-sectional evidence due to LLB is replicable. Second, there is preliminary evidence that financial development does not affect the median of the conditional long-run growth distribution. Third, if three very high-growth countries are removed from the LLB sample (Korea, Malta and Taiwan), the evidence that financial development has average positive causal effect on growth disappears. Fourth, if the country with the highest growth rate is removed from the sample (Korea), the evidence becomes mixed. Summing up, the cross-sectional results provided by LLB are sensitive to the presence of outliers (with Korea playing a fundamental role).

Acknowledgements Financial support from the FCT-Portugal is gratefully acknowledged. For useful comments and discussions, the author would like to thank Monica Andini, Santiago Budría, Ricardo Cabral, Günther Lang, Marco Pagano, Pedro Telhado Pereira, and the participants at "The Economics of Imperfect Markets" conference (Rome, 16–17 May 2008). The usual disclaimer applies.

References

Arias O, Hallock KF, and Sosa-Escudero W (2001) Individual Heterogeneity in the Returns to Schooling: Instrumental Variables Quantile Regression Using Twins Data. Empir Econ 26:7–40

Buchinsky M (1994) Changes in the U.S. Wage Structure 1963–1987: Application of Quantile Regression. Econometrica 62:405–458

Koenker R, and Bassett G (1978) Regression Quantiles. Econometrica 46:33–50

La Porta R, Lopez de Silanes F, Shleifer A et al. (1998) Law and Finance. J Polit Econ 106:1113–1155

Levine R (2003) More on Finance and Growth: More Finance, More Growth? Federal Reserve Bank of St. Luis Review 85:31–46

Levine R, Loayza N, and Beck T (2000) Financial Intermediation and Growth: Causality and Causes. J Monetary Econ 46:31–77

Lucas RE Jr (1988) On the Mechanics of Economic Development. J Monetary Econ 22:3–42

Miller MH (1998) Financial Markets and Economic Growth. J Appl Corporate Finance 11:8–15

Robinson J (1952) The Interest Rate and Other Essays. Macmillan, London

Schumpeter J (1912) Theorie der Wirtschaftlichen Entwicklung. Duncker & Humblot, Leipzig

Part II
Imperfections in Real Markets

Chapter 7
Investment, Productivity and Employment in the Italian Economy

Enrico Saltari, Giuseppe Travaglini, and Clifford R. Wymer

Abstract This paper analyzes the effect of institutional structure, regulations, technological progress, and labor market flexibility on productivity in the Italian economy within the framework of the representative agent model of Saltari and Travaglini (2007). The core model is shown to be too restrictive to provide a good representation of the Italian economy. Broadening the view of the way in which firms take account of the costs of changing the labor force and investment achieves a more satisfactory representation of the dynamics of the productive sector of the economy while still retaining the spirit of the core model. Institutional or market structures, regulations, and other factors are incorporated in the system through modifications to the production function, the demand and supply functions for labor. A full-information, Gaussian estimator of a differential equation system is used throughout. As the constraints on the system arise from both macro-economic theory and the institutional structure of the Italian economy, this estimator provides a much more stringent test of all the hypotheses embedded in the model than many other studies. The model provides a foundation for a study of the extent to which, over time, changes in regulations or market structure might allow firms to reallocate resources to take better advantage of the skills available in the labor force within the context of a segmented labor market with varying efficiencies. The model lends itself to a policy analysis of the effects of these changes on the workings of the labor market as the ease with which firms may change their labor force determine

E. Saltari
Department of Public Economics, Sapienza, University of Rome, Rome, Italy,
e-mail: Enrico.Saltari@uniroma1.it

G. Travaglini
Department of Economics and Quantitative Methods, Università di Urbino "Carlo Bo", Via Saffi 42, Italy,
e-mail: giuseppe.travaglini@uniurb.it

C. R. Wymer
Visiting Professor at the Department of Public Economics, Sapienza, University of Rome, Rome, Italy,
e-mail: wymer@mail.com

G. Calcagnini and E. Saltari (eds.), *The Economics of Imperfect Markets*, Contributions to Economics,
DOI: 10.1007/978-3-7908-2131-4_7,

the dynamics of the interaction between firms and labor and the path over time of labor and capital themselves.

Introduction

The aim of this study is to investigate the effect of the institutional structure, regulations, technological progress, and labor market flexibility on productivity in the Italian economy within the context of a tightly defined macro-economic model. The core model is based on the representative agent model of Saltari and Travaglini (2007).

The core model (called ST below) is derived from maximizing the intertemporal profit function of a firm with respect to the labor/capital ratio, with the value function determining investment, both subject to deterministic costs of adjustment. A simple function for real wages closes the model. The steady state may be derived from the first order conditions so that differentiating with respect to the parameters of the system allows both a comparative steady state analysis and an analysis of stability in the neighborhood of the steady state.

The core model assumes the value of the firm is normalized by capital stock which means it cannot be estimated as a dynamic system as it stands. Also, it did not allow differentiation between the different issues being investigated. For those reasons it was modified to allow aggregation over firms to the macro level and to incorporate costs of investment directly in the behavior function. The wage determination equation was reformulated as a simple nontatonnement process which helps differentiate demand and supply effects on the system. The Hamiltonian of this extended or augmented model (called STA below) provides first order conditions very similar to the core (ST) model and hence it has a similar steady state. The differential equations that form this model can be estimated directly by a full information procedure so all the constraints inherent in the theory are imposed within that procedure and hence there is full consistency between the estimated parameters and model and the theory. Moreover, the estimators use either the nonlinear model directly or, for linear or linearized differential equation models, a stochastically equivalent discrete model which is satisfied by the observations generated by the continuous system irrespective of the observation interval of the sample. Thus the properties of the parameters of the differential equation system are given directly by the nonlinear model or may be derived from the sampling properties of the discrete model.

The derivation of this model does not take account of the specific institutional structures in the economy nor of regulations imposed on firms or the labor market that affect the workings and flexibility of the labor market. Thus it still precludes investigation of some of the issues of concern. In order to address these issues, a more general causal model of the production sector was specified. This model (called STW below) again has a very similar steady state (if it exists) to the models above, but although it is based on optimizing the profit function of the firm subject to the usual constraints, it is not Hamiltonian and hence the question of its stability is much more complex.

The models in this study are derived from or based directly on economic theory, particularly the theory of the firm, and do not take account of the specific institutional or market structure within which the system operates. These institutional or market structures, regulations, and other factors may be incorporated in the system by appropriate modifications to the functions of the model such as, in this case, the production function, the demand and supply functions for labor, and the overall labor market function that brings together demand and supply to determine the wage rate (or it's rate of change). In a more general model, price determination could also be introduced.

The specific issues of interest are:

1. The effect of a segmented labor market on productivity where the different segments have different efficiencies. Over time, and with changes in regulations or market structure more generally, firms may be able to reallocate resources to take better advantage of the skills available in the labor force
2. The effect of institutions on the structure of the labor market, including the way in which it operates, and the impact of changes in regulations on the workings of the market, the ease or otherwise with which firms may change their labor force and hence the associated costs. Regulations affect the function that embodies the interaction between firms and labor as well as the costs embedded in the functions that determine labor and capital themselves
3. The effect of changes in technology on productivity and employment
4. The effect of the differential in efficiency of skilled and unskilled labor, and the extent to which firms can utilize skills, on the productivity and profitability of the firm.

Part of this study was to estimate and test the joint hypotheses underlying the core model using macroeconomic data of the Italian economy. In investigating the issues above, it is necessary to have some base model which can incorporate additional hypotheses and allow them to be tested with enough precision that they can be distinguished. It was found that when the core model was estimated subject to all the constraints imposed by the theory underlying the model, it was rejected by the data. This meant that alternative models, as much as possible in the spirit of the underlying core model, had to be developed and tested. Modifying the model by replacing the Cobb–Douglas production function of the core model by a CES improved the estimates but was not sufficient to give a model which could be estimated precisely enough for the purposes of this research. It was necessary to broaden the view of the way in which firms take account of the costs of changing both the labor force or investment, and hence in their optimal choice of technology, in order to achieve a more satisfactory representation of the dynamics of the productive sector of the economy. These results raise the question of whether some of the models being used in this field are justifiable.

A feature of this research is that the steady state of even the more complex models are essentially the same as the core model and are functions of the parameters of the system. Thus the effect of changes in those parameters may be derived immediately. The dynamic properties of the model written in terms of (logarithmic) deviations about the steady state may then be calculated.

The core model is given in Appendix 1. Section Augmented Saltari–Travaglini Model with Investment in the Objective Function, develops this model so it is suitable for econometric purposes. Some comments on the estimation procedure, and the estimates of the augmented (STA) core model, are given in Section Estimation. Section A More General Specification of Core Model: Saltari–Travaglini–Wymer Model, discusses variants of this model and gives estimates of the two major variants.

Augmented Saltari-Travaglini Model with Investment in the Objective Function

This model is based directly on Saltari and Travaglini (2007). The value of the firm is maximized taking into account the costs of changing employment and investment and assuming the production function is Cobb–Douglas with constant returns to scale. Let L be employment, K the fixed capital stock, and the labor/capital ratio $n = \frac{L}{K}$. It is assumed that the derivatives of employment and capital can be changed by the firm so let $z = \dot{n}$ and $I = \dot{K}$ with costs of adjustment c and h respectively. Initially I is considered as net investment but it could be defined as gross with a depreciation factor. In Saltari and Travaglini (2007) the size of the firm was normalized but in this study capital is made explicit; no distinction is made between firms increasing in size and an increase in the number of firms.

Let the value of the firm be

$$\max_{z,I} \int_t^{\infty} e^{-\rho s} \left\{ \left(An^{1-\alpha} - wn - \frac{c}{2}\left(\frac{z}{n}\right)^2 \right) K - \left(1 + \frac{h}{2} I\right) I \right\} \mathrm{d}s \qquad (7.1)$$

subject to the definitional equations above for the control variables. Function (7.1) may be written

$$\max_{z,I} \int_t^{\infty} e^{-\rho s} \left\{ \left(An^{1-\alpha} - wn - \frac{c}{2}\left(\frac{z}{n}\right)^2 \right) - \left(1 + \frac{h}{2} I\right) k \right\} K \mathrm{d}s \qquad (7.1a)$$

where $k = \frac{I}{K}$. This allows (7.1) to be interpreted both as the objective function of an individual firm at the micro level or the aggregate at the macro level on the assumption of the firm being a representative agent. For theoretical studies of a single firm, K is often assumed to be normalized to 1 for simplicity but that is unnecessary. The term inside {...} in (7.1a) is the value function of the single firm per unit capital; if the initial capital stock is normalized, I and k are the same and the final K in the expression disappears but otherwise I refers to the *level* of net investment by the single firm. Hence under normalization K disappears from the value function.

At the macro level, the value function is aggregated across firms to give a total capital stock K but in this case investment I, and costs of investment, must be interpreted as the aggregate level. Moving from micro to the macro level is not just a matter of multiplying the (normalized) value of the firm by the number of firms K but of noting that, because the model is no longer normalized and the interpretation of I, K becomes explicit in the value function itself via k. The first order conditions below apply to both interpretations.

It is useful (as a minor simplification) to transform the control variable by defining $\ell = \frac{\dot{n}}{n} = D\ln n$. This does not change the profit function but the constraint on the state variable n becomes $\dot{n} = \ell n$ and the inter-temporal objective function is optimized with respect to ℓ rather than z.

The Hamiltonian becomes

$$H = e^{-\rho t}\left\{\left(An^{1-\alpha} - wn - \frac{c}{2}\ell^2\right)K - \left(1 + \frac{h}{2}I\right)I\right\} + \nu_1 \ell n + \nu_2 I \tag{7.2}$$

Where required, it will be assumed $\nu_i = \mu_i e^{-\rho t}$ so $\dot{\nu}_i = \dot{\mu}_i e^{-\rho t} - \rho\mu_i e^{-\rho t}$.

The first order conditions are:

$$\frac{\partial H}{\partial \nu_1} = \dot{n} = \ell n, \tag{7.3}$$

$$\frac{\partial H}{\partial \nu_2} = \dot{K} = I, \tag{7.4}$$

$$\frac{\partial H}{\partial n} = e^{-\rho t}(-\dot{\mu}_1 + \mu_1\rho) = e^{-\rho t}\{A(1-\alpha)n^{-\alpha} - w\}K + e^{-\rho t}\mu_1\ell, \tag{7.5}$$

$$\frac{\partial H}{\partial K} = e^{-\rho t}(-\dot{\mu}_2 + \mu_2\rho) = e^{-\rho t}\left\{An^{1-\alpha} - wn - \frac{c}{2}\ell^2\right\}, \tag{7.6}$$

$$\frac{\partial H}{\partial \ell} = -e^{-\rho t}(c\ell K - \mu_1 n) = 0, \tag{7.7}$$

$$\frac{\partial H}{\partial I} = -e^{-\rho t}(1 + hI - \mu_2) = 0. \tag{7.8}$$

Thus

$$\mu_1 = \tfrac{c}{n}\ell K,\ \dot{\mu}_1 = \tfrac{c}{n}(\dot{\ell}K + \ell\dot{K} - \ell^2\dot{K}), \tag{7.7a}$$

$$\mu_2 = 1 + hI,\ \dot{\mu}_2 = h\dot{I}. \tag{7.7b}$$

From (7.5) and (7.6)

$$\dot{\mu}_1 = \mu_1(\rho - \ell) - \{A(1-\alpha)n^{-\alpha} - w\}K, \tag{7.5a}$$

and

$$\dot{\mu}_2 = \mu_2\rho - \left\{An^{1-\alpha} - wn - \frac{c}{2}\ell^2\right\}. \tag{7.6a}$$

If required, this reduces to a second order system in n and K. μ_1 is essentially the same as q in Saltari and Travaglini (2007). If $q^* = \frac{\mu_1}{K}$, (7.5a) becomes

$$\dot{q}^* = \rho q^* - A(1-\alpha)n^{-\alpha} - w - q^* D \ln K \text{ and } \ell = \tfrac{n}{c} q^* . \tag{7.5b}$$

Alternatively, for estimation purposes, (7.3), (7.4) and (7.7a) give

$$\dot{\ell} = \ell(\rho - k) - \frac{n}{c}\{A(1-\alpha)n^{-\alpha} - w\}, \tag{7.9}$$

and, similarly, (7.4), (7.6) and (7.8a) give

$$\dot{k} = k(\rho - k) - \frac{1}{hK}\left\{An^{1-\alpha} - wn - \frac{c}{2}\ell^2 - \rho\right\} \tag{7.10}$$

Assuming that wages are determined by marginal product of labor but are sticky, the model may be closed with a wage determination equation such as,

$$D \ln w = \gamma \ln\left(\frac{A(1-\alpha)n^{-\alpha}}{w}\right) + \lambda_w \tag{7.11}$$

where the numerator is the marginal product of capital and λ_w is the long run rate of growth of wages. The latter term is necessary for consistency in a model with growth; alternatively, a corresponding term could be introduced within the logarithm giving

$$D \ln w = \gamma \ln\left(\frac{A(1-\alpha)n^{-\alpha}}{we^{-\lambda_w/\gamma}}\right). \tag{7.11a}$$

It was found during estimation that a second order function, which gives a "humped" adjustment functions so that the peak adjustment to wages does not occur immediately, was preferable. Thus

$$D^2 \ln w = \gamma_1 \ln\left(\frac{A(1-\alpha)n^{-\alpha}}{w}\right) - \gamma_2(D \ln w - \lambda_w). \tag{7.12}$$

If investment is gross and capital depreciates at a fixed rate δ the capital equation (7.4) becomes

$$\dot{K} = I - \delta K \tag{7.4a}$$

and so (7.6) has an extra term $-\delta\mu_2 e^{-\rho t}$; hence (7.6a) becomes

$$\dot{\mu}_2 = \mu_2(\rho - \delta) - (An^{1-\alpha} - wn - \frac{c}{2}z^{\frac{2}{n}}). \tag{7.6b}$$

In order for the model to be a plausible representation of a developed economy, it is necessary to introduce growth in some form; for simplicity, technical progress was introduced into the production function by replacing A by $A_0 e^{\lambda_1 t}$ where λ_1 is the rate of technical progress.

The model has a steady state if there exists a solution of the form $x(t) = x^* e^{\mu_x t}$ for all variables. Let the rate of growth of the labor force be λ_2. The rate of growth of the capital stock is k^*, and as all terms in {...} in (7.10) must be independent of t, the first term in that expression gives $k^* = \lambda_1/(1-\alpha) + \lambda_2$; as the left hand side of (7.10) is zero, multiplying through by hK shows that for a steady state to exist ρ must equal to k^*. From (7.11) the steady state rate of growth of wages is $\lambda_1/(1-\alpha)$ so that in efficiency units, wages are constant. Thus for consistency $\lambda_w = \lambda_1/(1-\alpha)$. The term $\{A(1-\alpha)n^{-\alpha} - w\}$ in (7.9) is zero and hence the term $\{...\}$ in (7.10) becomes $\{A\alpha n^{1-\alpha} - \frac{c}{2}\ell^2 - \rho\}$ which again is independent of t.

Without costs of adjustment, the steady state solution of the model is given by wages w and the return on capital ρ being equal to the corresponding marginal products. With costs, the steady state levels are

$$n^* = \psi^{\frac{1}{1-\alpha}} \text{ and } w^* = A_0(1-\alpha)\psi^{-\frac{\alpha}{1-\alpha}}$$

where

$$\psi = \frac{1}{A_0\alpha}\left[\rho + \frac{c}{2}\left(\frac{\lambda_1}{1-\alpha}\right)^2\right]$$

The assumption of a Cobb–Douglas production function with constant returns to scale means that the steady state level of the capital stock is indeterminate and is a function of initial values. For a given steady state value of employment L^* there is a corresponding steady state level of capital stock $K^* = L^*/n^*$.

For analytical purposes, such as questions of stability either in a classical or nonclassical sense, it is useful to write the model in terms of deviations about the steady state, if it exists. The underlying model above has the nonautonomous form

$$Dy(t) = f\{y(t), t; \theta\} \tag{7.13}$$

where θ is the vector of parameters; under appropriate conditions, there is a transformation of variables that allows it to be written as the autonomous or non-autonomous system

$$Dx(t) = \phi\{x(t), t; \theta\}\,. \tag{7.14}$$

Let $x_\ell = \ell - \ell^*$, $x_k = k - k^*$, $x_\omega = D\ln w - \frac{\lambda_1}{1-\alpha}$, $x_n = \ln(n/n^*) + \frac{\lambda_1}{1-\alpha}t$, $x_w = \ln(w/w^*) - \lambda_w t$ and $x_K = \ln(K/K^*) - (\frac{\lambda}{1-\alpha} + \lambda_2)t$ be the (logarithmic) deviations from the steady state $\omega = D\ln w$. Thus

$$\dot{x}_\ell = (x_\ell + \ell^*)(\rho - x_k - k^*) - A_0\frac{1-\alpha}{c}\psi\left(e^{(1-\alpha)x_n} - e^{x_n + x_w}\right), \tag{7.15}$$

$$\dot{x}_k = (x_k + k^*)(\rho - x_k - k^*)$$
$$-\frac{1}{hK^*}e^{-x_K - k^* t}\left\{A_0\psi e^{(1-\alpha)x_n} - A_0(1-\alpha)\psi e^{x_w + x_n} - \frac{c}{2}\left(x_\ell + \frac{\lambda_1}{1-\alpha}\right)^2 - \rho\right\}, \tag{7.16}$$

$$\dot{x}_\omega = -\gamma_1\alpha x_n - \gamma_1 x_w - \gamma_2 x_\omega, \tag{7.17}$$

with three definitional equations

$$\dot{x}_n = x_\ell, \tag{7.18}$$

$$\dot{x}_K = x_k,$$

$$\dot{x}_w = x_\omega. \tag{7.19}$$

The first terms in (7.17) and (7.18) simplify if the steady state condition $\rho = k^*$ is imposed.

Linearizing in terms of deviations about the steady state, with $x_j = 0$ for all j, gives

$$\dot{x}_\ell = x_\ell(\rho - k^*) - x_k\ell^* + A_0\frac{1-\alpha}{c}\psi(\alpha x_n + x_w), \tag{7.20}$$

$$\dot{x}_k = x_k(\rho - 2k^*) + \frac{1}{hK^*}\left\{A_0\alpha\psi - \frac{c}{2}\left(\frac{\lambda_1}{1-\alpha}\right)^2 - \rho\right\}e^{-k^*t}x_K \tag{7.21}$$

$$+\frac{1}{hK^*}A_0(1-\alpha)\psi e^{-k^*t}x_w + \frac{c}{hK^*}\frac{\lambda_1}{1-\alpha}e^{-k^*t}x_\ell,$$

$$\dot{x}_\omega = -\gamma_1\alpha x_n - \gamma_1 x_w - \gamma_2 x_\omega, \tag{7.22}$$

$$\dot{x}_n = x_\ell, \tag{7.23}$$

$$\dot{x}_K = x_k, \tag{7.24}$$

$$\dot{x}_w = x_\omega. \tag{7.25}$$

As t becomes large, the exponential in t goes to zero.

Estimation

It is assumed throughout that at the macro-economic level the Italian economy can be represented by a continuous system as in (7.2) or (7.3)–(7.6) and (7.11) above, and the data used are discrete observations of the continuous trajectory at equidistant (quarterly) periods. The estimators used are all full-information maximum-likelihood and estimate the parameters of the system defined above using either the continuous model directly or a discrete models stochastically equivalent to that system. Thus the parameters of the estimated models are the same as the parameters of the specified differential equation system. Owing to the derivation of the first order conditions of the profit function (7.2) these models are heavily over-identified and thus provide a powerful test of the joint hypotheses inherent in (7.2). Similar comments apply to the models below.

Full-information maximum-likelihood estimators were used throughout, an exact discrete estimator of a linear (or linearized) system and a Gaussian estimator of a nonlinear system.[1] These are described in Wymer (2006) and a more general

[1] The programs used here are part of the WYSEA System Estimation and Analysis package. Specifically, they were an approximate discrete estimator (Resimul), the exact discrete estimator (Discon)

discussion of these techniques is in Wymer (1996, 2006). The properties of full-information maximum likelihood estimators of linear models are more developed than those for nonlinear models but a nonlinear estimator eliminates any bias arising from and provides an estimate of any biases. Moreover, linearization may sometimes lead to parameters becoming unidentified, or poorly identified in that the asymptotic standard errors become very large; this is less likely with a nonlinear estimator.

The data are described in the Data Appendix below.

Assuming that the data are generated by the process (7.2) or (7.9), (7.10) etc. above, the model with second order derivatives of n and K may be estimated directly.[2]

The model used for estimation is (7.9), (7.10), (7.11) or (7.12) in terms of $\ln(n)$, $\ln(K)$, and $\ln(w)$ but written as a first order system with $D\ln(n) = \ell$ and $D\ln(K) = k$, and $D\ln(w) = \omega$ where (7.12) is used. Although the model may be estimated in linear or nonlinear form, it was decided initially to linearize the system about sample means (that is, $\overline{\ell}$, $\overline{k}$, $\overline{\ln n}$, $\overline{\ln K}$, and $\overline{\ln w}$); this linear model may be estimated subject to all of the constraints inherent in the underlying theory as well as those arising from the linearization. Alternatively, the model could have been linearized about the steady state. In either case, the estimated parameters are those of the theoretical model. For simplification only, time t is defined to have mean zero; thus $\overline{t}$ drops out of the linearization.

The model linearized about sample means is:

$$\begin{aligned} D\ell &= (\rho - \overline{k})\ell - \overline{\ell}k - \frac{1}{c}\left\{(1-\alpha)\psi - e^{\overline{\ln w}+\overline{\ln n}}\right\}\ln n + \frac{1}{c}e^{\overline{\ln w}+\overline{\ln n}}\ln w + \frac{1}{c}\psi\lambda_1 t \\ &\quad + \overline{\ell k} - \frac{1}{c}\left\{\psi - (1-\alpha)\psi\overline{\ln n} - e^{\overline{\ln w}+\overline{\ln n}}(1 - \overline{\ln w} - \overline{\ln n})\right\} \end{aligned} \tag{7.26}$$

where $\psi = A_0(1-\alpha)e^{(1-\alpha)\overline{\ln n}}$,

---

and a nonlinear exact estimator (Escona). Eigenvalues of a linear system and Lyapunov exponents of a nonlinear system may also be calculated.

[2] Several attempts were made to estimate the underlying model (7.3), (7.4) and (7.11) with other estimators but the extent to which the model was not consistent with the data led to these being unsatisfactory. The first order conditions give a first order nonlinear differential equation model with endogenous (state) variables n, K and w and costate variables μ_1 and μ_2. Although the costate variables are unobserved this may be estimated as a two point boundary point model with $\mu_i\ (t + T) = 0$ for each observation point t and T is a given horizon relative to t as in Wymer (2006).

As the system is continuous, (7.3), (7.4) may be replaced by the second order process in n and K (7.9), (7.10) as all observations are consistent with the latter. This nonlinear model, with (7.11) or (7.12) can be estimated using a nonlinear continuous estimator or linearized and estimated with a linear estimator but subject to all of the constraints inherent in the underlying model and in the linearization. Both estimators were used during this study but only the results for the linearized model are given in this Section.

Table 7.1 Estimates of parameters

Parameter	Estimate	Asymptotic Standard Error
c	3.636	4.629
h	126.807	$1.00E{+}05$
ρ	0.016	0.004
A_0	3.840	24.780
α	0.185	1.663
γ_1	0.057	0.098
γ_2	0.196	4.866
λ_1	0.016	0.012
λ_2	−0.001	0.122
p	1.056	2.657

$$\begin{aligned} Dk &= (\rho - 2\overline{k})k + \frac{\phi}{h} e^{-\overline{\ln K}} \ln K - \frac{1}{h} e^{-\overline{\ln K}} \left\{ \psi - e^{\overline{\ln w} + \overline{\ln n}} \right\} \ln n \\ &+ \frac{1}{h} e^{\overline{\ln w} + \overline{\ln n} - \overline{\ln K}} \ln w - \frac{1}{h} A_0 e^{(1-\alpha)\overline{\ln n} - \overline{\ln K}} \lambda_1 t + \frac{c}{h} e^{-\overline{\ln K}} \overline{\ell} \ell \\ &+ \overline{k}^2 - \frac{1}{h} e^{-\overline{\ln K}} \left\{ \phi + \phi \overline{\ln K} - \left(\psi - e^{\overline{\ln w} + e^{\overline{\ln n}}} \right) \overline{\ln n} + e^{\overline{\ln w} + \overline{\ln n}} \overline{\ln w} + c \overline{\ell}^2 \right\} \end{aligned} \tag{7.27}$$

where $\phi = A_0 e^{(1-\alpha)\overline{\ln n}} - e^{\overline{\ln w} + \overline{\ln n}} - \frac{c}{2}\overline{\ell}^2 - \rho$,

$$D\omega = -\gamma_1 \alpha \ln n - \gamma_1 \ln w - \gamma_1 \lambda_1 t - \gamma_2 \omega + \gamma_1 \{\ln A_0 + \ln(1-\alpha)\} + \gamma_2 \frac{\lambda_1}{1-\alpha}, \tag{7.28}$$

$$Dn = \ell, \tag{7.29}$$

$$D \ln K = k, \tag{7.30}$$

$$D \ln w = \omega. \tag{7.31}$$

Full-information maximum-likelihood estimates of this model are given in Table 7.1.

The Chi-square value of the likelihood ratio test is 990.6 with 14° of freedom; the critical value at the 5% level is 23.7.

These estimates give some idea of the values of the parameters[3] of the core theoretical model but the asymptotic standard errors are large and the likelihood ratio test rejects the hypothesis that the model represents the system that generated the data. Almost all parameters are not significantly different from zero but the large asymp-

[3] To interpret these parameters, the mean values of the variables are approximately K = 3,000 (€ × bn), L = 20 (m), n = 0.007 (employees per unit capital), and w = 6 (€× '000 per employee per quarter). Real output, Y, used in the models below, is approximately 220 (€ bn per quarter).

totic standard errors show that the true values of the parameters could lie within a wide range. The parameter p is merely a scaling factor in the wage equation needed to equate (approximately) the mean marginal product of labor and the mean wage rate and has no economic significance.

Given the values of variables in the model, the cost of adjustment c of the labor/capital ratio seems particularly low. This may indicate a misspecification of the cost of adjustment term in the (discounted long-term profit) objective function of the firm.

It should be noted that the full-information estimation procedure used here imposes all the conditions implicit in the underlying theoretical model as defined in equations (7.26), (7.27) and (7.29) as well as imposing the constraints that arise in linearization. This provides consistent estimation of all parameters in the system subject to all constraints. The tight, highly theoretical, specification means that the parameter set used to represent the core equations of the economy is very small and undoubtedly this leads to the data rejecting this specification.

The properties of a Cobb–Douglas production function raise the question of whether it is justifiable and the most suitable for a model of this nature. While the labor/capital ratio is well-defined, the steady state level of capital (or of labor) is not; given an assumption about the level of one variable, for instance L^*, immediately provides the other as n^* is known. The use of this function is particularly restrictive and it has poor properties; in particular the elasticity of substitution is one. The CES is perhaps the simplest of production functions which have more satisfactory properties with the CES having an elasticity of substitution which is constant but not necessarily one and although the standard specification has constant returns to scale, that is not necessary. Comparing the two functions must take into account the way in which the functions enter each equation of the model; while the CES can, as a special case, exhibit constant returns to scale and in that sense be similar to a Cobb-Douglas, this is only one aspect of their relative properties and estimates of this, independent of the whole model, are likely to be biased.

This model was also estimated in nonlinear form (7.9)–(7.11) using a full-information Gaussian estimator and also as a two-point boundary point system (7.3)–(7.8) as indicated above. These estimates were not satisfactory and again reject the joint hypothesis that the observed data were generated by this system.

A More General Specification of Core Model: Saltari-Travaglini-Wymer model

Several suggestions can be made towards formulating a more representative model of the Italian economy while still retaining the strongly theoretical core. Although a number of suggestions can be made, for the purposes of this study only those that are broadly within the framework of the core model will be tested.

A CES production function has more plausible properties than the Cobb–Douglas from the viewpoint of the whole system. It is more general than the Cobb–Douglas but is amenable to analysis and, in models such as this, usually is consistent with a steady state (if that is considered important) and, subject to the specification of the whole system, provides a well defined steady state level of the capital stock as a function of parameters of the model. It can also be adapted more easily to investigate some of the issues discussed below.

Secondly, wage determination may be mis-specified. In the present model wages are assumed to adjust to the marginal product of labor and this imposes a strong constraints on the system and the parameters. A better representation may be that wages are determined by excess demand in the labor market. This process of prices adjusting to excess stocks has been found to provide a good explanation of price movements in other models: in macro models where the GDP deflator depends on excess demand for stocks of goods (inventories); with interest rates in monetary models; with copper prices to excess copper stocks in a commodity model, and similar results in other commodity markets.

A more general formulation within the same framework defines the value of the firm as

$$\max_{z,I} \int_t^{\infty} e^{-\rho s} \left\{ f(L,K) - wL - \frac{c}{2}z^2 - \left(1 + \frac{h}{2}I\right) I \right\} \mathrm{d}s \qquad (7.32)$$

subject to the definitional equations above for the control variables $z = \dot{L}$ and $I = \dot{K}$.

Thus the Hamiltonian is

$$H = e^{-\rho t} \left\{ f(L,K) - wL - \frac{c}{2}z^2 - (1 + \frac{h}{2}I)I \right\} + \nu_1 z + \nu_2 I. \qquad (7.33)$$

As above, let $\nu_i = \mu_i e^{-\rho t}$ so $\dot{\nu}_i = \dot{\mu}_i e^{-\rho t} - \rho \mu_i e^{-\rho t}$

The first order conditions are:

$$\frac{\partial H}{\partial \nu_1} = \dot{L} = z, \qquad (7.34)$$

$$\frac{\partial H}{\partial \nu_2} = \dot{K} = I, \qquad (7.35)$$

$$\frac{\partial H}{\partial L} = e^{-\rho t}(-\dot{\mu}_1 + \mu_1 \rho) = e^{-\rho t} \left\{ \frac{\partial f}{\partial L} - w \right\}, \qquad (7.36)$$

$$\frac{\partial H}{\partial K} = e^{-\rho t}(-\dot{\mu}_2 + \mu_2 \rho) = e^{-\rho t} \frac{\partial f}{\partial K}, \qquad (7.37)$$

$$\frac{\partial H}{\partial z} = -e^{-\rho t}(cz - \mu_1) = 0, \qquad (7.38)$$

$$\frac{\partial H}{\partial I} = -e^{-\rho t}(1 + hI - \mu_2) = 0. \tag{7.39}$$

Thus $\mu_1 = c\ell L$ and $\mu_2 = 1 + hkK$ and the model reduces to

$$\dot{\ell} = \ell(\rho - \ell) - \frac{1}{cL}\left(\frac{\partial f}{\partial L} - w\right), \tag{7.40}$$

and

$$\dot{k} = k(\rho - k) - \frac{1}{hK}\left(\frac{\partial f}{\partial K} - \rho\right). \tag{7.41}$$

If wages are assumed to be determined by demand and supply but again, as above, are sticky, an appropriate function (in logarithmic form) would be

$$\ddot{w} = g(L^d, L^s) - \alpha\dot{w} \tag{7.42}$$

where L^d is the demand for labor (defined as the inverse of the production function or derived from Hamiltonian optimization) and L^s is supply. The function $g(...)$ is defined to take account of the structure of the labor market and it's affect on wage determination. Thus this can be viewed as a non-tatonnement process which depends on excess demand and the structure of the labor market.

If the supply function is

$$L^s = L_0 w^{\beta_4} e^{\lambda_2 t}, \tag{7.43}$$

Equation (7.42) could then become

$$D^2 \ln w = \gamma_1 \ln\left(\frac{L^d}{L_0 e^{\lambda_2 t} w^{\beta_4}}\right) - \gamma_2(D \ln w - \lambda_w) \tag{7.44}$$

where the numerator is the demand for labor L^d defined as the inverse of the production function and the denominator is a supply function L^s where the labor force is defined to grow (or decline) at a steady rate $\lambda_2$and vary according to the real wage rate with elasticity β_4. The wage rate w is defined in units corresponding to the definition of L.

$L_0$is a parameter representing the base labor force (at $t = 0$) and λ_2 the rate of growth of the labor force. If w is real wages, then $\beta_4$is the elasticity of the supply of labor with respect to real wages; depending on the definition of wages in the model it may be necessary to correct for efficiency units in which case that factor becomes $(we^{-\lambda_1 t})^{\beta_4}$. Demand for labor presents more of a problem in the present model. A production function $Y = f(L, K)$ can be inverted to give $L = g(Y, K)$ which shows the amount of labor required to produce a given level of output Y using a given capital stock K. In a more complete macro model with output endogenous (perhaps as a function of aggregate demand) the numerator in (7.44) is just $L^d = g(Y, K)$.

The formulation in (7.32) in which the costs of adjusting labor is defined in terms of ℓ (or similarly in terms of $\dot{L}$) may not be satisfactory. The real costs, from the point of view of the firm, is in deviations of actual labor from the optimal level, that is $|L - L^d|$ and these costs may not be symmetric.

If the production function $f(K, L)$ is defined as CES then

$$Y = \beta_3[K^{-\beta_1} + (\beta_2 e^{\lambda_1 t} L)^{-\beta_1}]^{-1/\beta_1}, \tag{7.45}$$

so that

$$\frac{\partial f}{\partial L} = \beta_2 e^{\lambda_1 t} \beta_3 \left[1 + \left(\beta_2 e^{\lambda_1 t} \frac{L}{K}\right)^{\beta_1}\right]^{-\frac{1+\beta_1}{\beta_1}}, \tag{7.45a}$$

and

$$\frac{\partial f}{\partial K} = \beta_3 \left[1 + \left(\beta_2 e^{\lambda_1 t} \frac{L}{K}\right)^{-\beta_1}\right]^{-\frac{1+\beta_1}{\beta_1}}, \tag{7.45b}$$

and these are substituted into (7.40) and (7.41).

The steady state may be derived as above.

This model may be estimated directly in nonlinear form or linearized about sample means or the steady state. In all cases the estimator imposes all the constraints on the parameters of the system both from theory and, if linearized, from the linearization.

Full-information Gaussian estimates of the nonlinear model, again subject to all the constraints imposed by theory, are given in Table 7.2:

The elasticity of substitution, $1/(1+\beta_1)$, is 0.512 with asymptotic standard error 0.838.

Table 7.2 Estimates of parameters

Parameter	Estimate	Asymptotic standard error
c	6.908	65.354
h	−0.134	198.869
s	0.211	0.091
ρ	0.000	0.001
β_1	0.955	3.203
$\ln \beta_2$	0.047	21.696
$\ln \beta_3$	−0.752	21.450
β_4	0.392	2.314
γ_1	0.000	0.001
γ_2	0.691	0.159
λ_1	0.000	0.000
λ_2	0.023	0.023
$\ln(L_0)$	0.453	0.368

Variants of the this model, and full-information estimates of a linearized version, give broadly similar results. Again, the likelihood ratio test shows this model is inconsistent with the Italian economy generating the data so the joint hypotheses underlying the model must be rejected.

These results are consistent with other research in the field for other economies and must raise doubts whether such models can be justified. It is suggested that the constraints of the Hamiltonian optimization of the objective function which is the basis of these models is just too stringent to explain the dynamic behavior of a developed economy. In particular, the hypothesis that the costs of changing either labor or capital is a function of only the derivative (proportional or otherwise) of the control variables may be too simplistic or not robust enough to provide a satisfactory explanation of the behavior of the firm. For instance, rather than costs depending only on the derivative of the appropriate variable, for instance capital or employment, the discrepancy between current levels of employment and some medium term target may be more appropriate. As employment provides a flow of services, this deviation is the integral of any shortfall, or over-supply in those services; other factors are the discrepancy in current services and the rate of change of the control variable. This is a feature of control systems and is similar to the Phillips proposal of integral, proportional and derivative macro policies. While the objective function could be extended to incorporate these factors this rapidly becomes mathematically intractable.

Instead of introducing adjustment costs into the profit function, a two step optimization process may be a better representation of the behavior of a firm. The firm first optimizes an objective function to give the optimal medium to long run levels of capital and labor given output, wages, cost of capital etc., and then minimizes a cost function to take account of the deviation of the firm from it's optimal position and to allow for uncertainty as in Bergstrom (1984).

Let $\tilde{K} = ax(t)$, $\tilde{I} = \delta ax(t)$ be the optimal medium term or steady state levels of the capital stock $K(t)$ and investment $I(t)$ derived from Hamiltonian optimization as in (7.9)–(7.12) but without costs of adjustment; $x(t)$ is a vector of nonrandom functions of variables exogenous to the firm and a is a vector whose elements are functions of the parameters of the underlying objective function. As the values of $x(t)$ are not known with certainty, it is assumed implicitly that the firm views $x(t)$ as the conditional expectations of $x(t+s)$ for all $s > 0$, so $x(t+s), -\infty < t < \infty$ is treated as a martingale process.

In the second stage of the optimization, the firm minimizes the cost function

$$Q = \frac{1}{2}\int_t^{\infty} \left([\tilde{K}(s) - K(s)]^2 + c_1[\tilde{I}(s) - I(s)]^2 + c_2[\dot{I}(s)]^2\right) \mathrm{d}s \tag{7.46}$$

subject to

$$\mathrm{d}K(t) = I(t) - \delta K(t)dt.$$

The optimal function which minimizes Q is

$$\mathrm{d}I(t) = \gamma\alpha x(t) + \beta K(t) - I(t)dt + \zeta(\mathrm{d}t) \tag{7.47}$$

where

$$[\gamma\beta, -\gamma] = \left[0, \frac{-1}{c_2}\right] P, \ \alpha = \frac{\delta - \beta}{\delta} a,$$

and P is the non-negative definite second order matrix satisfying the Riccati equation

$$\begin{bmatrix} 1 & 0 \\ 0 & c_1 \end{bmatrix} + P \begin{bmatrix} -\delta & 1 \\ 0 & 0 \end{bmatrix} + \begin{bmatrix} -\delta & 1 \\ 0 & 0 \end{bmatrix} P - P \begin{bmatrix} 0 & 0 \\ 0 & 1/c_2 \end{bmatrix} P = 0.$$

In general, it is not necessary to calculate c_1, c_2 but these are implicit in the parameters α, β, γ.

The form of the cost function (7.46) may be modified to take account of deviations between actual labor being used and its optimal path. If both labor and capital are both subject to decisions of the firm, there are two optimal equations of the form (7.47) and the Riccati equations expand accordingly.

This minimization of adjustment costs provides a justification or alternative interpretation of the adjustment processes.

The model that results from these suggestions is:

$$\dot{\ell} = \alpha_1 \alpha_2 \ln \left(\frac{\partial f}{\partial L} / w \right) - \alpha_1 (\ell - \lambda_2), \tag{7.48}$$

$$\dot{k} = \alpha_3 \left[\alpha_4 \left(\frac{\partial f}{\partial K} - \rho \right) + \beta_5 - k \right], \tag{7.49}$$

and, as in (7.42),

$$D^2 \ln w = \gamma_1 \ln \left(\frac{L^d}{L_0 e^{\lambda_2 t} w^{\beta_4}} \right) - \gamma_2 (D \ln w - \lambda_1). \tag{7.50}$$

If there were perfect competition and no risk, β_5 would be the rate of growth of fixed capital formation and hence would be the rate at which firms expect output to grow. In this specification, the real interest rate or return on capital is constant and it cannot be distinguished from β_5.

In this formulation, the question arises of the point at which the partial derivatives should be evaluated; in equilibrium this is irrelevant but out of equilibrium it is not. In the model estimated here, the partial derivative of labor is evaluated at (L, K) to reflect the short term effect of the labor/capital ratio on changes in employment of the firm, but the partial derivative of capital in the investment equation is evaluated at (Y, K); this is relevant to the longer term development of the firm. For the CES production function as defined above, $\frac{\partial f}{\partial K} = \beta_3 \left(\frac{Y}{\beta_3 K} \right)^{1+\beta_1}$. Full-information Gaussian estimates of the nonlinear version of this model, subject to all the constraints in the specification of (7.32)–(7.42) are given in Table 7.3.

The usual Chi-square value of the likelihood ratio test cannot be calculated directly for a nonlinear model but based on a linearized version of this model it

Table 7.3 Estimates of parameters

Parameter	Estimate	Asymptotic standard error
ρ	0.0031	0.0100
β_1	0.8068	0.1672
$\ln\beta_2$	4.0189	0.3537
$\ln\beta_3$	−1.5648	0.1034
β_4	0.3380	3.9525
α_1	1.0870	0.0690
α_2	0.0109	0.0036
α_3	0.1102	0.0033
α_4	0.0081	0.0029
γ_1	0.0024	0.0007
γ_2	0.8450	0.0367
λ_1	0.0004	0.0012
λ_2	0.0029	0.0003
$\ln(L_0)$	3.8671	7.8336

is likely to be around 100 with 13° of freedom; the critical value at the 5% level is 22.4. It should be noted that the likelihood ratio test is biased towards rejection in small samples.

The elasticity of substitution, $1/(1+\beta_1)$, is 0.553 with asymptotic standard error 0.051. Note that the scale of β_2 depends on the relative magnitudes of capital and labor while the scale of L_0 depends on employment, wages and output.

All parameters have the expected sign but many are not significantly different from zero so the specification is still not satisfactory, but it should be noted that this is a much stricter test than is usually imposed in research with this class of models.

These models exclude the real interest rate, and feedbacks from price determination and output. The real interest rate, or the time discount factor, is assumed to be constant. In this model this is, in effect, represented by ρ but the investment function (7.33) includes an expected growth rate and risk premium; the combined factor is $-\alpha_3\rho+\beta_5$ but ρ and β_5 cannot be identified individually. Under these assumptions, the estimated value of ρ above is really the joint value.

The steady state of this model can be calculated as in Section Augmented Saltari–Travaglini Model with Investment in the Objective Function, and the dynamic properties derived from writing the model in terms of deviations about the steady state. Let the steady state paths be $X(t) = X^* e^{\nu_x t}$ so if $x = \ln X$, so (by definition) in the steady state $\dot{x} = \nu_x$ and $\ddot{x} = 0$. Substituting this and (7.45) into (7.48), (7.49) and (7.50) and equating powers of t gives

$$Y^* = \beta_3[K^{*-\beta_1} + (\beta_2 L^*)^{-\beta_1}]^{-1/\beta_1} \quad \text{or} \quad \left(\frac{Y^*}{\beta_3 K^*}\right)^{-\beta_1} = 1 + \left(\beta_2 \frac{L^*}{K^*}\right)^{-\beta_1}. \tag{7.51a}$$

The rate of growth of Y and K must be the same and equal to that of the employment term $\lambda_1+\lambda$. Hence $k^* = \lambda_1+\lambda_2$ and $\ell^* = \lambda_2$ but a steady state will exist only if the elasticity of wages in the labor supply function is zero. Under that assumption, from (7.48) the steady state growth rate of wages is λ_1. In addition,

$$\beta_2\beta_3\left[1+\left(\beta_2\frac{L^*}{K^*}\right)^{\beta_1}\right]^{-\frac{1+\beta_1}{\beta_1}} = w^*, \tag{7.51b}$$

$$\alpha_4\beta_3\left(\frac{Y^*}{\beta_3 K^*}\right)^{1+\beta_1} = \alpha_4\rho - \beta_5 + k, \tag{7.51c}$$

$$\frac{1}{\beta_2\beta_3}\left[Y^{*-\beta_1} - (\beta_3 K^*)^{-\beta_1}\right]^{-\frac{1}{\beta_1}} = L_0 w^{*\beta_4}. \tag{7.51d}$$

(7.51c) can be solved to give the capital/output ratio. With β_4 nonzero, (7.51d) would give $w^* = (L^*/L_0)^{\frac{1}{\beta_4}}$ and (7.51b)..L^* as a function of Y^*. With $\beta_4 = 0$, however, $L^* = L_0$ and (7.51b) gives w^*. Hence,

$$K^* = qY^* \text{ where } q = \beta_3^{-\frac{\beta_1}{1+\beta_1}}\mu^{\frac{1}{1+\beta_1}} \text{ and } \mu = \rho - (\beta_5 - \lambda_1 - \lambda_2)/\alpha_4, \tag{7.52a}$$

$$Y^* = \beta_2\beta_3 L_0[1-(\beta_3 q)^{-\beta_1}]^{\frac{1}{\beta_1}} \tag{7.52b}$$

$$w^* = \beta_2\beta_3[1-(\beta q)^{-\beta_1}]^{\frac{1+\beta_1}{\beta_1}} \tag{7.52c}$$

The model may now be rewritten in terms of (logarithmic) deviations about the steady state. If

$$x_L = \ln\frac{L}{L^* e^{\lambda_2 t}},\quad x_K = \ln\frac{K}{K^* e^{(\lambda_1+\lambda_2)t}},$$

$$x_w = \ln\frac{w}{w^* e^{\lambda_1 t}} \quad \text{and} \quad x_Y = \ln\frac{Y}{Y^* e^{(\lambda_1+\lambda_2)t}},$$

$$\ddot{x}_L = \alpha_1\alpha_2\left(-\frac{1+\beta_1}{\beta_1}\ln\left[1-(\beta_3 q)^{-\beta_1} + (\beta_3 q)^{-\beta_1}e^{\beta_1(x_L - x_K)}\right] - x_w\right) - \alpha_1\dot{x}_L, \tag{7.53a}$$

$$\ddot{x}_K = \alpha_3\left(\alpha_4\left[\beta_3^{-\beta_1}q^{-(1+\beta_1)}e^{(1+\beta_1)(x_Y - x_K)} - \rho\right] + \beta_5 - \dot{x}_K - (\lambda_1+\lambda_2)\right), \tag{7.53b}$$

$$\ddot{x}_w = \frac{\gamma_1}{\beta_1}\ln\left(\frac{1-(\beta_3 q)^{-\beta_1}}{e^{-\beta_1 x_Y} - (\beta_3 q)^{-\beta_1}e^{-\beta_1 x_K}}\right) - \gamma_1\beta_4(x_w + \ln w^*) - \gamma_2\dot{x}_w, \tag{7.53c}$$

$$x_Y = -\frac{1}{\beta_1}\ln\left((\beta_3 q)^{-\beta_1}e^{\beta_1 x_K} + \left[1-(\beta_3 q)^{-\beta_1}\right]^{-\frac{1}{\beta_1}}e^{-\beta_1 x_L}\right). \tag{7.53d}$$

Table 7.4 gives the steady state values calculated for the estimates given in Table 7.3 and assuming $t = 0$ at the mid-point of the sample, 1993 Q3.

The steady state levels are close to the mean values of the corresponding variables, and the actual values at the mid-point of the sample, apart from K^* which is low. This suggests that the estimated value of q, derived from the estimates of the underlying parameters in the model, is too low. The asymptotic standard errors are large but this is due to the large standard error of $\ln L_0$. If the steady state is calculated with a given value of L_0 the standard errors of $\ln Y^*$ and $\ln K^*$ are 0.36 and 0.28 respectively.

The core model was derived from the optimisation of the discounted present value of the firm with respect to investment and employment under the assumption of that prices are given and output is independent of demand. In a developed economy, however, a demand driven model may be more appropriate. If the theory is modified to allow monopolistic competition with firms having some control over prices, the value of the firm would be optimized subject to the production function by choosing the level of investment in the longer term, with output (or expected output) given, and (the change of) prices and employment in the shorter term. Thus the labor/capital ratio would be a short term control variable as in the core model, but this would be dependent on output and changes in fixed capital.

The introduction of prices into the system may lead to indeterminacy but, as a first approximation to the optimal solution, prices can be determined as a markup on marginal cost but this is not unconstrained. From a macro-economic point of view, relative domestic and foreign prices determine the mix between domestic output (including output for exports) and imports; excessive markups will lead to an increase in imports and decrease in exports.

This approach paves the way formulating a more representative model of the Italian economy while still retaining the strongly theoretical core.

A demand driven model still allows for innovation. While new products will create demand, at the macro level this may be just a matter of substitution or a fulfilment of a demand waiting for a solution. For instance, the creation of new drugs may fulfil a demand for improved health care, new telephone systems fulfil a demand for more efficient communications, and containerisation of shipping was a major step in decreasing transport costs.

It is in this model that institutional or market structures, and other factors such as regulations, may be incorporated in the system by appropriate modifications to the central functions of the model, in this case, the production function, the demand and supply functions for labor L^d and L^s, and the overall labor market function $g(.)$ as in (7.40)–(7.42).

In the present model the scaling factor A_0 or the parameters of the CES production function and the rate of technical progress λ_1 are considered fixed parameters in that they do not vary over time. This may be considered a first approximation as these parameters may not be constant but dependent on factors such as the distri-

Table 7.4 Estimates of steady state

Steady state	Estimate	Asymptotic standard error	Mean value
q	1.23	0.26	
$\ln Y^*$	5.95	7.89	5.40
$\ln K^*$	6.16	7.84	8.06
$\ln w^*$	1.79	0.39	1.81
$\ln L_0$	3.86	7.83	3.04

bution and degree of skills and education in the economy. Thus parameters that in the present model are considered fixed would become functions of a wider set of parameters and variables with the estimated values of the present parameters being some approximation to (say) the mean of these functions. For instance, if skills S were thought to affect the value of A_0 that parameter could be replaced by the time-variant expression

$$A_0 = h(A_0', S..; \theta)$$

where θ is a set of parameters. The function $h(.)$ must, of course, be specified explicitly; it is suggested that this be approached by setting out the properties required of $h(.)$ and finding more or less the simplest function which has these properties. The basic properties may be quite simple: how is the sign of h to vary with S; are there any limiting factors; what are the properties of the first, or second, order derivative of h with respect to S, and so on. Similar considerations apply to variations in $\lambda_1$or other parameters.

Another aspect of direct relevance to this study is the question of rigidities in the labor market and the effect of regulation on the market. In the present model the parameters γ_1, γ_2 in the wage equation can be taken as a nonspecific representation of such effects. If increased regulation does distort the labor market by increasing costs of adjustment, then the γ in the model will increase with regulation and the market adjust more slowly. The Employment Protection Legislation series produced by the OECD could be used (as an exogenous variable) for this purpose.

More generally, and with more difficulty, a CES or other production function could be extended to incorporate human capital measured by some proxy such as education. One approach here is to have a two tier production function with labor L and capital K forming the CES but with labor then defined as a Cobb–Douglas or geometric average of two (or more) parts such as

$$L_U, L_S, L_H$$

unskilled, skilled, and highly skilled.

For instance, let p be the proportion of skilled labor employed in the economy and assume that a Cobb–Douglas function representing aggregate labor or, equivalently, a geometric average of skilled and unskilled labor, is embedded in the CES production function. The labor term in the production function $(\beta_2 L e^{\lambda_1 t})$ may be replaced by the differentiated term

$$\left(\beta_{2s} p L e^{\lambda_{1s} t}\right)^p \left(\beta_{2u}(1-p) L e^{\lambda_{1u} t}\right)^{1-p}$$

or

$$(\beta_{2s} p)^p \left(\beta_{2u}(1-p)\right)^{1-p} L e^{[p\lambda_{1s} + (1-p)\lambda_{1u}]t}.$$

Conclusions

The purpose of this research was to develop and estimate the model of the productive sector of Saltari and Travaglini (2007), derived from the optimising the value of the firm subject to a Cobb–Douglas production function and taking into account costs of changing employment and fixed capital. The resulting model was rejected by the data as a representation of the Italian economy. A modified model, replacing the Cobb–Douglas production function by a CES and generalizing the cost functions for changes in employment and investment, but remaining well within the spirit of the core model, provided more satisfactory estimates but was still rejected when estimated with the same data. It must be noted that the models were estimated using full-information, maximum-likelihood procedures subject to all the constraints inherent in the theory. These estimation procedures, and the likelihood ratio test used in this paper, provide a particularly stringent test of the joint hypotheses that the model represents the system generating the data. It is considered, on the basis of experience with the estimation of macroeconomic models of other countries, that the Saltari–Travaglini–Wymer model above provides a sufficiently good basis to continue with the investigation of the issues that are to be addressed.

The immediate task is to derive the dynamical properties of the Saltari–Travaglini–Wymer model; these may well be aperiodic. The model will then be used to further the aims of this research project in investigating the effect of institutional structure, regulations, and labor market flexibility on the productive sector of the Italian economy.

Appendix 1. Saltari–Travaglini model. Formal Derivation via Hamiltonian Optimisation of a Profit Function

Let $n = \frac{L}{K}$, $z = \dot{n}$, and $I = \dot{K}$. Assume the costs of adjustment of n and I are c and h respectively. Initially I is considered as net investment but is later defined as gross.

The profit function is:

$$\psi(L, K; Y) = Y - wL - z_2 - \frac{c}{2}(z_1)^2 - \frac{h}{2}(z_2)^2 \tag{7.54}$$

where $z_1 = \dot{L}$, $z_2 = \dot{K}$, $k = D\ln(K)$, $\ell = D\ln(L)$.

It is assumed Y, K and w as well as the costs c and h to be defined as real.

$\lambda_1 =$ Harrod neutral technical progress (This could be defined as a stochastic trend if required).

$\lambda_2 =$ rate of growth of the labor force (or again defined as a stochastic trend).

Let investment be given by profit maximisation subject to a production function. In the short term, (1) labor could also be given by the same profit maximisation and the rate of change of the real wage rate a function of the excess demand for labor (that is demand minus supply) or, vice versa (2) if output is to be taken as demand determined, (very) short term labor requirements (L) could be determined by the inverse production function and the real wage rate a function of the marginal product of labor. The rate of time preference ρ is not assumed to be equal to the real interest rate in the formal model.

Hence,

$$\max_{k,\ell} \int_t^\infty e^{-\rho s}\psi(L, K; Y)\mathrm{d}s \tag{7.55}$$

s.t. $Y = f(L, K)$, $z_1 = \dot{L}$, $z_2 = \dot{K}$,
so the Hamiltonian becomes

$$H = e^{-\rho t}\left\{ f(L, K) - wL - z_2 - \frac{c}{2}(z_1)^2 - \frac{h}{2}(z_2)^2 \right\} + \nu_1 z_1 + \nu_2 z_2. \tag{7.56}$$

Where required, it will be assumed $\nu_i = \mu_i e^{-\rho t}$ so $\dot{\nu}_i = \dot{\mu}_i e^{-\rho t} - \rho\mu_i e^{-\rho t}$.

The first order conditions are:

$$\frac{\partial H}{\partial \nu_1} = \dot{L} = z_1 \tag{7.57}$$

$$\frac{\partial H}{\partial \nu_2} = \dot{K} = z_2 \tag{7.58}$$

$$\frac{\partial H}{\partial L} = e^{-\rho t}(-\dot{\mu}_1 + \mu_1\rho) = e^{-\rho t}\left(\frac{\partial f}{\partial L} - w\right) \tag{7.59}$$

$$\frac{\partial H}{\partial K} = e^{-\rho t}(-\dot{\mu}_2 + \mu_2\rho) = e^{-\rho t}\frac{\partial f}{\partial K} \tag{7.60}$$

$$\frac{\partial H}{\partial z_1} = -e^{-\rho t}(cz_1 - \mu_1) = 0 \tag{7.61}$$

$$\frac{\partial H}{\partial k} = -e^{-\rho t}(1 + hz_2 - \mu_2) = 0 \tag{7.62}$$

From (7.61) and (7.62)

$$\mu_1 = cz_1,\ \dot{\mu}_1 = c\dot{z}_1, \tag{7.63a}$$

$$\mu_2 = 1 + hz_2\ ,\dot{\mu}_2 = h\dot{z}_2. \tag{7.64a}$$

Hence, solving from (7.59) and (7.60),

$$\dot{z}_1 = -\frac{1}{c}\left(\frac{\partial f}{\partial L} - w\right) + \rho z_1, \tag{7.59a}$$

$$\dot{z}_2 = -\frac{1}{h}\left(\frac{\partial f}{\partial K} - h\rho z_2 - 1\right). \tag{7.60a}$$

These may be written as functions of $\ell = z_1/L$, $k = z_2/K$.

If wages are a (second order) distributed lag function of excess demand for labor, wage determination (in logarithmic form) would be something like

$$\ddot{w} = g(L^d, L^s) - \alpha\dot{w}. \tag{7.65}$$

Assume wage rates are determined by a nontatonnement process depending on excess demand and the structure of the labor market. The wage rate w is defined in units corresponding to the definition of L. The demand of labor that is relevant in the wage equation could be defined as the inverse of the production in the short term as in (7.55) or as derived from Hamiltonian optimization.

The supply function could be

$$L^s = \gamma_4 w^{\beta_6} e^{\lambda_2 t}. \tag{7.66}$$

The function $g(..)$ is defined to take account of the structure of the labor market and it's affect on wage determination.

The formulation in (7.56) in which the costs of adjusting labor is defined in terms of ℓ (or similarly in terms of $\dot{L}$) may not be satisfactory. The real costs, from the point of view of the firm, is in deviations of actual labor from the optimal level, that is $|L - L^d|$ and these costs may not be symmetric.

Data Appendix

The data used in this study are of the Italian economy, quarterly from 1980, Q2, to 2006, Q1. GDP and GNP, fixed capital, and total remuneration (wages) are defined as € bn (10^9), employment in millions of employees, any parameters of variables such as interest rates, rate of time preference, rates of growth, etc as rates per quarter in natural numbers (for instance, ten per cent per annum is represented throughout this study as 0.025). All real variables are defined with base year 2000 (so that the GDP deflator used in preparation of the data has mean value 1.0 in 2000).

All logarithms are to base e.

The stock of fixed capital is calculated from net capital formation (gross capital formation less fixed capital consumption or depreciation) divided by the GDP deflator.

The time trend has been defined with value 0.0 at the mid-point of the sample (so the mean of t is zero) to simplify linearization without affecting the properties of the model. If required, it is trivial to rebase the time trend by an appropriate adjustment of intercept terms in the model.

All series have been transformed to eliminate (to an approximation) the moving average process inherent in discrete data generated by a continuous system as discussed in Wymer (1972).

The data sources are:

- Real National Income account data: ISTAT, OECD
- Total employment: AMECO, European Commission

- Civilian Employment: AMECO, European Commission
- Short term interest rate: OECD
- EPL: OECD index
- Skilled and unskilled labor force: OECD index.

References

Bergstrom AR (1984) Monetary, fiscal and exchange rate policy in a continuous time model of the United Kingdom, Blackwell, Oxford, pp 183–206

Saltari E, Travaglini G (2007) Sources of productivity slowdown in european countries during 1990s. Discussion Papers in Economics, University of York, n.24

Wymer CR (1972) Econometric estimation of stochastic differential equation systems. Econometrica 40: 565–577

Wymer CR (1996) The role of continuous time disequilibrium models in macro-economics. Presented at the SEMECON conference on dynamic disequilibrium modelling, University of Munich, Germany, 30 August – 3 September 1993; also published in Barnett WA, Gandolfo G, Hillinger C (eds) Dynamic disequilibrium modelling (Cambridge University Press, Cambridge)

Wymer CR (1997) Structural non-linear continuous-time models in econometrics. MacroeconomicDynamics 1: 518–548

Wymer CR (2006) WYSEA: systems estimation and analysis reference and user guide

Chapter 8
The Macroeconomics of Imperfect Capital Markets: Whither Saving-Investment Imbalances?

Roberto Tamborini

Abstract Starting with Wicksell and until the heyday of Keynesian economics, inflation, unemployment and business cycles were thought and taught mainly as problems originating from "saving-investment imbalances" due to some form of malfunctioning of the capital market. Whereas modern studies of imperfect capital markets have greatly improved our understanding of capital market failures, their impact on macroeconomics has remained surprisingly limited. The macroeconomic consequences of saving-investment imbalances are still undeveloped in this literature. The most popular macroeconomic model to date – the so-called New Neoclassical Synthesis – dispenses with capital market imperfections altogether. The aim of this paper is to fill this gap. After an overview of the historical foundations and the current state of the macroeconomics of imperfect capital markets, the paper presents a competitive, flex-price model of saving-investment imbalances where deviations of the market interest rate from the Wicksellian natural rate generate (disequilibrium) business cycles. Then the model is extended to make the market interest rate endogenous and to allow preliminary considerations to be made about monetary policy and the control of the interest rate over the business cycle.

Introduction

> Starting with Wicksell [...] until Friedman revived the Quantity Theory, the saving-investment approaches dominated the field in this [Twentieth] century. All Keynesians, of whatever description, belong to this branch. The Stockholm School and the Austrians also descend from the Wicksell Connection. (Leijonhufvud 1981, p. 132).

Since the origins of macroeconomics and for a long time, inflation, unemployment and business cycles had been thought and taught mainly as *problems* related to intertemporal disequilibrium originating from "saving-investment imbalances" due

R. Tamborini
University of Trento, Department of Economics, Via Inama 5, 38100 Trento, Italy,
e-mail: roberto.tamborini@economia.unitn.it

G. Calcagnini and E. Saltari (eds.), *The Economics of Imperfect Markets*, Contributions to Economics,
DOI: 10.1007/978-3-7908-2131-4_8,

to some form of malfunctioning of the capital market. This approach to macroeconomics progressively fell by the wayside with completion of the Neo-Walrasian general-equilibrium paradigm, the rise of Monetarism, and finally the advent of the New Classical School with its method of dynamic stochastic general equilibrium.

At the same time, a robust and rigorous body of literature has grown devoted to explaining why capital markets may indeed fail in their allocation and coordination tasks. It is worth noting that some of the outstanding contributors to the modern theory of imperfect capital markets were motivated by the idea of giving firmer foundations to the original views of Wicksell and Keynes.

> For more than a decade now, I and several of my coauthors (...) have been exploring the thesis that it is imperfections in the capital market – imperfections that themselves can be explained by imperfect information – which account for many of the peculiar aspects of the behaviour of the economy which macroeconomics attempts to explain" (Stiglitz 1992, p. 269).
>
> [This] second strand of New Keynesian literature explores another path suggested by Keynes: that increased flexibility of prices and wages might exacerbate the economy's downturn. This insight implies that wage and price rigidity are not the only problem, and perhaps not even the central problem" (Greenwald and Stiglitz 1993b, p. 25).

However, whereas the study of imperfect capital markets has had far-reaching ramifications at the microeconomic level of analysis of markets, intermediaries and institutions, its impact on macroeconomics has remained surprisingly limited. As will be seen below, almost all the ingredients of a complete macro-theoretic menu are available, and yet the most popular macroeconomic model put forward to date – the so-called "New Neoclassical Synthesis" (NNS) – dispenses with capital market imperfections altogether. Thus, a clear divide has also emerged between the NNS and the earlier New Keynesian programme put forward by Stiglitz and co-authors.

The problem, however, is not only of interest for the history of thought. If the association of the NNS paradigm with the age of "Great Moderation" – the sustained growth and employment with low and stable inflation that blessed most of the industrialized world in the 1990s – induced the profession to believe that the right theoretical recipe had been found (Blanchard 2000), its inability to explain, predict and control the seeds of dramatic instability erupted in the world's best developed capital market with the new millennium suggests that the demise of capital market imperfections has turned out to be a hasty and unfortunate choice. Creeping "*financial imbalances* that build up disguised by a benign economic environment" (Borio and Lowe 2002, p. 1); italics added) have been detected as a major empirical regularity behind a significant sample of financial crises.

If this is true, however, it is also fair to say that the current state of development of the macroeconomics of imperfect capital markets, too, reveals some deficiencies. On the one hand, its microfoundations provide us with a rigorous taxonomy of the reasons why the market real interest rate may differ from the rate associated with intertemporal general equilibrium (IGE) of the economy (the Wicksellian "natural rate of interest") (e.g., Stiglitz 1982, 1992). This malfunctioning may result either in a form of rationing (the capital market does not clear at the market rate) or in a form of trading at false price (the capital market clears but the market rate differs from the natural rate). In either case, saving and investment will generally differ from the amount that would be consistent with IGE. On the other hand, with few exceptions, the macroeconomic consequences of saving-investment imbalances are still undeveloped in this literature. Ignoring intertemporal disequilibrium constitutes a major theoretical weakness because it is a *logical implication* in *any* theory based on the distinction between the market interest rate and the natural rate (see also Leijonhufvud 1981; Van der Ploeg 2005). Filling this gap is the main purpose of the paper.

Section The macroeconomics of imperfect capital markets – An overview, overviews the current state of the macroeconomics of imperfect capital markets. The section begins with a summary of the modern foundations of imperfect capital markets, and ends with the remark that these do not develop the implications of saving-investment imbalances that are inherent in capital market misallocations. Section Some macroeconomics of saving-investment imbalances – The baseline model, outlines an analysis of these implications. First, preliminary tools are introduced. Second, I present a general-equilibrium flex-price model directly comparable with the standard NNS model. Here, however, (exogenous) deviations of the market interest rate from the Wicksellian natural rate generate (disequilibrium) business cycles with Wicksell-Keynesian features. In Section Endogenizing the nominal interest rate, the model is extended in order to make the market interest rate endogenous following insights from both Wicksell and Keynes. This extension also allows for preliminary considerations about monetary policy and the control of the interest rate over the business cycle. Section Conclusions summarizes and concludes.

The Macroeconomics of Imperfect Capital Markets: An Overview

Brief Historical Foundations – Wicksell and Keynes

This paragraph simply sketches, with no claim to provide a detailed picture, some historical antecedents of the macroeconomics of imperfect capital markets. As the opening quotation indicates, Wicksell is the right and natural starting point.

As is well known, the role of what came to be known as "saving-investment imbalances" in the business cycle was put forward by Wicksell in his interest-rate theory of the general price level (GPL) and of "cumulative processes" (e.g., Wicksell 1898a, b). This was centred on the notion of the "natural rate of interest." It is worth quoting one of the key sentences once again

> At any moment in time in any income situation there is always a certain rate of interest, at which the exchange value of money and the general level of commodity prices have no tendency to change. This can be called *the normal rate of interest*; its level is determined by the current natural rate of interest, the real return on capital in production, and must rise or fall with this. If the rate of interest on money deviates downwards, be it ever so little, from this normal level, prices will, as long as the deviation lasts, rise continuously; if it deviates upwards, they will fall indefinitely in the same way (1898a, p. 82).

Therefore,

> In Wicksell's theory of the cumulative process, the maladjustment of the interest rate – the discrepancy between the market and the natural rate – is the central idea. It is also the idea that motivates the analysis of changes in the price level (or in nominal income) in terms of saving and investment. [. . .]. Use of the saving-investment approach to income fluctuations is predicated on the hypothesis that the interest rate mechanism fails to coordinate saving and investment decisions appropriately (Leijonhufvud 1981, p. 132).

The natural question raised by this view is how this maladjustment may happen. Interpretations here are more difficult, but it seems fair to point out two basic ideas. The first is the difference between a monetary economy and a barter or "corn economy." In the former, unlike the latter, capital is not self-lent in kind by households to themselves, but firms need to borrow funds in monetary form from households in order to pay for capital goods (e.g., Wicksell 1898b, p. 84). Second, there are intermediaries between savers and investors. As long as non-bank agents borrow and lend among themselves, the total amount of nominal purchasing power in the economy is redistributed but cannot (need not) increase. The capital market finds its equilibrium at the natural rate of interest as determined by the "forces of productivity and thrift" that equate saving and investment at full-employment of resources. Yet, as soon as the banking system (central bank and private banks) comes into play, the latter proposition no longer necessarily holds. A private bank is in a position to grant additional nominal purchasing power to any of its depositors' accounts with no one else in the economy undergoing an equivalent reduction. Likewise, a private bank can increase its own nominal purchasing (lending) power by borrowing from the central bank. Thus, the point is that the banking system as a whole might both expand the total nominal purchasing power in the economy and allocate it at terms that differ from those dictated by full-employment saving-investment equilibrium (e.g., Wicksell 1898b, p. 74, ff.).

Note that, from the viewpoint of modern analysis, the kind of market failure that Wicksell introduces is *not* in the form of rationing, but in the form of "trade at false price" (more on this distinction in paragraph 2.3 below). See Fig. 8.1: if the market interest rate r_t differs from the natural rate r^*_t and saving differs from investment, the capital market does clear at all times, with households and firms saving and investing, respectively, what they wish, as the banking sector steps in to fill the gap by hoarding (excess saving) or dishoarding (excess investment) reserves (Leijonhufvud 1981).

As to the motivation for banks to extend credit beyond (or below) saving-investment equilibrium, a possible explanation may be, in modern terms, *limited information*. In various passages, Wicksell warned that the critical challenge for monetary and banking policy lies in the natural interest rate being subject to unobservable shocks and fluctuations (e.g., 1898a, 82 ff.). If banks do not observe the natural rate directly, and are not immediately constrained in their ability to extend and contract their loans, the market interest may well deviate from the natural rate as long as banks are not induced to revise it in response to some indirect market signal. Such a signal is, in Wicksell's view, precisely the cumulative process of changes in the GPL.

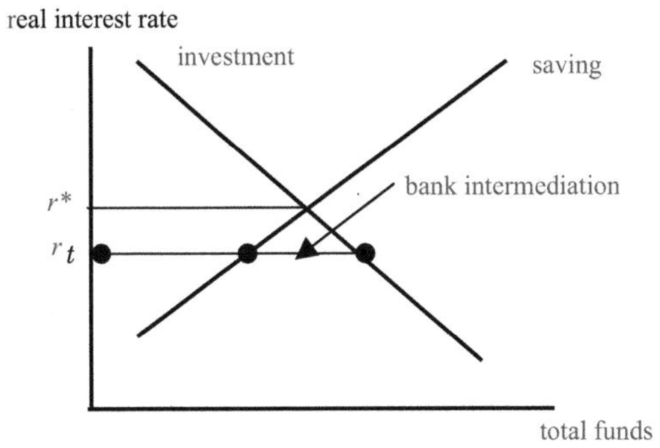

Fig. 8.1 A Wicksellian capital market

The debate on the business cycle in the first two decades of the twentieth century was largely dominated by Wicksellian ideas as re-elaborated by the Swedish, Austrian and Cambridge Schools (e.g., Boianovsky and Trautwein 2004, 2006). At that time it was understood that saving-investment imbalances – or the breakdown of Say's Law as Keynes put it – not only imply that today's supply of goods exceeds demand, but they also have an intertemporal nature, in that tomorrow's consumption and production plans will not match. Hence these imbalances are a major force behind the determination of the level of real and nominal variables as well as their (endogenous) fluctuations.

Keynes's first major theoretical work, the *Treatise on Money* (1930), was clearly developed along this line of reasoning, whilst the *General Theory* (1936) can be viewed as an attempt to recast the Wicksellian ideas in terms of real economic activity and employment. Ample textual evidence, in the *General Theory* (e.g., Bk. II) and after (Keynes 1937a–c), testifies that Keynes sought to explain unemployment equilibrium as a result of a mismatch between investment and saving due to a capital market failure. Yet Keynes was even more sceptical than Wicksell about the very existence of the natural rate of interest, and pointed to a different account of the capital market failure. This was related not to intermediaries but to the "monetary nature of the rate of interest." Uncertainty and the demand for money as store of value and as a speculative asset were brought to the forefront as the main causes driving a wedge between the market interest rate and the rate that, in the same given circumstances, would yield the full-employment saving-investment equilibrium. However, like Wicksell, Keynes did not introduce any form of rationing: the capital market eventually clears at a "false" interest rate leading to the unemployment equilibrium.

Throughout the first half of its parable, the "Keynesian revolution" was understood, explained and taught precisely as a departure from the neoclassical macroeconomics of general equilibrium theory on the grounds of capital markets. Keynes's discussion of the role of the labour market in the adjustment process in the event of excess saving, and in particular in light of the possibility that the real wage may not fall *enough* (1936, ch. 19), should be understood as a warning that there is no reason to expect that the misallocational effects of a "wrong" price of capital will necessarily be corrected through changes in the price of labor by market forces. Wage stickiness, though possibly a fact of real life, is a side issue in this theoretical picture. Indeed, the theoretical debate in the aftermath of the *General Theory* concentrated on the theory of the interest rate (see Moggridge 1987, pp. 201–367) with little or no reference to wage stickiness.

Modern Foundations of Imperfect Capital Markets

As recalled in the Introduction, an initial important impulse came from the scholars who were seeking to give better microeconomic foundations to Keynes's idea that capital market failures are the main source of macroeconomic fluctuations. However, with respect to Keynes's approach centred on outside uncertainty and the demand for money as store of value, which was subsequently embodied in the Neoclassical Synthesis, the modern foundations marked a significant shift towards inside uncertainty, that is asymmetric information (AI) and the related agency problems between lenders and borrowers. From this point of view, the general outlook is more Wicksellian than Keynesian. It is also worth adding that Keynes, and many of his followers, attached great importance to his notion of non-classic-probabilistic uncertainty underlying savers' and investors' behavior (e.g., 1937c) as the source of the endemic nature of the capital market failures. The new foundations are instead laid within the boundaries of classical probabilistic uncertainty and rational decision-making. They essentially rest on the following five points (e.g., Stiglitz 1982).

1. *Agents heterogeneity*: Markets exist and trades take place because agents differ. Traditional microeconomics concentrates on differences in preferences and/or endowments as inducements to trade; the economics of imperfect capital markets concentrates on differences in information endowments.
2. *Imperfect information*: Agents have free access to a *public information set* on relevant current and future state variables, which may be incomplete for the future variables (probabilistic risk); but they do not have free access to each other's *private information set* on individual payoff-relevant variables or actions.
3. *Incomplete markets*: Agents are constrained not to trade for goods to which they attach positive value. In particular, economies are studied where future contingent markets for consumption goods are absent. Note that the definition of AI implies another missing market, the market for private information.
4. *Sequential time and transactions*: Markets operate and trades take place in discrete "calendar" time periods. In each period, only spot transactions take place.
5. *The "special nature" of financial "goods"*: Capital markets handle "special goods", namely financial contracts. They are special for a number of reasons: (1) they are immaterial entitlements to *future* delivery of *money* payments, (2) the transaction involved is opened spot (the purchase of the entitlement), but is closed in the future (the delivery of the money payment), (3) the open

end of the transaction is dependent upon both general market states and specific individual states or actions of the party due to deliver the money payment.

Analyses of financial relationships under costly or asymmetric information produce results that as a rule imply some form of capital market failure. These results are often referred to as violations of the Modigliani-Miller theorem (Modigliani and Miller 1958) that demonstrates the irrelevance of financial factors in firms' real investment choices. Market failures emerge as a consequence of two possible responses of rational agents to imperfect information. One, in a context of pre-defined contracts, ex-ante asymmetry and adverse selection, is the uninformed party's use of the price of the financial transaction as an indicator of the hidden information about the other party (e.g., Stiglitz 1987). The other, in a context of ex-post asymmetry and moral hazard, is the design of financial contracts able to regulate the conflict of interests between the better informed and the worse informed party once the relationship is established (e.g., Hart 1995, Part II).

Looking at the macroeconomic level, the foregoing array of imperfect capital-market transactions have mostly been employed to deploy new building blocks regarding

- Investment in fixed capital (as a component of aggregate demand: e.g., Fazzari et al. 1988; Bond and Jenkinson 1996)
- Investment in working capital, in particular the wage bill (as a component of aggregate supply: e.g., Greenwald and Stiglitz 1988, 1993a)
- Financial factors in the business cycle (e.g., Bernanke and Gertler 1989; Bernanke et al. 1996; Gertler 1988; Gertler and Hubbard 1988; Kiyotaki and Moore 1997)
- Financial factors in growth (e.g., Demirguç-Kunt and Levine 2001; Allen and Gale 2001)
- Policy, especially monetary policy, implications (e.g., Bernanke and Blinder 1998; Greenwald and Stiglitz 1991, Gertler and Gilchrist 1993, Bernanke and Gertler 1995)

Hence it seems fair to say that *almost* a complete macroeconomic theory with imperfect capital markets is now available. For reasons of space, here my assessment of the state of the art will be limited to the first and second points, with some indirect considerations of the last.[1] These, in my view, are also the key issues on which the strengths and weaknesses of the theory should be assessed.

Underinvestment and Overinvestment

Following the taxonomy racalled in paragraph 2.1, let us first consider the class of models with rationing. This allocational failure entails that the capital market does not clear, that is, saving is not equal to investment at the market rate. A typical

[1] A more comprehensive overview can be found in Delli Gatti and Tamborini (2000).

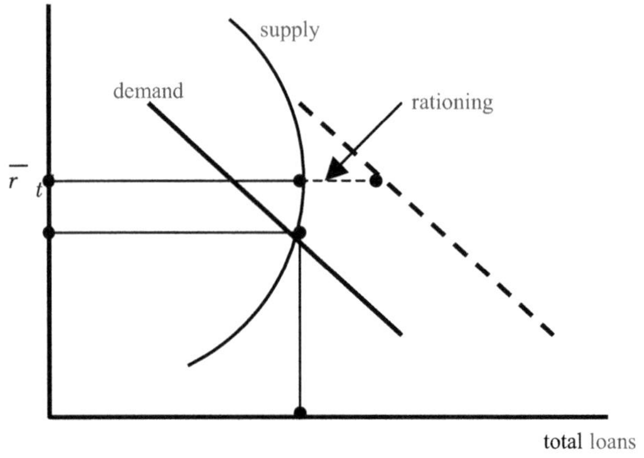

Fig. 8.2 Credit rationing in the Stiglitz–Weiss model

example is given by the Stiglitz-Weiss (1981) model of credit with AI and adverse selection (see Fig. 8.2)

This is a partial equilibrium model of the credit market which, however, includes an endogenous supply of funds vis-à-vis a conventional downward-sloping demand curve. The supply of funds comes from households' deposits and can be regarded as representative of savings. In a perfect market, intermediation (if any) would be neutral, and deposits (savings) would equal loans (investments) at the market-clearing interest rate. As a consequence of adverse selection, however, the supply curve of loans is backward-bending. This is because increasing the interest rate raises the unit return to loans on the one hand, but also raises the probability of default by borrowers on the other. Beyond a certain threshold of the interest rate, $\bar{r}_t$ the banks' expected profit bends backward and so does the supply of loans. With this supply curve in place, it may happen that the demand for loans exceeds supply at the maximum interest rate set by banks, and excess demand is rationed. The conclusion is that, at the interest rate set by banks, *notional* investment exceeds saving whereas *actual* investment is constrained to be equal to saving.

Alternatively, we may consider models with trading at false price, which is emphatically not to be confused with rationing. In this case the capital market clears, but the market interest rate differs from the natural rate. A useful example is provided by De Meza and Webb (1987). Like Stiglitz and Weiss they consider a credit market characterized by AI and adverse selection. This phenomenon, however, operates in the opposite way from that envisaged by Stiglitz and Weiss. There, increasing the interest rate crowds out low-risk projects, here it crowds in high-return projects. Thus the average quality of borrowers is higher than the quality of the marginal borrower. As a result, the banks' expected profit function, as well as the loan supply curve, are monotonically increasing with the interest rate, and a market-clearing equilibrium can be reached. However, De Meza and Webb demonstrate that the net present value of the project of the marginal borrower is negative. Their conclusion is that adverse selection may well generate excess investment by way of the bank sector. In other words, if the natural interest rate is the rate that drives the net present value of the marginal borrower to zero, we can also say that the equilibrium interest rate charged by banks is below the natural rate.[2]

Macroeconomic Implications

The first, in order of time and importance, macroeconomic projection of the study of imperfect capital markets concerns aggregate investment determination, with a particular emphasis on *underinvestment*, that is, investment below the perfect-market benchmark (e.g., Fazzari et al. 1988). Figure 8.3 depicts the main issues. The vertical axis measures the return to invested capital (however it is measured), and the horizontal axis measures total investment. A standard inverse relationship is considered. The first key point (the first violation of the Modigliani–Miller theorem) is that in AI capital markets *firms face different costs of capital* according to different sources even in the absence of exogenous risk. Typically, the cheapest cost of capital r_t is the risk-free opportunity cost of internal funds (in a risk-free market this would also be the single market rate). External funds, whether they be equity or debt (here we need not distinguish them), entail an extra cost r'_t due to the AI "lemon" premium that the market charges to cope with any of the AI risks recalled above.

In some circumstances, namely under rationing, the lemon premium becomes "infinite" (the second violation of the Modigliani–Miller theorem), and the corresponding investments cannot be financed at the given market conditions. This phenomenon may occur in the equity market (e.g., Leland-Pyle 1977; Myers-Majluf

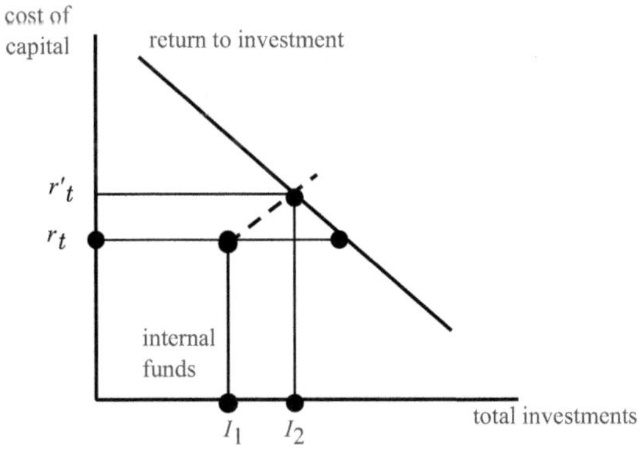

Fig. 8.3 Aggregate investement with capital market failures

[2] Thus this model can be viewed as a modern explanation of the role of banks in Wicksell's theory of saving-investment imbalances.

1984) as well as in the credit market (e.g., Jaffee and Stiglitz 1990; Stiglitz and Weiss 1981).

Consequently, total investment comes to depend on (1) the extent to which firms own internal funds, (2) the extent to which, and the cost at which, they have access to external funds. Therefore, two main phenomena characterize AI capital markets

- *Financial hierarchy* (or *pecking order*): Firms finance investment starting from the cheapest source of capital supply, and they resort to other sources only as the scale of, and the return to, investment increase sufficiently
- *Financial rationing*: Some classes of firms may have no access at all to some forms of capital supply; hence their ability to invest is constrained by their amount of internal resources, say I_1.

It is important to note that the two phenomena give rise to two different allocational situations. The former, generally, entails that total investment may be *less* than it would be in a perfect market, but nonetheless firms are *unconstrained* (i.e., they are *on* their efficient investment curve that they reach by combining different funds). The latter, by contrast, implies both a loss of total investment and that firms are constrained (i.e., they are *off* their efficient investment curve). In other words, in one case we have low but efficient investment at the margin, in the other we have a loss of efficient investments.

It is perhaps a clue to the Keynesian inspiration of this literature that its has largely focused on underinvestment, the cases of rationing being the most critical ones. On the other hand, if stagnations and recessions are recurrent evils that may be traced back to underinvestment, it is nonetheless striking that the most important episodes of large-scale underinvestment, starting from 1929 and ending in 2008, did follow episodes of overinvestment, with stock market bubbles and the subsequent crash landing of stock values (Borio and Lowe 2002). The most important Keynesian author who sought to explore capital market failures leading to overinvestment and complete boom-bust cycles was Minsky (1972, 1975). He should be credited with the introduction of the concepts of "financial fragility" and "financial accelerator" that have subsequently been reshaped with the modern tools of the New Keynesians (Bernanke and Gertler 1989, 1990; Bernanke et al. 1996). De Meza and Webb (1987) have drawn attention to the fact that AI may lead to overinvestment, and Tamborini (2001, ch. 8) has exemplified this case in a simple model of equity market *à la* Myers-Majluf. The compelling evidence for the role of overinvestment in the generation of recent financial crises has prompted further research extending towards the role of monetary policy (e.g., Cecchetti et al. 2000; Bernanke and Gertler 2001; Bordo and Jeanne 2002).

Whither Saving-Investment Imbalances?

More than two decades of active research in the field of imperfect capital markets have greatly improved our understanding of the actual working of these markets, and of their role in the life of market economies, either for the better of stability and growth or for the worse of instability and slumps. Nonetheless, the overall picture is still incomplete. The point is that in the presence of market imperfections, it is generally no longer the case that saving equals investment at the Wicksellian natural interest rate, that is, the interest rate which grants IGE (Stiglitz 1992). Yet we generally do not find explicit treatment of the supply side of the capital market, or of the intertemporal consistency between saving and investment.

Looking back at the evolution of the macroeconomics of imperfect capital markets, from its origins to its modern developments, we may be struck by a sort of paradox. Initially, the key issue was the macroeconomic consequences of saving-investment imbalances, in a theoretical context with relatively poor instruments of microeconomic and intertemporal analysis. Today, we have a rich and powerful theory of capital market failures at the microeconomic level, but their macroeconomic consequences are poorly developed. Exploring this neglected side of the modern macroeconomics of imperfect capital markets is the purpose of the subsequent parts of the paper.

Some Macroeconomics of Saving-Investment Imbalances: The Baseline Model

Preliminary Tools and Discussion

To begin with, let us consider an economy along its IGE path. The corresponding price vector includes the relative price of factors at each time t (the real wage rate and the real interest rate as dictated by real determinants). The problem is how the economy reacts when the real interest rate is "wrong." As usual, investment in t determines the capital stock for production in $t + 1$. The ensuing allocation scheme is exemplified in Table 8.1.

Consider the case that in t the market real interest rate exceeds the natural one. Excess saving arises, to which there corresponds excess supply in the output market in t, and, by intertemporal Walras Law, excess (planned) demand in $t + 1$. Note that the capital-market disequilibrium in t, if uncorrected, *must* have an intertemporal disequilibrium effect on the output and labour markets in $t + 1$ even though the

Table 8.1 Allocation scheme when the market real interest rate differs from the natural rate

	t		$t+1$	
	$R_t < R^*$	$R_t > R^*$	$R_t < R^*$	$R_t > R^*$
Capital market	$S_t < I_t$	$S_t > I_t$	$K_{t+1} > K_t$	$K_{t+1} < K_t$
Goods market	$AD_t > Y_t$	$AD_t < Y_t$	$AD_{t+1} < Y_{t+1}$	$AD_{t+1} > Y_{t+1}$

R = market real interest rate, R^* = natural interest rate, S = saving, I = investment, K = capital stock, AD = aggregate demand, Y = aggregate supply (potential output)

real wage is perfectly "right" with respect to the natural interest rate. As thoroughly explained by Leijonhufvud (1981), these are the two key logical implications of any saving-investment imbalance theory, namely

- "Unemployment will not converge to its natural level *unless* the interest rate goes to its natural level – (...) the latter condition will not always be fulfilled" (p. 135)
- "With the interest rate at the right level, market forces should make unemployment converge to the natural rate – otherwise not" (p. 136).

As a corollary, the fact that we may observe disequilibrium in one market, say the labour market, does not imply that the *problem* lies in that market. In a system of interrelated markets, "wrong signals" impinging on one market may well originate from elsewhere.

> The very nature of the problem associated with information asymmetries suggests that it is precisely in those markets which are in charge of coordinating intertemporal decisions that rigidities and inefficiencies are most common [Since] investment decisions are made on the basis of signals sent by these typically inefficient markets, it is only too natural to expect that they lead to distortions. As a result, the burden of adjustment will fall upon other markets (Fitoussi 2001, p. 24)

In order to develop these implications analytically, we can take the two alternative analytical routes exemplified in Section Underinvestment and Overinvestment, rationing or trading at false price. The first requires exploring different rationing schemes (e.g., Heijdra and van der Ploeg 2005) and non-market-clearing processes (e.g., Chiarella et al. 2005). Rationing schemes typically produce adjustments in quantities at the given rationing prices. A typical example is given by the "short-side-of-the-market" rule. If $R_t > R^*$, the rule states that households are rationed in saving in t and are rationed in consumption in $t+1$, whereas firms are only rationed in production in t. That is to say, households are forced to save in t, and consume in $t+1$, as much as it is determined by firms' investment in t, and production capacity in $t+1$, respectively. Likewise, in t firms can undertake as much investment as they wish, but they are forced to produce less.

With trading at false price, demand equals supply at all times, but the resulting vector of prices and quantities is different than in the IGE vector. Hence, there must be an allocational "error" arising at some point in the system. In general, we may expect a mix of adjustment in prices and quantities. Yet the mix has little to do with the degree of price flexibility. Rather, the eventual result depends first of all on the allocation scheme in the capital market.

Whereas the bulk of the modern literature on capital market failures deals with rationing, here I shall pursue the other route, which was instead common to both Wicksell and Keynes. Here I shall follow Tamborini (2007) based on Wicksell's hypothesis that the banking system sets the market interest rate and then *it fills any possible gap between investment and saving if the market rate differs from the natural rate* by lending or hoarding reserves.[3] If firms are on the long side of the market,

[3] Recall the model by De Meza and Webb mentioned in Section Underinvestment and Overinvestment.

$R_t < R^*$, they can actually invest more than households wish to save thanks to banks' additional loans. If households are on the long side, they are allowed to save as much as they wish by banks hoarding reserves. For the time being, the interest rate set by the banking system is kept exogenous, whereas it will be endogenized later on. On these assumptions, it can be shown that in a competitive, flex-price economy with optimizing, forward-looking agents, saving-investment imbalances with trades at the "false" interest rate in t imply a single, well-defined vector of output realizations to be accommodated by the goods market in t and $t + 1$. The related market-clearing paths of output and the GPL depend on technology, production capacity and price expectations. Yet the key point is that both deviate from the IGE path that would obtain with trade at the natural interest rate. Under suitable, though standard, conditions on the utility and production functions, *both output and the GPL* deviate upwards if $R_t < R^*$ and deviate downwards if $R_t > R^*$.

The Model

This subsection introduces a log-linear version of the above-mentioned model that focuses on unemployment upon the assumption that a unique, well-defined relationship (e.g., Okun Law) exists between output and unemployment.

Let us consider an economy with IGE characterized by the natural rate of unemployment (NAIRU) u as determined by a given combination of tastes, technology and the relative value of the real wage rate w with respect to the natural interest rate r. All the IGE variables (u, w, r) are assumed to be constant.[4] As discussed above, the actual unemployment rate at any time, u_t, differs from u to the extent that the market real interest rate, $i_t - \pi^e{}_{t+1}$, differs from r. Also recall that any saving-investment imbalance at time t implies a corresponding labour demand-supply imbalance at time $t + 1$. Hence there should be a *feed-forward effect* of current interest-gaps on *present and future* unemployment gaps. Therefore, looking at the time series of the two variables one may expect to detect (1) dependence of unemployment gaps on past interest-rate gaps, (2) some degree of (spurious) persistence of unemployment gaps due to dependence on the common interest-rate gap.[5] Consequently, the unemployment *out-of-equilibrium* dynamics can also be

[4] According to standard DSGE methodology these variables may change over time owing to random shocks to the underlying parameters. This feature is inessential for present purposes.

[5] As a matter of fact, recurrent estimates of the output/unemployment and inflation functions invariably find these features. See Orphanides and Williams (2002, 2006) and Caresma et al. (2005) for a survey. These empirical regularities are not easily accommodated within a model whose hallmark is the role of so-called *forward-looking* output and inflation functions, unless the model is filled with additional ad hoc "frictions" (Chiarella et al. 2005, chs. 1 and 8, offer a thorough discussion). However, the time structure of our equations 0-0 are not due to backward-looking behavior or other frictions. On the contrary, they result from the correct consideration of the *feed-foward* effects of saving-investment imbalances.

represented by a first-order linear equation like the following

$$u_{t+1} = u + \rho(u_t - u) + \alpha(i_t - \pi^e_{t+1} - r) \tag{8.1}$$

where $u_{t+1} \neq u$ as long as $(i_t - \pi^e{}_{t+1}) \neq r$, with some degree of persistence $0 < \rho < 1$. This may be called the "cap-lab" (CL) function since it relates the labour to the capital market.

The inflation rate at any point in time turns out to be governed by an expectation-augmented Phillips curve (PC), i.e.,

$$\pi_{t+1} = \pi^e_{t+1} - \beta(u_{t+1} - u) \tag{8.2}$$

where $\beta > 0$ denotes the responsiveness of nominal prices/wages to goods/labor markets deviations from steady state. It should be noted that this PC is consistent with flexible nominal wages and prices and a finite value of β, in that it describes how unemployment reacts to transitory inflation dynamics as long as $\pi_{t+1} \neq \pi^e{}_{t+1}$. In other words, this can be regarded as the non-vertical, out-of-equilibrium PC generated by a Lucasian flex-price aggregate supply function with "surprise inflation." Nominal rigidities affecting the value of β may exist as a matter of fact, but they are not necessary theoretically.

Finally, the model is closed by the determination of the expected inflation rate. As is well known, investors' expectation-formation was a matter of endless dispute in the older macroeconomic literature until the advent of the rational expectations hypothesis. In the context of this model, recourse to the rational expectations hypothesis would imply that agents know the steady-state values of the variables, which in turn depend on the inflation expectation itself. This is the notorious self-referentiality inherent in that hypothesis (see e.g., Evans and Honkapohja 2001). In order to have a flexible framework in which different expectation mechanisms can be assessed, I consider two co-existing hypotheses.

The first is a close antecedent of the modern rational expectations hypothesis, namely the concept of normal inflation rate. The concept of normal value of a variable was widely used as point of reference for expectations by Wicksell, Keynes and pre-Lucasian economists in general. Normality was generally referred to the long-run average value observed for a variable, which is also expected to prevail in the future in the states of rest of the system. For simplicity, this information about inflation is taken as a pre-determined (possibly zero) value π. If the belief that π is the normal inflation rate is correct, then π should result as the steady-state solution of inflation. If this happens, π is also the "long-run" rational expectation of the inflation rate. The second expectation mechanism is borrowed from the standard NNS model, namely that agents correctly anticipate next-period's inflation, that is, $E_t(\pi^e{}_{t+1} - \pi_{t+1}) = 0$, where E_t indicates the statistical expectation operator as of time t. These I would call "short-run" rational expectations.

Then, let a share δ of agents form "short-run" rational expectations, while the complementary share believes in the return to normality. As a result, the variable $\pi^e{}_{t+1}$ in (1) and (2) should be replaced with

$$\delta\pi_{t+1} + (1 - \delta)\pi \tag{8.3}$$

After substituting for inflation expectations, the CL–PC equations form a system of two first-order difference equations with two endogenous variables $[u_t, \pi_t]$, one time-varying exogenous variable, i_t, and three exogenous constants $[u, \pi, r]$. The system can conveniently be transformed in terms of two endogenous gaps $[\hat{u}_t \equiv u_t - u,\ \hat{\pi}_t \equiv \pi_t - \pi]$, and one exogenous gap $(\hat{i}_t = i_t - i)$, where $i \equiv r + \pi$. The latter is the "non-accelerating-inflation rate of interest" (NAIRI) or the nominal value of the natural rate at the normal inflation rate. This expression is exactly equivalent to the difference between the market real interest and the natural rate, but it is more convenient in the present context. Therefore we have the following non-homogenous system

$$\hat{u}_{t+1} = \rho' \hat{u}_t + \alpha' \hat{i}_t \tag{8.4}$$

$$\hat{\pi}_{i+1} = -\beta' \hat{u}_{i+1} \tag{8.5}$$

where

$$\alpha' = \alpha \frac{1-\delta}{1-\delta(1+\alpha\beta)}, \quad \rho = \rho \frac{1-\delta}{1-\delta(1+\alpha\beta)}, \quad \beta = \frac{\beta}{1-\delta}$$

Steady State

The first and most important result is that, for any constant initial value $\hat{i}_0 \neq 0$, the system admits of a solution where

$$\hat{u} = \frac{\alpha'}{1 \quad \rho'} \hat{i}_0 \tag{8.6}$$

$$\hat{\pi} = -\frac{\beta' \alpha'}{1-\rho'} \hat{i}_0 \tag{8.7}$$

Then it is easily seen that the system achieves the steady state with zero endogenous gaps $[\hat{u}_t = 0,\ \hat{\pi}_t = 0]$ if and only if $\hat{i}_0 = 0$. The condition $\rho' \in [0,\ 1]$ also entails that if $\hat{i}_0 \neq 0$, unemployment and inflation converge monotonically to, and remain locked in, the values given by (8.6) and (8.7), with *both unemployment and inflation being inefficiently high or low*, and *being inconsistent with their IGE values*. This is in fact the analytical solution of the general implication of saving-investment imbalances discussed above (see the quotations from Leijonhufvud 1981; Fitoussi 2001). Note, however, that non-zero gaps is a general property of non-homogenous systems, and we have a non-homogenous system because of the assumption that the nominal interest rate is exogenously given. This assumption will be relaxed later on.

The model also captures the essence of Wicksell–Keynes cumultative processes. Suppose, as Wicksell did, that $\hat{i}_0 < 0$, and the initial steady state is one with constant price level. Then, our result means that the price level would indefinitely rise at a constant rate (Wicksell 1898b, pp. 77–78). Wicksell correctly considered these price changes a major disequilibrium phenomenon which should be carefully understood and curbed, though they may occur in perfectly competitive goods and labor markets (in which case the NAIRU u would simply be zero). Wicksellian cumulative processes are a disequilibrium phenomenon in a precise sense: *expectations of a return to normality are systematically falsified.* While all markets clear at all times, the "error" generated by trading at the "false" interest rate in the capital market shows up as an expectational error about inflation. As was clear to Wicksell himself, and to the Swedish school in general (e.g., Boianovski and Trautwein 2004, 2006), this fact raises the problem of how expectations are possibly revised, and how the revision mechanism impinges upon the dynamic process. This problem will be reconsidered later on.

What is important to stress at this juncture is that this is a radically different interpretation of the role of changes in the GPL with respect to the NNS. In the NNS model "it is only [...] with sticky prices that one is able to introduce the crucial Wicksellian distinction between the actual and the natural rate of interest, as the discrepancy between the two arises only as a consequence of a failure of prices to adjust sufficiently rapidly" (Woodford 2003, p. 238). By contrast, Wicksell cast his theory in a competitive, flex-price framework, and he argued that interest rates should be brought under policy control not because prices do not move enough, but because unfettered interest rates may force prices to move out-of-equilibrium. On the other hand, changes in the GPL are a means to re-equilibrate the economy only if, and to the extent that, they induce the nominal interest rate to close the gap with the natural rate (Wicksell 1898a, pp. 80 ff). Sticky prices may be introduced into the picture as a matter of realism, yet they are not necessary theoretically.

On the other hand, Wicksell did not pay sufficient attention to the real side of the disequilibrium cumulative process, which was unveiled by Keynes's theory of effective demand.[6] Consider now the case that $\hat{i}_0 > 0$. The system converges to a steady-state unemployment rate above the NAIRU (the unemployment level given by the "right" relative price of labour to capital). This result may be regarded as a characterization of Keynes's concept of "involuntary unemployment" (with a caveat to be discussed below). Given the "false" market real interest rate, not all workers ready to work at the IGE real wage rate will ever be employed. Since no structural parameter has changed that justifies a change in the real wage rate, the unemployment gap is entirely due to the interest-rate gap. Note also, that the much debated β parameter of the PC function is not so much crucial *per se* as it is in connection with the parameter δ regulating expectation formation. Insofar as the interplay between β and δ fulfills the convergence condition $\rho' \in [0,\ 1]$, the system does not change its qualitative properties. However, for any given δ, the system tends towards instability as β *increases*: that is, the PC function becomes steeper – a well-known argument

[6] "While Wicksell had refused to use his theory of cumulative processes for the explanation of industrial fluctuations, [it was] Lindahl [who] wanted to extend Wicksell's approach into a general theory of business cycle" (Boianovsky and Trautwein 2006, p. 8). Lindahl (1939) in fact included unemployment in his analysis, foreshadowing the modern distinction between cyclical and structural unemployment (Lindahl 1939, p. 11).

by Keynes (1936, ch. 19). On the other hand, the unemployment gap is associated with less-than-expected inflation, a well-known argument against the consistency of "involuntary unemployment" as a steady-state.

System's Dynamics and the Role of Expectations

First of all, the coefficients of the steady-state values of $\hat{u}$ and $\hat{\pi}$ increase with δ in absolute value, that is, short-run forward-looking expectations are *deviation-amplifying* in steady state. Moreover, the system will converge to the steady state only if δ is bounded

$$\delta < \left(\frac{1-\rho}{1-\rho+\alpha\beta}\right) < 1$$

As δ exceeds this threshold, unemployment and inflation will take divergent trajectories. This possibility was well understood and feared by both Wicksell, in the event of self-sustained inflation (e.g., Wicksell (1922, XII, n.1)) and Keynes, in the event of bottomless deflation (1936, ch. 19). As long as $\hat{i}_0$ remains positive or negative, investors anticipate the ensuing rise or fall in the inflation rate. As a consequence, the positive or negative gap of the market real interest rate relative to the natural rate is amplified, and so are the unemployment and inflation gaps along the adjustment path.

As $\delta \to 1$, the system jumps to a steady state where $\hat{u} = 0$, $\hat{\pi} = \hat{i}_0$. On the one hand, there are no real effects, on the other, the sign of the relationship between $\hat{i}_0$ and $\hat{\pi}$ is inverted (low (high) interest rate generates excess deflation (inflation)). This replicates a well-known result in the modern theory of monetary policy established by McCallum (1986). As he stressed, this result is consistent with the Fisher equation. In fact, if one takes the Fisher equation as a basis for inflation expectations, then $\pi^e{}_{t+1} = i_t - r$. However, *starting* from the Fisher equation is not a correct rendition of models of saving-investment imbalances, in which the Fisher equation should eventually be the *ending* point of the adjustment of a *disequilibrium* process. Indeed, as can be seen from our treatment, McCallum's conclusion is valid only within the limits of uniformly held short-run rational expectations, but there is no trajectory leading the system to the Fisher equation when the starting point is at $\delta < 1$.

Endogenizing the Nominal Interest Rate

So far the nominal interest rate has been treated as an exogenous variable. Our next step will be to close the model with an adjustment equation of the nominal interest rate i_t that endogenizes the dynamics of the interest rate gap after an initial shock. The focus will be on *endogenous market mechanisms*, which means that monetary policy is, for the time being, left in the background. This choice can be justified for two reasons. The first is that there are various theories of *market* interest rate determination in the context of saving-investment imbalances that should be considered in order to have a broader view of this phenomenon. The second is that the almost exclusive shift of monetary policy analysis towards interest-rate control that has occurred in the last few years has hidden from view the fundamental fact that there exist other channels of interest rate determination in addition to, or in the place of, direct control of the central bank.

For the sake of comparison, I will consider three different specifications inspired by the alternative theories of the interest rate put forward by the founders of the saving-investment imbalance approach: (1) a Wicksellian bank mechanism, (2) a "dynamic" Keynesian LM equation, (3) a "speculative" LM equation. Let me first point out that, from an analytical point of view, "endogenizing" the nominal interest rate means that, whereas the baseline model with exogenous interest rate was a non-homogeneous system, we may expect that a well-specified interest-rate equation transforms the system into a homogenous one. This class of systems generally admits of zero-gaps steady states, that is, complete stabilization. It should therefore be borne in mind that complete stabilization can be the outcome of *any* interest-rate equation that endogenizes the nominal interest rate properly.

A Wicksellian Bank Mechanism

The well-known Wicksellian idea is that the out-of-equilibrium nominal interest rate is procyclical with the GPL (e.g., 1901, Bk. II, 1898b). This was a well-established fact even before the inception of inflation-target rules by central banks.[7] In Wicksell's view the reason is that banks raise or lower their nominal lending rate to the extent that the GPL increases above or decreases below what is considered its normal level. This process may be driven by the need of banks to keep their loans balanced with real reserves during the expansion (contraction) of the demand for funds and of the GPL. More simply, banks may have a real interest target and index the nominal rate accordingly. These two explanations have, however, different theoretical implications in the present context. As explained in Section The Macroeconomics of Imperfect Capital Markets: An Overview, the key to interest-rate gaps essentially consists in information about the natural rate. Hence, the former explanation of banks' behaviour hinges on a limited informational requirement, in that banks need not know what the natural rate is at each point in time, which is consistent with the idea that the *nominal* interest rate may assume wrong values. The latter explanation instead requires an informational hypothesis about the relationship between the target real interest rate of banks and the natural rate, which implies the possibility that the *real* interest rate set by banks may be wrong.

[7] At the time when Wicksell was writing, there was already clear evidence that nominal interest rates would tend to move together with the GPL (see e.g., the diagrams in 1898a) – a phenomenon later labelled the "Gibson paradox" by Keynes. Wicksell argued that this phenomenon would not contradict his theory, but that it was instead to be explained as the ongoing adjustment process of nominal interest rates towards a new level consistent with the steady-state level of prices.

It will be convenient to work with a general formulation nesting more specific ones, like the following

$$i_{t+1} = \phi(i_t + \gamma(\pi_{t+1} - \pi^e_{i+1})) + (1-\phi)(r^b + \pi_{t+1}) \tag{8.8}$$

This interest-rate equation (IR) states that, starting from a nominal interest rate in t, its law of motion depends on (1) the share ϕ of "adaptive" banks that do not have (information on) an explicit real interest target, (2) their "indexation" sensitivity γ to excess current inflation with respect to its expected level, (3) the share $(1-\phi)$ of banks which have the real interest target r^b and simply index the nominal rate to it.

As to inflation expectations, let us assume the same structure as the rest of the private sector, namely

$$\pi^e_{t+1} = \delta\pi_{t+1} + (1-\delta)\pi \tag{8.9}$$

Now, defining $\hat{r} \equiv r^b - r$ as the possible informational error of banks which have a real interest target, equation (8) can easily be transformed in terms of the baseline model's gaps, i.e.,:

$$\hat{i}_{i+1} = \phi\hat{i}_t + (1-\phi)\hat{r} + \eta\hat{\pi}_{t+1}$$

where $\eta \equiv 1 - \phi + \gamma\phi(1-\delta)$

This formulation indicates that, as a result of the law of motion of the interest rate (8.8), interest-rate gaps evolve endogenously according to (1) one-period lag in proportion to the share of banks with no real-interest target, $\phi\hat{i}_t$, (2) the indexation elasticity to the inflation gap, η. This evolution of interest-rate gaps may however have a drift, $(1-\phi)\hat{r}$, that is, the incidence of banks' misinformation about the natural rate in proportion to the share of banks with a real-interest target. On adding this equation to the baseline system in gaps (4)–(5) we obtain the CL–PC–IR non-homogeneous system of three first-order difference equations in the three endogenous gaps $[\hat{u}_{t+1}, \hat{\pi}_{t+1}, \hat{i}_{t+1}]$, and one exogenous constant $\hat{r}$:

$$\begin{bmatrix} \hat{u}_{t+1} \\ \hat{\pi}_{t+1} \\ \hat{i}_{t+1} \end{bmatrix} = \begin{bmatrix} \rho' & \alpha' \\ -\rho'\beta' & -\alpha'\beta' \\ -\rho'\beta'\eta & \phi - \alpha'\beta'\eta \end{bmatrix} \begin{bmatrix} \hat{u}_t \\ \hat{i}_t \end{bmatrix} + \begin{bmatrix} 0 \\ 0 \\ 1-\phi \end{bmatrix} \hat{r} \tag{8.10}$$

Let us concentrate on conditions for the system to achieve a zero-gaps steady state.

1. *The system admits of a zero-gaps steady state only if* $(1-\phi)\hat{r} = 0$. Hence, a Wicksellian bank mechanism is potentially able to self-correct the interest-rate gaps that may trigger saving-investment imbalances. However, this potential stabilization role may be jeopardized by the incidence of banks' misinformation about the *real* rate ($\hat{r} \neq 0$). If one looks at the modern economics of imperfect capital markets, a "false" *real* interest rate is the typical result. This suggests that if banks take the market real interest rate as their target, these capital market failures undermine the system's intertemporal stability. For this component to be neutralized, it should happen that, vis-à-vis inflation, banks let nominal rates rise but do not engage in real-interest targeting ($\phi = 1$).

2. *In the perfect information case* ($\phi = 0$, $\hat{r} = 0$) *the system's stability requires that the share* δ *of short-run rational forecasters be bounded.* This result is similar to the case of exogenous interest rate as discussed in Section Some Macroeconomics of Saving-Investment Imbalances: The Baseline Model. As $\delta \to 1$, the steady state is no longer stable. More in detail, we have that unemployment is insensitive to interest-rate gaps ($\rho' = 0$, $\alpha' = 0$) but the latter are nonconvergent ($\phi - \alpha'\beta'\eta = 1$). The reason for this is simple and can be understood from the interest-rate gap equation (8.9): if all banks just anchor the nominal interest rate to the (true) natural rate ($\phi = 0$), the fact that all them also have short-run rational expectations ($\delta = 1$) implies that they always see the inflation rate at the level they expected to, so that the correction mechanism of the *nominal* interest-rate gaps stops working. Paradoxically, the system falls back in exactly the same situation as the one with exogenous interest-rate gap: if a nominal gap occurs, it becomes permanent, unemployment is unaffected, but inflation deviates from the initial normal rate permanently.
3. *In the limited information, long-run rational-expectations case* ($\phi = 1$, $\delta = 0$), Stability requires that banks' sensitivity γ to inflation gaps is bounded:

$$\gamma < \frac{(1 - \rho^{1/2})^2}{\alpha\beta} \tag{8.11}$$

Under this condition, the Wicksellian bank mechanism is self-stabilizing: as the nominal interest rate converges to the NAIRI, unemployment converges to the NAIRU and the return-to-normality hypothesis of the inflation rate is fulfilled. Hence the steady state can be characterized as a rational-expectations equilibrium. Notably, the nominal interest rate converges to the NAIRI even though this variable (and hence the natural rate) is not made explicit in the interest-rate equation. Yet this result should be carefully understood: it hinges on the generalized belief in the normal inflation rate π. To be precise, what the model actually says is that *any belief concerning the normal inflation rate consistently held by all agents is self-fulfilling.*

The economic meaning of the boundedness condition on γ can be understood by noting that $\gamma\alpha\beta$ measures how one point of interest-rate gap that triggers α points of unemployment gap is self-corrected through the response γ of the nominal interest rate to the β points of inflation gap generated by the unemployment gap. As is intuitive, a stabilizing adjustment mechanism requires that γ should be smaller, the larger are α and β. As γ increases, the system first takes an oscillatory path and then becomes unstable.

The Dynamic LM

The monetary theory of the interest rate put forward by Keynes's *General Theory*, and transposed into the LM equation, offers a different account of the way in which the nominal interest rate can be endogenized within the saving-investment imbalances framework: an account where money supply and its real value play the key role.

It is clear that the standard specification of the LM equation, which is static in nature, cannot be used to address the problem of saving-investment imbalances, which is intrinsically dynamic (Leijonhufvud 1983). I have thus devised a "dynamic LM" equation for the nominal interest rate in the following way. Let us start from the textbook LM function which represents the nominal interest rate as a function increasing in current real income and decreasing in real money supply. [8] If μ_y and μ_i are the income and interest-rate elasticities of money demand, then $1/\mu_i \equiv \lambda$ and $\mu_y\lambda$ are the elasticities of the interest rate relative to real money supply and real income, respectively. This theory implies that the interest rate will be constant over time as long as real income and real money supply are constant. Assuming a log-linear relationship φ between output (income) and unemployment via production function, and starting from a given interest rate in t, a simple dynamic equation consistent with this theory is the following:

$$i_{i+1} = i_t - \varphi(u_{t+1} - u_t) - \lambda(\hat{m}_{t+1} - \pi_{t+1}) \tag{8.12}$$

where $\hat{m}_{t+1}$ is the growth rate of money supply.

We can now easily re-express this equation in terms of gaps with respect to the NAIRI, the NAIRU and the normal inflation rate, i.e.,:

$$\hat{i}_{i+1} = \hat{i}_t - \varphi(\hat{u}_{t+1} - \hat{u}_t) - \lambda((\hat{m}_{t+1} - \pi) - \hat{\pi}_{t+1}) \tag{8.13}$$

Adding (8.13) to the baseline model we obtain the CP-PC-LM system, with three endogenous gaps $[\hat{u}_{t+1}, \hat{\pi}_{t+1}, \hat{i}_{t+1}]$ and one exogenous variable

$$\begin{bmatrix} \hat{u}_{t+1} \\ \hat{\pi}_{t+1} \\ \hat{i}_{t+1} \end{bmatrix} = \begin{bmatrix} \rho' & \alpha' \\ \rho'\beta' & \alpha'\beta' \\ -\lambda\rho'\beta' + \varphi(1-\rho') & 1 - \alpha'(\lambda\beta' + \varphi) \end{bmatrix} \begin{bmatrix} \hat{u}_t \\ \hat{i}_t \end{bmatrix} + \begin{bmatrix} 0 \\ 0 \\ \lambda \end{bmatrix} (\hat{m}_{t+1} - \pi) \tag{8.14}$$

Hence, the conditions for the system to achieve the zero-gap steady state can now be summarized as follows.

1. *The system admits of a zero-gap steady state only if* $(\hat{m}_{t+1} - \pi) = 0$. Therefore, the message is that a plain dynamic LM function can provide a self-correcting mechanism of interest-rate gaps conditional upon money supply growing at the

[8] The typical LM function is obtained by starting from a log-linear money demand function,

$$m_t^d = \mu_y y_t - \mu_i i_t$$

Equating money demand to real money supply, $m_t - p_t$, the equilibrium interest rate is

$$i_t = (\mu_y / \mu_i) y_t - (1 / \mu_i)(m_t - p_t)$$

normal inflation rate. To put it differently, the implied self-correcting mechanism is such that the system can converge to the NAIRU as well as to the inflation rate dictated by the growth rate of money supply

2. *The share δ of short-run rational forecasters should be bounded.* This replicates the results obtained in the other versions of the model
3. *If all agents hold the long-run expectation of the normal inflation rate ($\delta = 0$), the interest-rate elasticities to unemployment and real money supply should satisfy the boundary condition*

$$\lambda\varphi \leq \rho / \alpha \tag{8.15}$$

The only relevant point is that the system's behaviour now crucially hinges on the relationship between the parameters of the LM function. In particular, stability implies an inverse relationship between the two. On the other hand, the smaller is λ, the smoother is the interest rate dynamics and the longer is the whole adjustment process.

The Speculative LM

The last alternative determination of the nominal interest rate to be examined ensues from one of the many criticisms raised against the textbook LM version of Keynes's theory of the interest rate. The thrust of this criticism is that one major element in that theory, the "speculative motive" of the demand for money, has gone completely astray (Leijonhufvud 1981). A truly "speculative" component of money demand should be related to *expected movements* of the interest rate relative to its future value, say i^e. Speculators substitute bonds for money whenever they expect capital gains, i.e., a rise in bond prices or else a fall in the market interest rate. Therefore, this component should enter the usual representation of money demand as a negative function of $(i_t - i^e)$ (Leijonhufvud 1981, p. 146). The dynamic LM should therefore be rewritten as follows

$$i_{t+1} = i^e - \varphi(u_{t+1} - u_t) - \lambda(\hat{m}_{t+1} - \pi_{t+1}) \tag{8.16}$$

This specification implies that as long as unemployment and real money supply are constant, speculation keeps the market interest rate aligned with its value expected by speculators i^e.

For brevity I do not report here the analytical results of the new model. Attention should be drawn to the point that (8.16) reintroduces an exogenous constant, i^e, into the model. The consequence is that now the zero-gaps steady state can only be attained if $i^e = i$. That is to say, if the speculators' expected interest rate is the NAIRI, then the market interest rate does convergence to the NAIRI, *otherwise it does not.* In the former case, the convergence and stability conditions are slightly different than in the plain LM case. But this is not the main point, which is instead that now the determination of the nominal interest rate has, again, a crucial informational requirement, that is, i^e.

The scenario under limited information, $i^e \neq i$ resembles the initial one with exogenous nominal interest rate (Section Some Macroeconomics of Saving-Investment Imbalances: The Baseline Model), and, again, it seems to have genuine Keynesian features, in that if $i^e > i$, "involuntary unemployment" arises because the speculative demand for money prevents the market interest rate from falling enough. The fundamental cause is that speculators do not adjust their expected rate to the lower NAIRI. On the other hand, the market interest rate stabilizes at a value lower than i^e expected by speculators, who should therefore keep on anticipating capital losses in the bond market which prevent them from buying bonds. It is tempting to see here a possible manifestation of the liquidity trap (clearly any further increase in the money growth rate would be useless). If this is the case, it seems necessary to conclude that the liquidity trap cannot be regarded as an extreme case in the Keynesian pathology but is indeed *the* Keynesian pathology! Are therefore Pigou and Modigliani vindicated? Not exactly. A methodological point made by Leijonhufvud in the "Wicksell Connection" (1981) applies here, namely that the pathological states of the system are not due to structural parameters but to particular combinations of events and the way in which they are processed by markets. In fact, the pathology we have found is not related to anomalous liquidity preference (the relevant parameter is always the same) but to an informational/expectational error. The implications concerning the relevance of the problem are quite different.

On the one hand, this scenario, being fraught with expectational errors, can hardly be considered a genuine steady state. This finding probably frustrates the Old Keynesians' search for "involuntary unemployment equilibria." On the other hand, it is also challenging in that it points out at least one case in which, in a well-specified sense, a purely market-driven interest rate may put the system on the wrong track. Moreover, it is difficult to see where the system can be driven from here, since the corrections of the underlying errors may prove far from smooth and painless.

A Glance at Monetary Policy

Though monetary policy falls outside the scope of the present paper, it is worth drawing some implications from previous analyses with a view to further research on monetary policy issues.

The results yielded by the different versions of the model of saving-investment imbalances elicit a conception of monetary policy as a visible hand possibly keeping the interest rate on the right track. In the framework of saving-investment imbalances, however, Keynesian, Monetarist as well as New Keynesian monetary policies share the common shortcoming that they do not consider (or explicitly rule out) these phenomena.

From the Wicksellian point of view, we have seen that, although a spontaneous adjustment mechanism may be at work through banks' interest-rate policy, it may well fall short of delivering full stabilization due to (1) misinformation about the natural rate of banks which seek to target it, (2) excessive weight placed upon short-run anticipation of the inflation rate. A third, more subtle, problem is that, even when the system is self-adjusting, the ending rate of inflation is the rate that agents believe to be the normal rate. Wicksell and his followers were aware of, and worried about, each of these wedges driven into the clockwork by the banking system (see e.g., Boianovsky and Trautwein 2004, 2006). Thus Wicksell realized that price stability (but one might say economic stability at large, as seen above) would require *two* conditions: connecting the nominal interest rate to changes in the GPL in a stabilizing way, *and* anchoring inflation expectations to a norm against which erratic GPL movements should be gauged. A crucial role for the central bank has emerged as "manager of expectations" (Woodford 2003, pp. 15–17). Hence Woodford is right when he stresses the remarkable modernity of this Wicksellian view of central banking and its consistency with the modern theory and practice of monetary policy rules. However, the underlying model is substantially different, and so are some key indications for monetary policy.

Keynes, too, brought monetary policy to the forefront, with more long-lasting success than Wicksell, one should say. However, having embedded saving-investment imbalances and misguided interest rates in a different framework, Keynes set the stage for the resurgence of a view of monetary policy, centered upon the quantity control of liquidity supply, that for about fifty years substantially departed from Wicksell's road. The most important lessons to be learned are two. The first is that a Keynesian LM interest-rate equation does not seem, per se, sufficient to explain a steady state with involuntary unemployment. If the real balance effect operates, the economy seems to be endowed with a reliable self-stabilizing mechanism. The second is that the most important role for monetary policy is more Friedmanite than Keynesian. Apart from accelerating and smoothing the adjustment process, little scope is left for money supply. Far more important is the point that the steady-state inflation, the rate in which agents have reason to believe in the long run, is the one dictated by the growth rate of money. Overall, these implications amount to the Monetarist interpretation of the Old Synthesis (see also Leijonhufvud 1981).

The real threat to this optimistic view "only" comes from the market's misperception of the long-run value of the interest rate. This threat parallels the one we have seen in the case of Wicksellian banks. The result is similar, in that the system is driven out of equilibrium, while monetary policy becomes impotent.

This last conclusion may sound like an additional argument in support of the general endorsement of interest-rate control strategies by all main central banks in the world – in the Neo-Wicksellian spirit highlighted by Woodford. Indeed, it is almost trivial to observe that a Wicksellian interest-rate mechanism like (8.8) is substantially similar to a rule of inflation targeting with interest-rate smoothing, where ${\pi^e}_{t+1}$ is replaced with the central banks' target (Svensson 1997). Thus, one may interpret (8.8) as the reduced form of a set of inter-bank relationships whereby the central bank drives the interest rate on loans, with the anchor of expected inflation being explicitly set by the central bank.

As to the Wicksellian pedigree of the Taylor rule, it is indeed easy to see that it consists of the Wicksellian bank mechanism plus the sensitivity of the interest rate to output gaps. However, since the latter are correlated with inflation gaps, an interest-rate equation like (8.8) can also be interpreted as the reduced form of a Taylor rule. An immediate implication is that the so-called "Taylor principle" – that is, the requirement that the inflation-gap parameter be greater than 1 (Woodford 2001) – is neither necessary nor sufficient. For particular combinations of very low persistence (ρ) and/or very high elasticity (α) of output gaps with respect to interest-rate gaps, $\gamma > 1$ might even turn out to be destabilizing. On the other hand, once the relevant stability condition has been verified, $\gamma < 1$ may well be sufficient.

Finally, specific consideration should be made of the prescription that the Taylor rule should be pegged to the natural rate of interest (Woodford 2003, ch. 4). This prescription stands in sharp contrast with our previous findings, which warn that managing the interest rate with a natural-rate target may be dangerous. Wicksell himself was well aware that the crucial challenge for monetary (and banking) policy lies in the natural interest rate being subject to unobservable shocks and fluctuations (1898a, pp. 82 ff.). Keynes (1937a, b) was even more radical, casting doubts on the existence itself of a single, general-equilibrium real interest rate. In a recent study published by the ECB, one reads that

> from the empirical point of view, the "natural" real interest rate is unobservable. The estimation of the natural real interest rate is not straightforward and is associated with a very high degree of uncertainty (Garnier and Wihelmsen 2005, p. 6).

If the central bank has complete and immediate information about the NAIRI, it can and should immediately adjust the nominal interest rate to offset any change in the NAIRI as it arises. If the central bank does not have this information, and if it happens to peg the nominal interest rate to the wrong NAIRI, then the Taylor rule would drive the system out of equilibrium, like the Wicksellian misinformed banks or the Keynesian speculators that the central bank is supposed to keep on the right track. Hence, unless we can be highly confident that central banks are better (perfectly) informed than the market about the natural rate of interest, "adaptive" rules, using step-by-step adjustments of the interest rate vis-à-vis observable conditions in the economy are preferable in that they produce adjustment paths which are generally slower, but safer.[9]

Conclusions

Let me summarize the main findings of this exploration of the old and new macroeconomics of imperfect capital markets. The idea of the founders of this approach to macroeconomics, Wicksell and Keynes above all, was that some form of malfunctioning of the capital market and the consequent saving-investment imbalances were

---

[9] This line of research is actively pursued, for instance, by Orphanides and co-authors (Orphanides and Williams 2002, 2006).

the keys to both the determination of the current level of output and prices and of their fluctuations over time. The modern foundations of imperfect capital markets have greatly improved the microeconomic level of analysis, but saving-investment imbalances still lack appropriate development at the macro-level. The aim of this paper has been to signal the problem and exemplify a model that can deal with saving-investment imbalances.

The model proposed represents a competitive, flex-price economy populated by forward-looking, optimizing households and firms that freely choose their levels of savings and investments in a capital market where the market real interest rate may differ from the natural rate (interest-rate gap). The allocation scheme that has been chosen is that of trading at false price, that can be detected in Wicksell's approach as well as in some modern contributions. In this scheme, when saving differs from investment the banking sector fills the gap by hoarding or dishoarding reserves.

The first main conclusion is that as long as the interest-rate gap persists, neither unemployment nor the GPL can remain on their IGE paths. This outcome reflects persistent intertemporal disequilibrium, and it occurs even though no other frictions or rigidities are present in economy. This conclusion stands in sharp contrast with current mainstream macroeconomics, where there are no capital market imperfections, the economy is always on its IGE path, fluctuations are only exogenously driven, and all relevant problems (excess movements in quantities) may only arise due to price stickiness. Nominal wage-price stickiness is not the only problem, wage-price flexibility is not the only solution.

A second set of conclusions can be drawn from analyses of different hypotheses that make the nominal interest rate endogenous. The Wicksellian hypothesis that banks index their nominal rate with excess inflation (with respect to the normal rate) has the potential role to stabilize the system, that is, to achieve a zero-gap steady state along the IGE path. A major finding in this respect is that this potential role is under threat if (1) banks have limited or wrong information about the natural rate, *and* (2) they engage in the natural-rate targeting. Since a typical result of the modern literature on capital market failures is that the *real* interest rate is wrong, the recommendation is that banks let their nominal rates rise with prices but do not aim at the real-rate target.

Analysis of a Keynesian capital market based on the monetary determination of the interest rate by way of a "dynamic" LM function leads to similarly mixed conclusions. A dynamic LM function represents a stabilizing mechanism for the nominal interest rate provided that exogenous money supply grows at the same rate as the normal inflation rate, which in fact is realized in the steady state. Under these conditions, the economic system is probably more robust than the Old Keynesians (and Keynes?) believe(d), and the mere existence of the interest elasticity of money demand is not an impediment. On the other hand, if we introduce a wrong "speculative component" – that is, an expected interest rate that is too high with respect to the equilibrium one – the adjustment mechanism breaks down and the economy is trapped in a high unemployment state (in which, however, both the expected interest rate and inflation rate are not realized).

Overall, we have seen that business cycles triggered by saving-investment imbalances *are benign* as long as the system embodies an endogenous mechanism that drives the nominal interest rate to close the gaps with the NAIRI. This is the main message as far as monetary policy is concerned. The current approach based on interest-rate rules is consistent with this perspective. However, the underlying macro-model has to be different from those currently employed in order to capture the features of intertemporal disequilibrium cycles. To mention just one point, the warning against natural-rate targeting, and the plea for simple adaptive rules, extends from private banks to the central bank.

If, against this background, we look at the evidence showing that the natural interest rate is a volatile variable difficult to measure and transmit to capital markets, and that saving-investment imbalances are detectable behind all major boom-bust episodes, we can conclude that reassessment of the macroeconomics of imperfect capital markets may be timely. Further elaborations of saving-investment analysis that can be indicated include the following:

- Keynes (1937) and Lindahl (1939), New Keynesians *à la* Greenwald and Stiglitz (1993), and Woodford on passing (2003, ch. 5), would add that the deviations of the market real interest rate from the natural rate do not leave the capital stock unaffected (which is a straightforward implication of the fact that saving-investment imbalances impinge upon aggregate demand, employment and output). If the capital stock changes over the cycle, then the real return to capital also changes. Thus, as Woodford recognizes, we (or the agents in the economy) out of the steady state face *three* interest rates: the market real interest, the actual real return to capital, and the natural interest rate. Yet all this blurs the notion of a given natural rate of interest independent of the cycle to which the economy should return, and we are led back to the question of the normative anchorage of the belief in a particular natural rate.
- A somewhat more radical perspective would add behavioural finance as a repertoire of causes for the mispricing of firms' investments and consequent misbeliefs in the natural interest rate.
- Neo-Hicksians (e.g., Amendola and Gaffard 1998) stress that "technological shocks" (possibly underlying the volatility of the NAIRI) are as such non existent (e.g., they remain ideas in the mind of entrepreneurs) until they are "validated" by financial means; in this perspective, *changes* in the NAIRI are not independent of monetary policy and the market interest rate.

Acknowledgements I wish to thank Axel Leijonhufvud, Vela Velupillai, Edoardo Gaffeo, Andrea Fracasso, Ronny Mazzocchi and Hans Michael Trautwein for helpful discussions and comments. Financial support is acknowledged to the Italy-Germany Inter-Univeristy "Vigoni Programme," 2006–2007.

References

Allen F, Gale D (2001) Comparing financial systems. MIT Press, Cambridge MA

Amendola M., Gaffard JL (1998) Out of equilibrium Clarendon Press, Oxford

Bernanke B, Blinder A (1988) Credit, money, and aggregate demand, Papers and Proceedings of the American Economic Association. Am Econ Rev 78:435–439

Bernanke B, Gertler M (1989) Agency costs, net worth and business fluctuations. Am Econ Rev 79:14–31

Bernanke B, Gertler M (1990) Financial fragility and economic performance. Q J Econ 105:87–114

Bernanke B, Gertler M (1995) Inside the black box: the credit channel of monetary policy transmission. J Econ Perspectives 9:27–42

Bernanke B, Gertler M (2001) Should central banks respond to movements in asset prices?, Papers and Proceedings of the American Economic Association. Am Econ Rev 91:253–257

Bernanke B, Gertler M, Gilchrist S (1996) The financial accelerator and the flight to quality. Rev Econ Stat 78:1–15

Blanchard OJ (2000) What do we know about macroeconomics that Fisher and Wicksell did not know?. Q J Econ 115:1375–1409

Blanchard OJ, Galì J (2005) Real wage rigidity and the new Keynesian model. MIT Department of Economics, Working Paper Series, 05–28

Boianovsky M, Trautwein M (2004) Wicksell after Woodford, Paper presented at the History of Economics Society meeting, Toronto, June

Boianovsky M, Trautwein M (2006) Price expectations, capital accumulation and employment: Lindahl's macroeconomics from the 1920s to the 1950s. Camb J Econ 17:1–20

Bond S, Jenkinson T (1996) The assessment: investment performance and policy. Oxf Rev Econ Pol 12:1–33

Bordo MD, Jeanne O (2002) Boom-busts in asset prices, economic instability, and monetary policy. NBER Working Paper, 8966

Borio C, Lowe P (2002) Asset prices, financial and monetary stability: exploring the Nexus. BIS Working Papers, 114

Caresma JC, Gnan E, Ritzberger-Gruenwald D (2005) The natural rate of interest. concepts and appraisal for the Euro area. Monetary Policy and the Economy, Austrian National Bank, Q4

Cecchetti SG, Genberg H, Lipsky J, Wadwhani S (2000) Asset prices and central bank policy, Internationa Centre for Monetary and Banking Studies, London

Chiarella C, Flaschel P, Franke R (2005) Foundations for a disequilibrium theory of the business cycle. Cambridge University Press, Cambridge UK

De Meza D, Webb DC (1987) Too much investment: a problem of asyymetric information. Q J Econ 102:181–192

Delli Gatti D, Tamborini R (2000) Imperfet capital markets: a new macroeconomic paradigm?. In: Backhouse R, Salanti A (eds) Macroeconomics and the real world, vol II. Oxford University Press, Oxford

Demirguç-Kunt A, Levine R (eds) (2001) Financial structure and economic growth. MIT, Cambridge MA

Evans GW, Honkapohja S (2001) Learning and expectations in macroeconomics. Princeton University Press, Princeton

Fazzari S, Hubbard RG, Petersen B (1988) Financing constraints and corporate investment. Brookings Papers Econ Activ 1:141–206

Fitoussi JP (2001) Monetary policy and the macroeconomics of soft growth. In: Leijonhufvud A (ed) Monetary theory and policy experience. Palgrave, London

Garnier J, Wihelmsen B (2005) The natural real interest and the output gap in the Euro area. A joint estimation. European Central Bank, Working Paper Series, 546

Gertler M (1988) Financial structure and aggregate activity: an overview. J Money Credit Bank 20:559–588

Gertler M, Gilchrist S (1993) The role of credit market imperfections in the monetary transmission mechanism: arguments and evidence. Scand J Econ 93:43–64

Gertler M, Hubbard RG (1988) Financial factors in business fluctuations. In: Federal Reserve Bank of Kansas City. Financial Market Volatility, Kansas City

Greenwald BC, Stiglitz JE (1988) Imperfect information, finance constraints and business fluctuations In: Kohn M, Tsiang SC (eds) Finance constraints, expectations and macroeconomics. Clarendon Press, Oxford

Greenwald BC, Stiglitz JE (1990) Macroeconomic models with equity and credit rationing. In: Hubbard RG (ed) Information, capital markets and investment., Chicago University Press, Chicago

Greenwald BC, Stiglitz, JE (1991) Towards a new paradigm in monetary economics. Cambridge University Press, Cambridge

Greenwald BC, Stiglitz JE (1993a) Financial market imperfections and business cycles. Q J Econ 108:77–113

Greenwald BC, Stiglitz JE (1993b) New and old Keynesians. J Econ Perspectives 7:23–44

Hart O (1995) Firms, contracts and financial structure. Clarendon Press, Oxford

Jaffee D, Stiglitz J (1990) Credit rationing. In: Friedman BM, Hahn FH (eds) Handbook of monetary economics. North Holland, Amsterdam

Keynes JM (1930) A treatise on money. Macmillan, London

Keynes JM (1936) The general theory of employment, interest and money. Macmillan, London

Keynes JM (1937a) Alternative theories of the rate of interest. Econ J 47:241–252

Keynes JM (1937b) The ex-ante theory of the rate of interest. Econ J 47:663–669

Keynes JM (1937c) The general theory of employment. Q J Econ 14:109–123

Kiyotaki N, Moore J (1997) Credit cycles. J Polit Econ 105:211–248

Leijonhufvud A (1981) The Wicksell connection. variations on a theme. In: Information and coordination: essays in macroeconomic theory. Oxford University Press, New York

Leijounhufvud A (1983) What was the matter with IS-LM?. In: Fitoussi JP (ed) Modern macroeconomic theory. Blackwell, Oxford

Lindahl E (1939) Studies in the theory of money and capital. George Allen and Unwin, London

Leland H, Pyle D (1977) Informational asymmetries, financial structure and financial intermediation. J Finance 32:371–387

McCallum BT (1986) Some issues concerning interest rate pegging, price level indeterminacy, and the real bills doctrine. J Monetary Econ 17:135–160

Minsky HP (1972) An exposition of a keynesian theory of investment. In: Can it happen again? essays on instability and finance. Sharpe, New York, 1982

Minsky HP (1975) John Maynard Keynes. Basic Books, New York

Modigliani F, Miller M (1958) The cost of capital, corporation finance and the theory of investment. Am Econ Rev 48:261–277

Moggridge D (ed) (1987) The collected writings of John Maynard Keynes, vol XIV, Part II, 2nd ed. Macmillan, London

Myers M, Majluf N (1984) Corporate financial decisions when firms have information that investors do not have. J Financ Econ 13:187–220

Orphanides A, Williams JC (2002) Robust monetary policy rules with unknown natural rates. Brookings Papers Econ Activ 2:63–118

Orphanides A, Williams JC (2006) Inflation targeting under imperfect knowledge. CEPR, Discussion Paper Series, 5664

Stiglitz JE (1982) Information and capital markets. In: Sharpe WF, Cootner CM (eds) Financial economics. Prentice Hall, New Jersey

Stiglitz JE (1987) The causes and consequences of the dependence of quality on price. J Econ Lit 25:1–48

Stiglitz JE (1992) Capital markets and economic fluctuations in capitalist economies. Paper and Proceedings of the European Economic Association. Eur Econ Rev 36:269–306

Stiglitz JE, Weiss A (1981) Credit rationing in markets with imperfect information. Am Econ Rev 71:393–410

Stiglitz JE, Weiss A (1992) Asymmetric information in credit markets and its implications for macroeconomics. Oxf Econ Papers 44:694–724
Svensson L (1997) Inflation forecast targeting. implementing and monitoring inflation targets. Eur Econ Rev 41:1111–1147
Tamborini R (2001) Mercati finanziari e attività economica Padova: CEDAM
Tamborini R (2007) Back to Wicksell? Some lessons for practical monetary policy Money, macro and finance conference. University of Birmingham, 12–14
Van der Ploeg F (2005) Back to Keynes?. CEPR. Discussion Paper Series 4897
Wicksell K (1898a) Interest and prices. Macmillan, London, 1936
Wicksell K (1898b) The influence of the rate of interest on commodity prices, In: Lindahl E (ed) Wicksell: Selected papers in economic theory. Allen and Unwin, London, 1958
Wicksell K (1922) Vorlesungen ueber Nationaloekonomie, Band 2. Gustav Fischer, Jena
Woodford M (2001) The taylor rule and optimal monetary policy. Princeton University, mimeo
Woodford M (2003) Interest and prices. Foundations of a theory of monetary policy. Princeton University Press, Princeton

Chapter 9
The Effects of Uncertainty and Sunk Costs on Firms' Decision-Making: Evidence from Net Entry, Industry Structure and Investment Dynamics

Vivek Ghosal

Abstract This paper presents selected evidence on the impact of uncertainty and sunk costs on firms' decisions related to entry and exit, and investment expenditures. Evidence from a large sample of US manufacturing industries shows that greater uncertainty about profits significantly *lowers* net entry as well as investment. The negative effects are most pronounced in industries that are dominated by small firms and have high sunk costs. We note some implications for policy related to antitrust, employment and economic stabilization.

Introduction

This paper presents empirical evidence on the effects of uncertainty and sunk costs on firms' decisions related to entry and exit, and investment. The theoretical background is spelled out in the real-options models highlighted in Dixit (1989), Dixit and Pindyck (1994) and numerous contributions since then. Theory shows that the presence of uncertainty and sunk costs imply an option value of waiting and are likely to be important determinants of firms' entry, exit and investment decisions. While the theory is well developed, empirical evaluation of these models, particularly in the context of entry and exit, is somewhat limited.

A second channel that may affect outcomes relates to potential financial market frictions (Greenwald and Stiglitz, 1990; Williamson, 1988). This literature suggests that the presence of uncertainty and sunk costs may exacerbate financing constraints, which in turn may affect entry and exit decisions as well as firms' investment decisions.

The empirical industrial organization literature has established several stylized facts about firms' entry and exit dynamics: (a) the typical entering (exiting) firm is small compared to incumbents; (b) incumbent larger firms are older with higher survival probabilities; and (c) there is significant turnover of firms even in mature

V. Ghosal
Georgia Institute of Technology, Atlanta, GA, 30318, USA
e-mail: vivek.ghosal@econ.gatech.edu

G. Calcagnini and E. Saltari (eds.), *The Economics of Imperfect Markets*, Contributions to Economics,
DOI: 10.1007/978-3-7908-2131-4_9, © Springer Physica-Verlag Berlin Heidelberg 2010

industries (Caves, 1998; Sutton, 1997). Given these findings, it is important to identify the forces that drive intertemporal dynamics of industry structure. While the role played by technology has been extensively researched in the literature (Caves, 1998; Sutton, 1997), other key forces identified in theory, such as uncertainty, have been somewhat neglected in the empirical literature.

In contrast, the empirical literature on examining firms' investment decisions under uncertainty is relatively more developed: see, for example, Lensink et al. (2001), Carruth et al. (2001) and Ghosal and Loungani (1996, 2000). This literature shows that greater uncertainty tends to reduce investment, therefore supporting the theoretical predictions in general.

The evidence I present on the impact of uncertainty and sunk costs is based on a large sample of US SIC 4-digit manufacturing industries over 1958–92. The empirical evidence I present shows that: (1) periods of greater uncertainty, especially in conjunction with higher sunk costs, results in a reduction of the number of small establishments and firms, and marginally higher industry concentration; and (2) lower investment, particularly in industries that have a greater fraction of small businesses. On average, large establishments appear virtually unaffected.

The paper is organized as follows. In Sect. 2 I briefly discuss the underlying models related to option-value and financing-constraints. Evidence on the entry and exit patterns, and the volatility of firms is presented in Sect. 3. Section 4 highlights some evidence on the impact of uncertainty on investment. Section 5 concludes with some implications for public policy.

Role of Uncertainty and Sunk Costs

In this section I summarize specific aspects of two distinct literatures that provide us with a framework for examining firms' entry and exit and investment decisions under uncertainty. Since there are numerous reviews of this literature, my discussion below is very brief. Carruth et al. (2001), Ghosal (2007), Ghosal and Loungani (2006, 2007), Lensink et al. (2001), for example, present summaries of different aspects of this literature.

Real-Options Literature

In the real-options literature, Dixit (1989) provides a broad framework to study time-series variations in entry, exit and the number of firms.[1] Dixit shows that uncertainty

[1] Pakes and Ericson (1998), Hopenhayn (1992), among others, study firm dynamics under firm-specific uncertainty and evaluate models of firm dynamics under active v. passive learning. These class of models can be better subjected to empirical evaluation using micro-datasets. Since our data is at the industry level, we are not in a position to evaluate the predictions of these models.

and sunk costs imply an option value of waiting for information and this increases (decreases) the entry (exit) trigger price. During periods of greater uncertainty, entry is delayed as firms require a premium over the conventional Marshallian entry price, and exit is delayed as incumbents know they have to re-incur sunk costs upon re-entry.[2]

Our industry level data only contains information on the total number of firms and establishments. I do not have data on gross industry entry and exit flows (these data are not generally available over the long time period I conduct some of the analysis). Therefore, for our empirical analysis, we would like to know whether, during periods of greater uncertainty, the entry trigger price is affected more or less than the exit trigger? The numerical simulations in Dixit and Pindyck (Chaps. 7 and 8) show that increase in uncertainty given sunk costs results in the entry trigger price increasing by more than the decrease in the exit trigger price. Therefore, greater uncertainty results in *negative net entry* and an industry is expected to show a decrease in the number of firms.[3] The results in Dixit (1989) and the numerical simulations in Dixit and Pindyck (1994) also show that the effect is conditioned on the level of sunk costs. The greater are the sunk costs, the greater is the effect of uncertainty.

Following the above insights provided by theory, I present empirical evidence on the impact of uncertainty and sunk costs on net entry, firm volatility and investment. There is an important data feature that needs to be grappled with. As is well known, the within-industry firm size distribution is typically highly skewed. Our data displayed in Fig. 9.1 reveals this to be the typical characteristic. Previous studies show that (a) entrants are typically small compared to incumbents and have high failure rates, (b) typical exiting firm is small and young, and (c) larger firms are older with higher survival rates.[4] The implications of size distribution can be summarized as

[2] Caballero and Pindyck (1996) examine the intertemporal path of a competitive industry where negative demand shocks decrease price along existing supply curve, but positive shocks may induce entry/expansion by incumbents, shifting the supply curve to the right and dampening price increase. Their evidence from a sample of U.S. manufacturing industries shows that sunk costs and industry-wide uncertainty cause the entry (investment) trigger to exceed the cost of capital.

[3] The above models assume perfect competition. Models of oligopolistic competition (e.g. Dixit and Pindyck, p. 309–315) highlight the dependence of outcomes on model assumptions and difficulties of arriving at clear predictions. As in models of perfect competition, the entry price exceeds the Marshallian trigger due to uncertainty and sunk costs, preserving the option value of waiting. But, for example, under simultaneous decision making, neither firm may wants to wait for fear of being preempted by its rival and losing leadership. This could lead to faster, simultaneous, entry than in the leader-follower sequential entry setting. Thus fear of pre-emption may necessitate a faster response and counteract the option value of waiting.

[4] In Audretsch (1995, p. 73–80), mean size of the *entering* firm is seven employees, varying from 4 to 15 across 2-digit industries. Audretsch (p. 159) finds 19% of *exiting* firms have been in the industry less than 2 years with mean size of 14 employees; for exiting firms of all ages, the mean size is 23. Dunne, Roberts and Samuelson (1988, p. 503) note that about 39% of firms exit from one Census to the next and entry cohort in each year accounts for about 16% of an industry's output. While the number of entrants is large, their size is tiny relative to incumbents. Data indicate similar pattern for exiters.

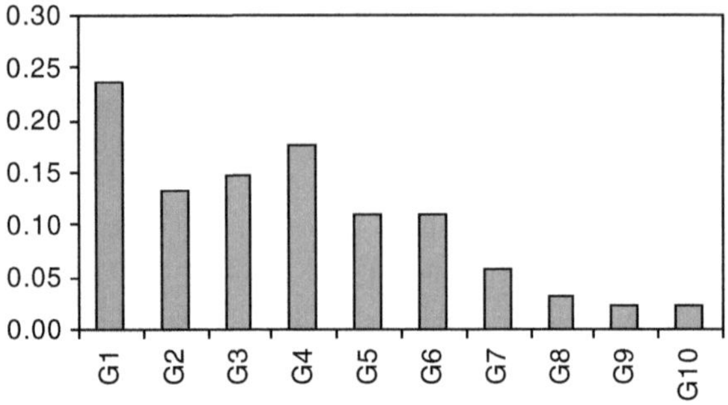

Fig. 9.1 Establishments by size, 1982. The figure represent the establishment size distribution for the typical SIC 4-digit industry (i.e., the average across the industries SIC 4-digit industries in our sample) for the Census year 1982. The establishment size groups correspond to the following number of employees (in parentheses). G1 (1–4); G2 (5–9); G3 (10–19); G4 (20–49); G5 (50–99); G6 (100–249); G7 (250–499); G8 (500–999); G9 (1,000–2,499); and G10 (2,500 or more). The vertical axis indicates the share of the number of establishments for that group in the industry total. Our data contain similar information for the other Census years (1963, 1967, 1972, 1977, 1987, 1992) in our sample and skewed size distribution pattern displayed above is observed for the other Census years (see Ghosal (2007) for additional discussion)

follows. Entry cohorts typically consist of relatively small firms, and exit cohorts of young and small firms. Based on the results discussed earlier, periods of greater uncertainty will delay entry more than exit, resulting in negative net entry. In other words, we can expect a decrease in the number of smaller firms. Further, based on the previous discussion, this effect will be larger when sunk costs are higher. Larger firms are more likely to show greater inaction regarding exit. Since data shows that entrants are rather small, entry of large firms is typically not an important consideration. Overall, we expect greater inaction in large firm net entry (little/no entry and lower exits) during periods of greater uncertainty.

Regarding firms' investment outlays, in general we expect investment to decrease with greater uncertainty (Dixit and Pindyck, 1994). This negative effect is expected to be more pronounced when sunk capital costs are higher and for smaller businesses. Lensink et al. (2001), Leahy and Whited (1996), Ghosal and Loungani (1996, 2000) and Carruth et al. (2001) present extensive discussion of various aspects of the uncertainty-investment relationship.

Financing Constraints Literature

Greenwald and Stiglitz (1990) model firms as maximizing expected equity minus expected cost of bankruptcy and examine scenarios where firms may be equity or borrowing constrained. A key result is that greater *uncertainty* about profits exacerbates information asymmetries, tightens financing constraints and lowers capital outlays. Since uncertainty increases the risk of bankruptcy, firms cannot issue equity to absorb the risk. Brito and Mello (1995) extend the Greenwald-Stiglitz framework to show that small firm survival is adversely affected by financing constraints. Second, higher *sunk costs* imply that lenders will be more hesitant to provide financing because asset specificity lowers resale value implying that collateral has less value (Williamson, 1988). Lensink et al. (2001) provide a lucid discussion of financing constraints in the related context of investment behavior. In short, periods of greater uncertainty, in conjunction with higher sunk costs, increase the likelihood of bankruptcy and exacerbate financing constraints. Incumbents who are more dependent on borrowing and adversely affected by tighter credit are likely to have lower probability of survival and expedited exits. Firms more likely to be adversely affected are those with little/no collateral, inadequate history and shaky past performance. Similarly, entry is likely to be retarded for potential entrants who are more adversely affected by the tighter credit conditions. Thus, periods of greater uncertainty, and in conjunction with higher sunk costs, are likely to accelerate exits and retard entry; i.e., negative net entry.

There exists an important literature which suggests that financial market frictions are more likely to affect smaller firms. These include Cabral and Mata (2003), Cooley and Quadrini (2001), Evans and Jovanovic (1989), Fazzari et al. (1988) and Gertler and Gilchrist (1994). Overall, for smaller firms, periods of greater uncertainty are likely to increase exits and lower entry, and the industry will experience loss of smaller firms, or negative net entry. This effect will be magnified in high sunk cost industries.

The effect on investment will be similar: smaller firms, via the financing constraints channel, are more likely to see a reduction in their investment outlays during periods of greater uncertainty.

Real-Options Versus Financing Constraints

As noted above, both the real-options and the financing constraints channels indicate similar qualitative effects of uncertainty on firms entry and exit, and investment, decisions. That is, a reduction in the industry number of firms or a reduction in investment during periods of greater uncertainty is consistent with both the channels described above. Unfortunately, with industry-level data, it appears rather difficult to disentangle the two channels. Access to firm-specific data, and using good proxies for sunk capital costs and potential financing constraints, may help us assess the relative importance of these two channels. This is left for a future research.

Uncertainty and the Dynamics of Net Entry

In this section I present evidence on: (1) *cross-industry* volatility of establishments; and (2) the *within-industry* intertemporal dynamics of the number of establishments. The data appendix provides information about the sources of data.

Data reveals wide differences across industries in the degree of volatility of firms and establishments. Caves (1998) and Sutton (1997), for example, document this and dwell on the underlying determinants. They mainly point to technological forces as the key driver of this volatility. Based on our discussion in Sect. 2 of the effects of uncertainty on firms' entry and exit decisions, I present some evidence on the extent to which uncertainty might be an important determinant of the volatility of firms and establishments.

As noted in the data appendix, our data contain information on the number of firms and the number of establishments in an industry. To provide a perspective on the number of establishments relative to the number of firms, for each industry I calculate the ratio: the number of establishments divided by the number of firms. Across our sample of industries, the median value of this ratio is 1.1, and the 75th and 90th percentile values are 1.3 and 1.6. Therefore, even at the 90th percentile value of this distribution, there is a rough equivalence between firm and establishment. The underlying data shows that small businesses are overwhelmingly single-establishment, medium sized businesses tend to be largely single-establishment or a very small number of establishments, and large firms typically tend to be multi-establishment. Therefore, the vast majority of multi-establishment firms are the larger firms. I utilize this observation to study the effect of uncertainty on small and large business dominated industries, where the size metric is the number of employees per establishment. While we have data on the within-industry size distribution of firms, the Census of Manufactures does not provide data on the within-industry size distribution of firms.

To examine the determinants of the volatility of the number of establishments, I estimate the following equation:

$$\begin{aligned} \ell n\sigma(ESTB)_i &= \ell n\alpha_0 + \alpha_1 \ell n\sigma(\pi)_i + \alpha_2 \ell n\Phi_i + \alpha_3 \ell nR\ \&\ D_i \\ &\quad + \alpha_4 \ell nADVT_i + \alpha_5 \ell nGRS_i + \ell n\upsilon_i, \end{aligned} \tag{9.1}$$

where "i" indexes industry, *ln* denotes natural logarithm, σ(ESTB) is the standard deviation of the number of establishments, $\sigma(\pi)$ measures profit uncertainty, Φ is a measure of sunk capital costs (see data appendix for construction), R&D is the research and development intensity as a proxy for technology, ADVT is advertising-intensity, GRS is industry growth and υ the random error term. The latter three variables are some of the standard control variables (see Ghosal (2006) for a more detailed discussion)

Industry profits are measured by: π = [(Sales Revenue-Variable Costs)/(Sales Revenue)]. To measure uncertainty, I use an industry profit forecasting equation. The residuals from this equation contain the unpredictable component of profits. The variance of the residuals measure uncertainty. This basic procedure is common in the literature: see Lensink et al. (2001), Carruth et al. (2001), Ghosal and Loungani (1996, 2000) and Ghosal (2006, 2007) and the references there. The profit forecasting equation can take many incarnations: see, for example, Ghosal (2006), Ghosal and Loungani (2000) and Lensink et al. (2001). The forecasting equation that I present here to provide a flavor of the results is:

$$\Pi_{i,t} = \lambda_0 + \sum_k \theta_k \Pi_{i,t-k} + \sum_m \zeta_m SALES_{i,t-m} + \sum_n \gamma_n UNEMP_{t-n} + \varepsilon_{i,t}, \quad (9.2)$$

where UNEMP is economy-wide unemployment rate designed to control for macroeconomic conditions. Using this, I obtain the measure of profit uncertainty $\sigma(\pi)_{\mathrm{i}}$.

The profit uncertainty variable $\sigma(\pi)$ may be endogenous in (1) due to the linkages between market structure and movements in prices. Given this, I estimate (1) using OLS as well as Instrumental Variables methods and conduct Hausman tests. For IV estimation, the main instrumental variable used is industry-specific energy prices.

The results from estimating (1) are presented in Table 9.1. The estimates of $\sigma(\pi)_{\mathrm{i}}$ are negative and highly significant. The results for the sunk cost measure Φ(W) indicate the same pattern. Given the standard errors, the Φ(W) effect is somewhat smaller than the $\sigma(\pi)$ effect. Overall, higher profit uncertainty leads to lower endemic volatility of the number of establishments in an industry. This points to lower net entry and churning in industries that have structurally greater uncertainty – which is in our analysis is measured as the unforecastable component of industry profits. Given that the estimated (1) is log-linear (non-linear in levels), the estimates show that a combination of uncertainty and sunk costs exacerbate the effects. The implied quantitative effects are large and economically meaningful.

Next, I examine the *within-industry* intertemporal dynamics of the total number of establishments.

Table 9.1 Cross-industry volatility of the number of establishments (1) $\ell n\sigma(ESTB)_i = \ell n\alpha_0 + \alpha_1 \ell n\sigma(\pi)_i + \alpha_2 \ell n\Phi_i + \alpha_3 \ell nR\ \&\ D_i + \alpha_4 \ell nADVT_i + \alpha_5 \ell nGRS_i + \ell n\upsilon_i$

	A. OLS	B. IV
Intercept	1.983*	0.122
	(0.013)	(0.964)
$\sigma(\pi)_{\mathrm{I}}$	−1.044*	−1.492*
Profit uncertainty	(0.001)	(0.020)
$\Phi(\mathrm{W})_{\mathrm{I}}$	−0.815*	−0.757*
Weighted sunk cost Index	(0.001)	(0.001)
$\mathrm{R\&D_i}$	−0.122*	−0.118*
R&D intensity	(0.014)	(0.015)
$\mathrm{ADVT_i}$	−0.058	−0.067
Advertising intensity	(0.139)	(0.129)
$\mathrm{GRS_i}$	0.040	−1.781
Growth of sales	(0.993)	(0.664)
Adj-R^2	0.405	0.387
Hausman test	NA	(0.684)

1. The p-values (two-tailed) from heteroscedasticity-consistent standard errors are in parentheses. For p-values < 0.001, they are indicated as 0.001. An asterisk * indicates significance at least at the 10% level. The number for the Hausman test is the p-value for the χ^2 test. All samples contain 266 industries.
2. The instrument for IV estimation (col. B) is the standard deviation of industry-specific real energy price.

The measure of profits and the equation to measure industry-specific profit uncertainty is the same as in (2). The procedure of constructing a within-industry time-series in uncertainty is quite different. The steps are as follows. First, for each industry in the sample, I first estimate (2) using annual data over the entire sample period 1958–1994. The residuals represent the *unsystematic* components. Second, the standard deviation of residuals, $\sigma(\Pi)_{\mathrm{i,t}}$, are the measure of uncertainty. The industry structure data are for the five-yearly Censuses 1963, 1967, 1972, 1977, 1982, 1987 and 1992. The standard deviation of residuals over, e.g., 1967–1971 serves as the uncertainty measure for 1972; similarly, the standard deviation of residuals over 1982–1986 measures uncertainty for 1987, and so on. Using this procedure I get seven time-series observations on $\sigma(\Pi)_{\mathrm{i,t}}$. The within-year cross-industry statistics for $\sigma(\Pi)$ shows a relatively high standard deviation compared to the mean value indicating large cross-industry variation in uncertainty. Key to our empirical analysis, the data show significant variation in uncertainty within-industries over time. More details on these measures and summary statistics can be found in Ghosal (2007).

The dynamic panel data model estimated is given by:

$$
\begin{aligned}
ESTB_{i,t} = {} & \beta_i + \beta_1\sigma(\Pi)_{i,t} + \beta_2 TECH_{i,t} + \beta_3\Pi_{i,t} + \beta_4 GROW_{i,t} \\
& + \beta_5 AESTB_t + \beta_6 ESTB_{i,t-1} + \varepsilon_{i,t},
\end{aligned}
\tag{9.3}
$$

where ESTB is the number of establishments in an industry in a Census year "t", $\sigma(\Pi)$ is profit uncertainty constructed as noted earlier, TECH is a measure of technical progress proxies by industry-specific total factor productivity growth,[5] Π is the level of industry profits, GROW is industry sales growth, and AESTB is the total number of establishments in all of U.S. manufacruting designed to capture aggregated macroeconomic (in this case, manufacturing-wide) effects. The variables ESTB, $\sigma(\Pi)$, Π, GROW and AESTB are measured in logarithms; these coefficients are therefore interpreted as elasticities. TECH (total factor productivity) is not measured in logarithms as it can be negative or positive. Ghosal (2007) contains detailed description of the construction of the variables and the justification for these controls.

Since the dynamic panel data model contains a lagged dependent variable, it needs to be instrumented. In addition, the industry variables related to $\sigma(\Pi)$, GROW and TECH are all likely to be endogenous, jointly-determined in industry equilibrium. Lagged values of the respective variables, as well as AESTB, are used as instruments. I also use variables constructed at the durable and non-durable levels of aggregation as instruments. Ghosal (2007) provides justification of these instruments.

Table 9.2 presents the estimates. In the discussion of the results, I only focus on the uncertainty related effects. The Hausman test statistics show that the

[5] See Ghosal (2007) for construction of the TFP measure. This is the standard TFP measure corrected for cyclical factor utilization (Basu, 1996).

Table 9.2 Impact of uncertainty on the number of establishments by size category (3) $ESTB_{i,t} = \beta_i + \beta_1\sigma(\Pi)_{i,t} + \beta_2 TECH_{i,t} + \beta_3\Pi_{i,t} + \beta_4 GROW_{i,t} + \beta_5 AESTB_t + \beta_6 ESTB_{i,t-1} + \varepsilon_{i,t}$

	A. Size: All	B. Size: ≥ 500 Large	C. Size: < 500 Small	D. Size: < 100 Smaller	E. Size: < 50 Smallest
$\sigma(\Pi)_{i,t}$	−0.172*	0.093	−0.178*	−0.268*	−0.308*
	(0.001)	(0.258)	(0.001)	(0.001)	(0.001)
$TECH_{i,t}$	−1.737*	0.492	−1.809*	−2.943*	−3.418*
	(0.057)	(0.729)	(0.074)	(0.028)	(0.015)
$\Pi_{i,t}$	0.089	0.421*	0.029	0.001	0.042
	(0.504)	(0.029)	(0.849)	(0.995)	(0.837)
$GROW_{i,t}$	−0.041*	−0.304*	−0.017	0.012	0.004
	(0.094)	(0.001)	(0.521)	(0.726)	(0.924)
$AESTB_t$	0.002*	0.001	0.002*	0.003*	0.004*
	(0.001)	(0.778)	(0.001)	(0.002)	(0.001)
$ESTB_{i,t-1}$	0.252*	0.261*	0.261*	0.233*	0.208*
	(0.001)	(0.001)	(0.001)	(0.005)	(0.016)
Panel Obs.	1335	1335	1335	1335	1335
Hausman test	0.001	0.001	0.001	0.001	0.001

1. Estimation is via the instrumental variables method; instruments are described in Sect. 3. *p-values* (two-tailed test) computed from heteroscedasticity-consistent standard errors are in parentheses. An asterisk * indicates significance at least at the 10% level.
2. Hausman test statistics (only the *p-value* is reported) easily reject the null that the industry-specific variables were pre-determined.
3. As noted in Sect. 3, ESTB, $\sigma(\Pi)$, Π, GROW and AESTB in (3) are measured in *logarithms*; these coefficients can be interpreted as elasticities. TECH is not measured in logarithms; thus the magnitude of these coefficients cannot be directly compared to others.
4. Variable definitions: $\sigma(\Pi)$ is profit margin uncertainty; TECH is technical change as measured by TFP growth; Π is profit margin; GROW is sales growth; AESTB is the total number of establishment in U.S. manufacturing. The size measure relates to the number of employees in an establishment. The last column, for example, contains industries that are relatively dominated by establishments with less than 50 employees.

industry-specific explanatory variables are best treated as jointly-determined. The estimated coefficients on the uncertainty variable shows that greater uncertainty reduces the number of establishments in the industry, and, based on the estimates across the establishment size sub-samples, all of the negative effect is arising from the industries where there is a preponderance of small businesses. The greater is the small establishment dominance, for example moving from sample Size < 500 to Size < 50, the greater is the negative effect of uncertainty. Note that the uncertainty variable is measured in logarithms, so the estimated coefficients are interprerted as elasticities. In industries that are dominated by large establishments (sample: Size ≥ 500), uncertainty has no impact on the number of establishments.

In Sect. 2 it was noted that greater sunk capital costs would exacerbate the effects of uncertainty. Table 9.3 presents estimates of the effect of uncertainty on the number of establishments by size groups as well as by high versus low sunk cost sub-samples. If we look at the estimates in row 1 (Size: All), we see that the negative

Table 9.3 Impact of uncertainty and sunk costs on the number of establishments by size category only the uncertainty coefficients are reported

	A. Low sunk costs	B. High sunk costs
Size: All	0.138	−0.314*
	(0.194)	(0.007)
Size: ≥ 500	0.075	−0.110
Large	(0.708)	(0.421)
Size: < 500	0.135	−0.286*
Small	(0.206)	(0.062)
Size: < 100	0.127	−0.531*
Smaller	(0.254)	(0.017)
Size: < 50	0.102	−0.622*
Smallest	(0.377)	(0.012)
Panel Obs.	310	305

1. Equation (9.3) was estimated for high and low sunk cost sub-samples. Only the uncertainty coefficients are presented. The estimated equations contain all the control variables noted in Table 9.2.
2. As in Table 9.2, estimation is via the instrumental variables method. The *p-values* (two-tailed test) computed from heteroscedasticity-consistent standard errors are in parentheses. An asterisk * indicates significance at least at the 10% level.
2. In column A, the combination "USED and RENT and DEPR greater than 50th percentile" constitutes the low sunk cost sample. In column B, the combination "USED and RENT and DEPR less than 50th percentile" constitutes the high sunk cost sub-sample. See data appendix and Ghosal (2007) for more details about the sunk costs measures.

effect of uncertainty is arising only in the high sunk-cost industries. None of the estimates of uncertainty are significant in column A. This implies that irrespective of establishment size, greater uncertainty has no effect in industry sub-samples where sunk costs are low. In contrast, as we look down the estimates in column B, we see that uncertainty has no effect on large establishments (Size > 500) even when sunk costs are high. As we examine the estimates for the smaller size groups, we find that the estimated elasticities get much larger. Given the estimated standard errors, the differences between the Size < 500 and Size < 50 is highly significant and the point estimate for the elasticity is almost double.

Overall, the estimates from Tables 9.2 and 9.3 reveal that greater uncertainty results in negative net entry and the vast majority of this effect is concentrated in the relatively small establishments. Large establishments are unaffected.

Uncertainty and Investment Expenditures

The final set of results we examine relate to the effect of uncertainty on investment. As noted earlier, there is a relatively large empirical literature that shows that greater uncertainty tends to reduce investment. While I present estimates for the overall effect, the main focus here is to note the results that reveal the role played by establishment (firm) size in the relationship between uncertainty and investment. The estimated investment equation is given by:

$$\left(\frac{I}{K}\right)_{i,t} = \eta_0 + \eta_1\sigma(\Pi)_{i,t} + \eta_2\left(\frac{CF}{K}\right)_{i,t} + \eta_3\left(\frac{CF}{K}\right)_{i,t-1} + \eta_4 AINV_t$$
$$+ \eta_5 AINV_{t-1} + \eta_6\left(\frac{I}{K}\right)_{i,t-1} + \omega_{i,t}, \qquad (9.4)$$

where $\sigma(\Pi)$ measures uncertainty, (I/K) is current investment divided by begining of year capital stock, (CF/K) is current year cashflow divided by begining of year capital stock, and AINV is economy-wide aggregate investment. All variables are measured in logarithms. For more details about such estimated investment equations, see Chirinko (1993), Chirinko and Schaller (1995), Ghosal and Loungani (2000) and the references there.

Since the above investment equation is estimated using annual data on all the variables, the following procedure is used for measuring profit uncertainty $\sigma(\Pi)$. First, for each industry, a profit forecasting equation is estimated over the entire sample period. The residuals contain the *unsystematic* (or unforecastable) components. Second, collect the residuals over five-year overlapping periods (1960–1964, 1961–1965, 1962–1966, ...) and the standard deviation of the residuals over the 5-year periods are the measure of uncertainty $\sigma(\Pi)$. For example, the standard deviation of residuals over 1960–1964 serve as the observation on uncertainty for the year 1965. This procedure provides an industry-specific time-series on $\sigma(\Pi)$. Alternative forecasting equations are used to obtain $\sigma(\Pi)$. A general specification is (2) given earlier. An alternate specification is a more basic autoregressive-distributed lag specification where industry profits Π are regressed on their own lags as well as current and lagged values of the economy-wide unemployment rate. As before, $\sigma(\Pi)$ is treated as endogenous. The two instruments used are energy prices and the Federal Funds Rate. The link between both of these variables and economic activity, prices and profitability are well documented.

Next, the following information is used to classify industries into small and large business dominated groups. Using the US Small Business Administration classification (see data appendix, and Ghosal and Loungani, 2000), the industries are segmented into two groups: (a) SMALL and (b) OTHER (i.e., not small). The SMALL sub-sample is further refined using the Census establishment size distribution data. As an illustration, the size metric of "100 workers" is used to represent a small firm (this is in contrast to the SBA size metric of 500 workers). The sub-sample "SMALL and Size(100)" is created consisting of industries that are SMALL and also satisfy the constraint that the percentage of establishments with more than 100 employees is "greater than or equal to" 0.9037 (50th percentile value).

Table 9.4 presents the estimates. Since the equation is estimated in logarithms, the coefficient estimates are interpreted as elasticities. For the full sample (col. A), periods of greater uncertainty about profits leads to a decrease in investment. Across columns B, C and D, the main conclusion is that the negative impact of uncertainty

Table 9.4 Impact of uncertainty on investment (4) $\left(\frac{I}{K}\right)_{i,t} = \eta_0 + \eta_1\sigma(\Pi)_{i,t} + \eta_2\left(\frac{CF}{K}\right)_{i,t} + \eta_3\left(\frac{CF}{K}\right)_{i,t-1} + \eta_4 AINV_t + \eta_5 AINV_{t-1} + \eta_6\left(\frac{I}{K}\right)_{i,t-1} + \omega_{i,t}$

	A. ALL	B. SBA SMALL	C. SBA SMALL and Size(100)	D. SBA OTHER (Not SMALL)
$\sigma(\Pi)_{it}$	−0.267*	−0.344*	−0.881*	−0.240*
	(0.038)	(0.093)	(0.360)	(0.041)
$(CF/K)_{it}$	0.248*	0.324*	0.360*	0.216*
	(0.021)	(0.041)	(0.086)	(0.024)
$(CF/K)_{it-1}$	0.137*	0.042	−0.033	0.177*
	(0.022)	(0.045)	(0.092)	(0.025)
$(I/K)_{it-1}$	0.510*	0.500*	0.512*	0.515*
	(0.018)	(0.045)	(0.110)	(0.019)
$AINV_{it}$	0.080*	0.110*	0.129*	0.070*
	(0.014)	(0.029)	(0.066)	(0.016)
$AINV_{it-1}$	0.022*	−0.001	−0.059	0.030*
	(0.016)	(0.033)	(0.078)	(0.018)
Panel Obs.	8910	2457	1080	6453
Industries	330	91	40	239
Adj-R^2	0.2855	0.2632	0.1123	0.2964

1. $\sigma(\Pi)_{it}$ and $(I/K)_{it-1}$ are treated as endogenous. The instruments include (a) energy price and federal funds rate uncertainty; (b) three lags of aggregate investment; and (c) lags two and three of industry cash-flow and investment.
2. All variables are measured in logarithms. All specifications are estimated with industry fixed-effects. Heteroscedasticity-consistent *standard errors* are in parentheses. An asterisk * indicates statistical significance at least at the 10% level.

on investment is the greatest for the "SBA SMALL and Size(100)" sub-sample. Given the standard errors, the effect on the smallest size group is statistically significant compared to the "SBA SMALL" group. The key findings, therefore, are that the sign of the investment-uncertainty relationship is negative, and the quantitative negative impact is substantially greater in the small firm dominated industries. Ghosal and Loungani (2000) present additional results with alternative measures of profit uncertainty and further refinements of the size classification; the key inferences remain intact.

Discussion and Some Implications for Public Policy

The evidence presented here indicates that greater uncertainty about profits appears to significantly *lower* net entry as well as investment. The effects are most pronounced in industries that are dominated by small firms and have high sunk costs. Some complementary evidence on the effect of uncertainty on industry structure is provided by Ghosal (1995, 1996). The empirical results in these two papers show that industries with greater uncertainty have significantly lower number of firms and greater output concentration (as measured by the industry four-firm concentration ratio). The quantitative effect on the number of firms is greater than the effect on industry concentration. Taken together, these results seem to indicate indicate that greater uncertainty creates a barrier-to-entry leading to less smaller firms and a more concentrated industry structure.

There is also an older literature that examined firms' input choices under uncertainty: for example, Hartman (1976) and Holthausen (1976). These theoretical papers, however, do not model the real-options or financing constraints channels. These papers rely on firms' risk-preferences (often risk-aversion) and technology to derive the impact of demand uncertainty on the capital-labor input mix. Empirical evaluation of these models by Ghosal (1991, 1995) shows that greater uncertainty about demand tends to increase firms' capital-labor ratio. Both the theoretical models as well as the empirical results on the input-mix are probably best viewed as firms' longer-run response to greater uncertainty. In contrast, the more recent theoretical models that explore the real-options channel, and the empirical evidence presented in this paper, are to be viewed as firms' short-run response to greater uncertainty.

The "big-picture" inferences from the evidence presented here on the impact of uncertainty and sunk costs on net entry and investment outlays are broadly consistent with a number of other studies, including Bloom et al. (2008), Chirinko and Schaller (2008) and Driver and Whelan (2001). Estimates in Chirinko and Schaller, for example, provide evidence that the irreversibility premium is both economically and statistically significant. Bloom, Bond and van Reenen show that uncertainty increases real option values making firms more cautious when investing or disinvesting, and that the cautionary effects of uncertainty are large. They conclude that the responsiveness of firms to any given policy stimulus may be much weaker in periods of high uncertainty.

Our findings could be useful in several areas. First, they may provide guidance for antitrust. Analysis of entry is an integral part of antitrust and competition law enforcement guidelines. Sunk costs are typically explicitly considered as a barrier to entry, but uncertainty is typically not considered at all or de-emphasized. Our results suggest that uncertainty compounds the sunk cost barriers, retards entry and lowers the survival probability of smaller incumbents. Therefore, uncertainty could be an added consideration in the forces governing market structure. Second, determinants of M&A activity is an important area of research; see Jovanovic and Rousseau (2001) and the references there. If periods of greater uncertainty lowers the probability of survival and increases exits, it may have implications for reallocation of capital. For example, do the assets exit the industry or are they reallocated via M&A? It may be also be useful to explore whether uncertainty helps explain part of M&A waves. Third, Davis et al. (1996) find that job destruction/creation decline with firm size/age. Cooley and Quadrini (2001) and Cabral and Mata (2003) suggest that small firms may have greater destruction (exits) due to financial frictions. Our results provide additional insights: periods of greater uncertainty, in combination with higher sunk costs, appear to significantly influence small firm turnover.

Data Appendix

Complete details about the data used can be found in Ghosal and Loungani (1996, 2000) and Ghosal (2006, 2007). I provide a brief description below of the sources and variables. The data are for the US manufacturing sector and at the SIC 4-digit level of disaggregation. The source of the industry time-series data are the Annual Survey of Manufactures ("NBER-CES Manufacturing Industry Database," by Eric Bartelsman, Randy Becker and Wayne Gray, and available at www.nber.org). These data are on a wide range of industry-specific variables related to costs, inputs (materials, energy) used, price deflators, investment, capital stock, sales, wages, among others. I collected industry-specific data from the 5-year Census of Manufactures on: (a) number of firms; (b) number of establishments; (c) size distribution of establishments (d) four-firm concentration ratio; (e) intensity of used capital; (f) intensity of rental capital; (g) percent depreciation of capital. We also have industry-specific data from the US Small Business Administration reports (The State of Small Business: A Report of the President, 1990.) The Small Business Administration classifies a small business as one that employs 500 workers or less. An industry is classified as "consistently small business dominated" if at least 60% of industry employment is in firms with fewer than 500 employees over 1979, 1983 and 1988.

Abstracting from depreciation considerations, sunk capital costs correspond to the non-recoverable component of entry capital investment $\Phi = (r - \varphi)K$, where K is the entry capital requirement, r the unit price of new capital and φ the resale price (or scrap value) of this capital. Obtaining data on φ is extremely difficult implying that we can't measure Φ directly for our industries. Instead, we pursue an alternative approach to measuring sunk costs. We adopt the methodologies outlined in Kessides (1990) and Sutton (1991) to obtain *proxies* for sunk capital costs. The extent of sunk capital outlays incurred by a potential entrant will be determined by the durability, specificity and mobility of capital. While these characteristics are unobservable, one can construct proxies. Following Kessides we construct the following three measures. Let RENT denote the fraction of total capital that a firm (entrant) can rent: RENT = (rental payments on plant and equipment/capital stock). If a potential entrant can lease capital, then sunk costs are correspondingly lower. Let USED denote the fraction of total capital expenditures corresponding to used capital goods: USED = (expenditures on used plant and equipment/total expenditures on new and used plant and equipment). Availability of used capital goods at lower prices reduces the embedded sunk costs. Finally, let DEPR denote the share of depreciation payments: DEPR = (depreciation payments/capital stock). Higher depreciation makes capital less sunk; in the limiting scenario if capital lives only for one period, then sunk costs, which arise from the non-depreciated component of capital, are negligible. We create the following three measures: Φ(RENT) = (1/RENT); Φ(USED) = (1/USED); and Φ(DEPR) = (1/DEPR). High Φ(RENT) indicates low-intensity rental market, implying higher sunk costs. High Φ(USED) signals low-intensity used capital market, implying higher sunk costs. High Φ(DEPR) indicates that capital decays slowly, implying higher sunk costs which arise from the undepreciated portion of capital. We collected data to construct Φ(RENT), Φ(USED), Φ(DEPR) and Φ(EK) for the Census years 1972, 1982 and 1992. Collecting these for some of the additional (particularly, earlier) years presented problems due to changing industry definitions and many missing data points. Our data revealed fairly high correlation (between 0.6 and 0.9) for the sunk cost proxies across the different years, indicating a fair degree of stability in these measures.

References

Audretsch D (1995) Innovation and industry evolution. Cambridge, MIT Press
Basu S (1996) Procyclical productivity: increasing returns or cyclical utilization? Q J Econ 719–751
Bloom N, Bond S van Reenen J (2008) Uncertainty and investment dynamics. Rev Econ Stud 74(2):391–415
Brito P, Mello A (1995) Financial constraints and firm post-entry performance. Int J Ind Organiz 543–565
Caballero R, Pindyck R (1996) Investment, uncertainty and industry evolution. Int Econ Revlinebreak 641–662
Cabral L, Mata J (2003) On the evolution of the firm size distribution: facts and theory. Am Econ Rev 1075–1090
Carruth A, Dickerson A, Henley A (2001) What do we know about investment under uncertainty? J Econ Surv 14:119–154
Caves R (1998) Industrial organization and new findings on the turnover and mobility of firms. J Econ Lit 1947–1982
Chirinko R, Schaller H (1995) Why does liquidity matter in investment equations? J Money Credit Banking 27:527–548
Chirinko R (1993) Business fixed investment spending: modeling strategies, empirical results, and policy implications. J Econ Lit 31:1875–1911
Chirinko R, Schaller H (2008) The irreversibility premium. Chicago University of Illinois at Chicago
Cooley T, Quadrini V (2001) Financial markets and firm dynamics. Am Econ Rev 1286–1310
Davis S, Haltiwanger J, Schuh S (1996) Job creation and destruction. Cambridge, MIT Press
Dixit A (1989) Entry and exit decisions under uncertainty. J Polit Econ 620–38
Dixit A, Pindyck R (1994) Investment under uncertainty. Princeton, Princeton University Press
Driver C, Whelan B (2001) The effect of business risk on manufacturing investment. J Econ Behav Organiz 44:403–412
Dunne T, Roberts M, Samuelson L (1988) Patterns of entry and exit in US manufacturing industries. Rand J Econ 495–515
Evans D, Jovanovic B (1989) An estimated model of entrepreneurial choice under liquidity constraints. J Polit Econ 808–827
Fazzari S, Hubbard G, Petersen B (1988) Financing constraints and corporate investment. Brookings Pap Econ Act 141–195
Gertler M, Gilchrist S (1994) Monetary policy, business cycles, and the behavior of small manufacturing firms. Q J Econ 309–340
Ghosal V (1991) Demand uncertainty and the capital-labor ratio: evidence from the US manufacturing sector. Rev Econ Stat 73:157–161
Ghosal V (1995) Input choices under uncertainty. Econ Inq 142–158
Ghosal V (1995) Price uncertainty and output concentration. Rev Ind Organiz 10:749–767
Ghosal V (1996) Does uncertainty influence the number of firms in an industry? Econ Lett 30: 229–37

Ghosal V, Loungani P (1996) Product market competition and the impact of price uncertainty on investment. J Ind Econ 217–228
Ghosal V, Loungani P (2000) The differential impact of uncertainty on investment in small and large businesses. Rev Econ Stat 338–343
Ghosal V (2006) Endemic volatility of firms and establishments. USA, Georgia Institute of Technology
Ghosal V (2007) Small is beautiful but size matters: the asymmetric impact of uncertainty and sunk costs on small and large businesses. USA, Georgia Institute of Technology
Greenwald B, Stiglitz J (1990) Macroeconomic models with equity and credit rationing. In: Hubbard, R Glenn (ed.) Asymmetric information, corporate finance, and investment. Chicago, University of Chicago Press, pp 15–42
Hartman R (1976) Factor demand with output price uncertainty. Am Econ Rev 66:675–681
Holthausen D (1976) Input choices under uncertain demand. Am Econ Rev 66:94–103
Hopenhayn H (1992) Entry, exit and firm dynamics in long run equilibrium. Econometrica 1127–1150
Jovanovic B, Rousseau P (2001) Mergers and technological change. Mimeo, Chicago, University of Chicago
Kessides I (1990) Market concentration, contestability and sunk costs. Rev Econ Stat 614–622
Leahy J, Whited T (1996) The effect of uncertainty on investment: some stylized facts. J Money Credit Banking 28:64–83
Lensink R, Bo H, Sterken E (2001) Investment, capital market imperfections, and uncertainty. Edward Elgar, London
Pakes A, Ericson R (1998) Empirical implications of alternate models of firm dynamics. J Econ Theory 1–45
Stiglitz J, Weiss A (1981) Credit rationing in markets with imperfect information. Am Econ Rev 393–410
Sutton J (1991) Sunk costs and market structure. Cambridge, MIT Press
Sutton J (1997) Gibrat's legacy. J Econ Lit 40–59
Williamson O (1988) Corporate finance and corporate governance. J Finance 567–591

Chapter 10
Investment and Trade Patterns in a Sticky-Price, Open-Economy Model

Enrique Martínez-García and Jens Søndergaard

Abstract This paper explores a two-country DSGE model with sticky prices à la Calvo (1983) and local-currency pricing. We analyze the investment decision in the presence of adjustment costs of two types, i.e., capital adjustment costs (CAC) and investment adjustment costs (IAC). We compare the investment and trade patterns with adjustment costs against those of a model without adjustment costs and with (quasi-) flexible prices. We show that having adjustment costs results into more volatile consumption and net exports series, and less volatile investment. We document three important facts on US trade dynamics: (1) the S-shaped cross-correlation between real GDP and the real net exports share, (2) the J-curve between terms of trade and net exports, and (3) the weak and S-shaped cross-correlation between real GDP and terms of trade. We find that adding adjustment costs tends to reduce the model's ability to match these stylized facts. Nominal rigidities cannot account for these features either.

Introduction

Adjustment costs on capital accumulation often feature in modern international macro models of the business cycle. The Q theory of investment with adjustment costs (developed among others by Lucas and Prescott 1971, and Abel 1983) formalizes the idea that investment becomes more attractive whenever the value of a unit of additional capital is higher relative to its acquisition cost. However, while there is broad agreement on the importance of investment for trade, there is less clarity on the role that adjustment costs play in these models.

E. Martínez-García
Federal Reserve Bank of Dallas, 2200 N. Pearl Street, Dallas, TX 75201, USA,
e-mail: enrique.martinez-garcia@dal.frb.org

J. Søndergaard
Monetary Assessment and Strategy Division, Monetary Analysis, Bank of England, Threadneedle Street, London EC2R 8AH, UK,
e-mail: jens.sondergaard@bankofengland.co.uk

G. Calcagnini and E. Saltari (eds.), *The Economics of Imperfect Markets*, Contributions to Economics,
DOI: 10.1007/978-3-7908-2131-4_10,

In the standard international real business cycle model (IRBC) of Backus, Kehoe and Kydland (BKK) (1995, p. 340), the connection between investment and trade is rather straightforward: "resources are shifted to the more productive location (...). This tendency to 'make hay where the sun shines' means that with uncorrelated productivity shocks, consumption will be positively correlated across countries, while investment, employment, and output will be negatively correlated. With productivity shocks that are positively correlated, (...), all of these correlations rise, but with the benchmark parameter values none change sign."

Heathcote and Perri (2002) elaborate further on this point, explaining that a domestic productivity shock causes domestic investment to increase by much more than the increase in foreign consumption, so the domestic country draws more resources from abroad and the domestic trade deficit widens at the same time as domestic output is raising. Hence, as in the data, the IRBC model implies that the trade balance is countercyclical. Engel and Wang (2007) use a richer model with adjustment costs and durable goods, and find that their IRBC framework can also deliver a countercyclical trade balance.

Raffo (2008, p. 21), however, notes that the IRBC model accounts for this empirical pattern "due to the strong terms of trade effect generated by the change in relative scarcity of goods across countries." This prediction on terms of trade is counterfactual for most countries. Furthermore, consumption volatility in BKK (1992, 1995) and Heathcote and Perri (2002) tends to be noticeably lower than in the data. As our work shows, models that do match the real US GDP volatility generate too much investment volatility, while attaining an excessively smooth consumption series.

The role of the Q theory extension in open economy models requires further consideration. While capital accumulation provides a powerful mechanism to smooth consumption intertemporally that diminishes the benefits of trade, capital adjustment costs are likely to induce smoother investment patterns and a more volatile consumption series. Therefore, costly adjustments on capital could enhance the appeal of trade. The Q extension arises from a long tradition on investment theory, but it definitely has implications for the model's ability to generate incentives to trade as well as empirically-consistent consumption and investment paths.

Another strand of the international macro literature has emphasized the role of deviations of the law of one price (LOOP) that lead to a misallocation of expenditures across countries and, in turn, to sizable effects on trade. The international new neoclassical synthesis (INNS) model is built around the assumptions of monopolistic competition among firms, price stickiness à la Calvo (1983) and local-currency pricing (LCP) to force a breakdown of the LOOP. An influential paper in this strand of the literature is Chari, Kehoe and McGrattan (CKM) (2002), which also incorporates a form of adjustment costs. Their paper, however, focuses on the behavior of the real exchange rate rather than on trade dynamics.

We believe that the CKM (2002) paper, by its own right a Q theory extension of the INNS model, raises the issue of how adjustment costs interact with deviations of the LOOP to affect the trade patterns implied by the model. The cost function that CKM (2002) use is not necessarily the only one being proposed either. Christiano, Eichenbaum and Evans (CEE) (2005) have popularized an alternative adjustment cost specification, recently advocated by Justiniano and Primiceri (2008) among others, linked to investment growth rates instead of the investment-to-capital ratio.[1]

To our knowledge, the trade predictions of the Q-INNS model with complete international asset markets have not been consistently evaluated against: (1) different specifications of the adjustment cost function (including the case without adjustment costs), and (2) an approximation of the flexible price environment conventionally assumed in the Q-IRBC literature. In this paper, we develop a two country DSGE model with the distinctive features of the Q-INNS model precisely to help us understand the role of adjustment costs and nominal rigidities on trade. We also examine whether there is any interaction between deviations of the LOOP and adjustment costs that can affect the dynamics of net exports. In other words, this paper aims to provide a broader assessment of whether the Q theory extension of the INNS model can simultaneously be reconciled with the empirical evidence on investment and trade.

We focus our analysis on several important features of the international business cycle data summarized in Table 10.1. First, investment is around three times more volatile than real GDP, while consumption and the net exports share are significantly less volatile. All series tend to be quite persistent. Second, the trade balance is countercyclical. This feature is quite robust across countries, as corroborated by the empirical evidence provided by Engel and Wang (2007). Among 25 OECD countries, they find that the mean correlation between real GDP and the real net exports share is -0.24 and the median is -0.25.

Third, as noted by Ghironi and Melitz (2007) and Engel and Wang (2007), the cross-correlation between real GDP and the real net exports share is S-shaped. Fourth, there is evidence of the J-curve in the cross-correlation between ToT and net exports; a relationship extensively discussed in BKK (1994). Finally, the data

Table 10.1 Stylized facts in the US data

Variable	Std. Dev.	Autocorr.	x_{t-4}	x_{t-2}	x_{t-1}	x_t	x_{t+1}	x_{t+2}	x_{t+4}
			Cross-correlation of real GDP with						
GDP	1.54	0.87	0.31	0.70	0.87	1.00	0.87	0.70	0.31
Investment	5.21	0.91	0.29	0.66	0.84	0.94	0.88	0.75	0.37
Consumption	1.24	0.87	0.51	0.79	0.87	0.85	0.69	0.51	0.16
Net exports	0.38	0.83	−0.46	−0.51	−0.52	−0.48	−0.38	−0.22	0.11
ToT	1.72	0.69	−0.14	−0.05	−0.01	0.07	0.16	0.18	0.20
			Cross-correlation of ToT with						
Net exports			−0.15	−0.18	−0.14	−0.03	0.14	0.25	0.35

Data Sources: The Bureau of Economic Analysis and the Bureau of Labor Statistics. For more details, see the description of the dataset in the Appendix. Sample period: 1973q1–2006q4 (except for ToT, which covers only 1983q3–2006q4)

[1] CEE (2005) and Justiniano and Primiceri (2008) are closed economy models. For an application in an open economy model, see e.g., Martínez-García and Søndergaard (2008b).

shows a weak cross-correlation between real GDP and ToT. This feature is quite robust across countries, as confirmed by the empirical evidence provided by Raffo (2008). For 14 OECD countries plus the EU-15, he finds that the mean correlation between real GDP and ToT is 0.08 and the median is 0.11. We also document that the cross-correlation between real GDP and ToT is S-shaped.

Equilibrium Conditions

Our baseline is a two-country stochastic general equilibrium model with monopolistic competition, sticky prices and LCP. We posit the existence of a deterministic, zero-inflation steady state (with zero net exports). We log-linearize the equilibrium conditions around this zero-inflation steady state and report them here. We refer the interested reader to Martínez-García and Søndergaard (2008a, b) for a description of the model from its first principles, and for details on the derivation of the steady state and the log-linearization. As a notational convention, any variable identified with lower-case letters and a caret on top will represent a transformation (expressed in log deviations relative to its steady state) of the corresponding variable.

Consumption and Investment Decisions

Aggregate consumption in both countries evolves according to a pair of standard Euler equations,

$$\widehat{c}_t \approx \mathbb{E}_t\left[\widehat{c}_{t+1}\right] - \sigma\left(\widehat{i}_t - \mathbb{E}_t\left[\widehat{\pi}_{t+1}\right]\right), \tag{10.1}$$

$$\widehat{c}_t^* \approx \mathbb{E}_t\left[\widehat{c}_{t+1}^*\right] - \sigma\left(\widehat{i}_t^* - \mathbb{E}_t\left[\widehat{\pi}_{t+1}^*\right]\right), \tag{10.2}$$

where $\sigma > 0$ ($\sigma \neq 1$) is the elasticity of intertemporal substitution, $\widehat{c}_t$ and $\widehat{c}_t^*$ denote consumption, $\widehat{i}_t$ and $\widehat{i}_t^*$ are the nominal short-term interest rates (which are also the instruments of monetary policy), $\widehat{p}_t$ and $\widehat{p}_t^*$ are the consumption-price indexes (CPIs), and $\widehat{\pi}_{t+1} \equiv \widehat{p}_{t+1} - \widehat{p}_t$ and $\widehat{\pi}_{t+1}^* \equiv \widehat{p}_{t+1}^* - \widehat{p}_t^*$ stand for CPI inflation in both countries.[2] Under complete international asset markets, the *perfect international risk-sharing condition* implies that,

$$\widehat{c}_t - \widehat{c}_t^* \approx \sigma \widehat{rs}_t, \tag{10.3}$$

[2] As a matter of notation, the superscript "$*$" distinguishes the foreign country from the domestic country.

where the real exchange rate is defined as $\widehat{rs}_t \equiv \widehat{s}_t + \widehat{p}_t^* - \widehat{p}_t$. Consequently, domestic consumption becomes relatively high whenever it is relatively "cheap" (that is, whenever there is a real depreciation).

Capital accumulation evolves according to the following laws of motion,

$$\widehat{k}_{t+1} \approx (1-\delta)\,\widehat{k}_t + \delta\widehat{x}_t, \tag{10.4}$$

$$\widehat{k}_{t+1}^* \approx (1-\delta)\,\widehat{k}_t^* + \delta\widehat{x}_t^*, \tag{10.5}$$

where the parameter $0 < \delta < 1$ denotes the depreciation rate of capital. Investment decisions depend on the technological rate at which aggregate investment goods in either country, $\widehat{x}_t$ and $\widehat{x}_t^*$, can be transformed into new capital, $\widehat{k}_{t+1}$ and $\widehat{k}_{t+1}^*$. The technological constraints on new capital can be summarized with an adjustment cost function, which we normalize to be equal to one in levels and zero in its first derivative whenever evaluated at the steady state.[3]

In a model without adjustment costs (NAC), the rate of transformation of investment into new capital is one-to-one. Hence, the real shadow value of an additional unit of capital (or marginal Q) is equal to one, implying that,

$$\widehat{q}_t = \widehat{q}_t^* \approx 0. \tag{10.6}$$

Naturally, $\widehat{q}_t$ and $\widehat{q}_t^*$ denote the marginal Q in each country in log deviations. Then, the investment decision can be conventionally summarized as,

$$(1-(1-\delta)\,\beta)\,\mathbb{E}_t\left(\widehat{r}_{t+1}^k\right) \approx \widehat{i}_t - \mathbb{E}_t\left(\widehat{\pi}_{t+1}\right), \tag{10.7}$$

$$(1-(1-\delta)\,\beta)\,\mathbb{E}_t\left(\widehat{r}_{t+1}^{k*}\right) \approx \widehat{i}_t^* - \mathbb{E}_t\left(\widehat{\pi}_{t+1}^*\right), \tag{10.8}$$

where $\widehat{r}_{t+1}^k$ and $\widehat{r}_{t+1}^{k*}$ denote the real rental rates on capital in both countries. The parameter $0 < \beta < 1$ is the subjective intertemporal discount factor. The real Fisherian interest rates on the right-hand side of (10.7)–(10.8) give us the opportunity cost of investing in capital. The left-hand side, in turn, reflects the real rental rate on capital adjusted to account for capital depreciation over time. In other words, households keep investing in capital until a point where the marginal return of investing in an additional unit of capital equals its marginal cost.

The Q theory extension of the model means that (10.6) does no longer hold true, and this forces us to revisit our notion of the marginal returns to investment. In this regard, we consider the capital adjustment cost (CAC) function favored by CKM (2002) and the investment adjustment cost (IAC) function preferred by CEE (2005) to make the marginal Q no longer equal to one. Under the CAC specification, we obtain that the marginal Q is,

[3] Even though the adjustment cost function affects the rate of transformation of investment goods into new capital, this normalization implies that log-linear equations (10.4) and (10.5) are invariant to any such adjustment cost specification.

$$\widehat{q}_t \approx \chi\delta\left(\widehat{x}_t - \widehat{k}_t\right), \tag{10.9}$$

$$\widehat{q}_t^* \approx \chi\delta\left(\widehat{x}_t^* - \widehat{k}_t^*\right), \tag{10.10}$$

which is a function of the contemporaneous investment-to-capital ratio, i.e., $\widehat{x}_t - \widehat{k}_t$ and $\widehat{x}_t^* - \widehat{k}_t^*$. The parameter $\chi \geq 0$ regulates the degree of concavity of the CAC function around the steady state, since $-\frac{\chi}{\delta}$ is the second-order derivative of the function whenever evaluated at the steady state.

Under the IAC specification, the marginal Q is related to investment growth,

$$\widehat{q}_t \approx \kappa\left[\left(\widehat{x}_t - \widehat{x}_{t-1}\right) - \beta\mathbb{E}_t\left(\widehat{x}_{t+1} - \widehat{x}_t\right)\right], \tag{10.11}$$

$$\widehat{q}_t^* \approx \kappa\left[\left(\widehat{x}_t^* - \widehat{x}_{t-1}^*\right) - \beta\mathbb{E}_t\left(\widehat{x}_{t+1}^* - \widehat{x}_t^*\right)\right]. \tag{10.12}$$

The parameter $\kappa \geq 0$ regulates the degree of concavity of the IAC function around the steady state, since $-\kappa$ is the second-order derivative of the function whenever evaluated at the steady state. Using the law of motion for capital in (10.4) and (10.5) we re-write (10.11) and (10.12) in terms of the investment-to-capital ratio as,

$$\begin{aligned}\widehat{q}_t \approx & -\kappa\left(1-\delta\right)\left(\widehat{x}_{t-1} - \widehat{k}_{t-1}\right) + \kappa\left(1 + \left(1-\delta\right)\beta\right)\left(\widehat{x}_t - \widehat{k}_t\right) \\ & - \kappa\beta\mathbb{E}_t\left(\widehat{x}_{t+1} - \widehat{k}_{t+1}\right),\end{aligned} \tag{10.13}$$

$$\begin{aligned}\widehat{q}_t^* \approx & -\kappa\left(1-\delta\right)\left(\widehat{x}_{t-1}^* - \widehat{k}_{t-1}^*\right) + \kappa\left(1 + \left(1-\delta\right)\beta\right)\left(\widehat{x}_t^* - \widehat{k}_t^*\right) \\ & - \kappa\beta\mathbb{E}_t\left(\widehat{x}_{t+1}^* - \widehat{k}_{t+1}^*\right).\end{aligned} \tag{10.14}$$

Under both adjustment cost functions, we can write the marginal Q as a function of the investment-to-capital ratio. The difference between the two specifications, as can be seen here, is that the CAC case links the marginal Q only to the contemporaneous investment-to-capital ratio while the IAC case introduces a more complex relationship that also depends on the past and the expectations for the future of the investment-to-capital ratio.[4]

We cannot ignore the time-variation of these marginal Q's when computing the marginal returns to investment in capital. The opportunity cost for investment is still given by the Fisherian real interest rate. However, the investment decision under the CAC specification implies that,

$$\left(1 - \left(1-\delta\right)\beta\right)\mathbb{E}_t\left(\widehat{r}_{t+1}^k\right) - \widehat{q}_t + \beta\mathbb{E}_t\left[\widehat{q}_{t+1}\right] \approx \widehat{i}_t - \mathbb{E}_t\left(\widehat{\pi}_{t+1}\right), \tag{10.15}$$

$$\left(1 - \left(1-\delta\right)\beta\right)\mathbb{E}_t\left(\widehat{r}_{t+1}^{k*}\right) - \widehat{q}_t^* + \beta\mathbb{E}_t\left[\widehat{q}_{t+1}^*\right] \approx \widehat{i}_t^* - \mathbb{E}_t\left(\widehat{\pi}_{t+1}^*\right), \tag{10.16}$$

[4] In the extreme case where there are no adjustment costs of either type, i.e., either $\chi = 0$ or $\kappa = 0$, then $\widehat{q}_t = \widehat{q}_t^* = 0$ for all t. Then, we are back to the NAC case described in (10.6).

while investment under the IAC specification implies that,

$$(1-(1-\delta)\beta)\,\mathbb{E}_t\left(\widehat{r}^{\,k}_{t+1}\right)-\widehat{q}_t+(1-\delta)\beta\mathbb{E}_t\left[\widehat{q}_{t+1}\right]\approx\widehat{i}_t-\mathbb{E}_t\left[\widehat{\pi}_{t+1}\right], \quad (10.17)$$

$$(1-(1-\delta)\beta)\,\mathbb{E}_t\left(\widehat{r}^{\,k*}_{t+1}\right)-\widehat{q}^*_t+(1-\delta)\beta\mathbb{E}_t\left[\widehat{q}^*_{t+1}\right]\approx\widehat{i}^*_t-\mathbb{E}_t\left[\widehat{\pi}^*_{t+1}\right]. \quad (10.18)$$

Equations (10.15)–(10.16) and (10.17)–(10.18) point out that the marginal benefits of investing in an additional unit of capital should include the properly discounted capital gains between the shadow cost of acquiring capital today, $\widehat{q}_t$ or $\widehat{q}^*_t$, and the shadow value of capital tomorrow, $\widehat{q}_{t+1}$ or $\widehat{q}^*_{t+1}$ (factoring the rate of time preference and the depreciation of capital).

Efficient Factor Use and Market-Clearing Conditions

The factors of production (capital and labor) are homogeneous within a country and factor markets are perfectly competitive, so factor prices equalize within a country.[5] Since the production function is assumed to be homogeneous of degree one (constant returns-to-scale), then all local firms choose the same capital-to-labor ratio. This yields an efficiency condition linking the aggregate capital-to-labor ratios to factor price ratios as,

$$\widehat{k}_t-\widehat{l}_t\approx\widehat{w}_t-\widehat{r}^{\,k}_t, \quad (10.19)$$

$$\widehat{k}^*_t-\widehat{l}^*_t\approx\widehat{w}^*_t-\widehat{r}^{\,k*}_t, \quad (10.20)$$

where $\widehat{w}_t$ and $\widehat{w}^*_t$ denote the real wages, while $\widehat{l}_t$ and $\widehat{l}^*_t$ stand for labor employment in both countries. Equations (10.19) and (10.20) establish a link between the real rental rates on capital and the real wages. The market clearing conditions in the labor markets can be fully characterized with the labor supply equations (the intratemporal first-order conditions) from the households' problem,

$$\widehat{w}_t\approx\frac{1}{\sigma}\widehat{c}_t+\varphi\widehat{l}_t, \quad (10.21)$$

$$\widehat{w}^*_t\approx\frac{1}{\sigma}\widehat{c}^{\,*}_t+\varphi\widehat{l}^*_t. \quad (10.22)$$

The parameter $\varphi > 0$ denotes the inverse of the Frisch elasticity of labor supply. Implicitly, we assume that consumption and labor are additively separable in preferences.

[5] It should be noted that while capital is immobile at the aggregate level, the varieties on which it is build are all tradable.

From the supply-side, we can express aggregate output in each country as a function of aggregate labor and aggregate capital,

$$\widehat{y}_t \approx \widehat{a}_t + (1-\psi)\widehat{k}_t + \psi\widehat{l}_t, \tag{10.23}$$
$$\widehat{y}_t^* \approx \widehat{a}_t^* + (1-\psi)\widehat{k}_t^* + \psi\widehat{l}_t^*. \tag{10.24}$$

where the labor share in the production function is captured by the parameter $0 < \psi \leq 1$. The productivity shocks, $\widehat{a}_t$ and $\widehat{a}_t{}^*$, follow a symmetric $AR(1)$ process of the form,

$$\widehat{a}_t = \rho_a \widehat{a}_{t-1} + \varepsilon_t^a, \tag{10.25}$$
$$\widehat{a}_t^* = \rho_a \widehat{a}_{t-1}^* + \varepsilon_t^{a*}, \tag{10.26}$$

where ε_t^a and ε_t^{a*} are zero mean, possibly correlated, and normally-distributed innovations with a common standard deviation $\left(\text{i.e., } \sigma\left(\varepsilon_t^a\right) = \sigma\left(\varepsilon_t^{a*}\right)\right)$. The persistence of the process is regulated by the parameter $-1 < \rho_a < 1$. From the demand-side, we can derive the following complementary expressions for aggregate output,

$$\widehat{y}_t \approx \eta\widehat{t}_t^W + (1-\gamma_x)\widehat{c}_t^W + \gamma_x\widehat{x}_t^W, \tag{10.27}$$
$$\widehat{y}_t^* \approx -\eta\widehat{t}_t^W + (1-\gamma_x)\widehat{c}_t^{W*} + \gamma_x\widehat{x}_t^{W*}, \tag{10.28}$$

which depend on weighted averages for world consumption, $\widehat{c}_t^W \equiv \phi_H\widehat{c}_t + \phi_F\widehat{c}_t^*$ and $\widehat{c}_t^{W*} \equiv \phi_F\widehat{c}_t + \phi_H\widehat{c}_t^*$, and for world investment, $\widehat{x}_t^W \equiv \phi_H\widehat{x}_t + \phi_F\widehat{x}_t^*$ and $\widehat{x}_t^{W*} \equiv \phi_F\widehat{x}_t + \phi_H\widehat{x}_t^*$. We denote world terms of trade as $\widehat{t}_t^W$, implying that an increase in $\widehat{t}_t^W$ shifts consumption and investment spending away from the foreign goods and into the domestic goods. We discuss the role of $\widehat{t}_t^W$ more extensively in the next section. Equations (10.27) and (10.28) coupled with (10.23)–(10.24) give us an aggregate clearing condition for the goods markets.

We define the steady state investment share as $\gamma_x \equiv \frac{(1-\psi)\delta}{\left(\frac{\theta}{\theta-1}\right)\left(\beta^{-1}-(1-\delta)\right)}$ and the consumption share as $\gamma_c \equiv 1-\gamma_x$. The parameter $\eta > 0$ is the elasticity of intratemporal substitution between the home and foreign bundles of varieties, while $\theta > 1$ defines the elasticity of substitution across varieties produced within the same country.[6] The share of the home goods in the domestic aggregator for consumption and investment is ϕ_H, while the share of foreign goods is $\phi_F = 1 - \phi_H$. We define the shares in the foreign aggregator symmetrically (see, e.g., Warnock 2003).

[6] The mark-up charged by any monopolistically competitive firm, $\frac{\theta}{\theta-1}$, is a function of the elasticity of substitution across varieties.

Inflation Dynamics

Firms supply the home and foreign markets and set their prices under LCP. Furthermore, firms enjoy monopolistic power in their own variety. Frictions in the goods markets are modeled with nominal price stickiness à la Calvo (1983). In this environment, the inflation dynamics can be partly summarized with the following pair of Phillip curves,

$$\widehat{\pi}_t \approx \beta \mathbb{E}_t \left(\widehat{\pi}_{t+1}\right) + \Phi \begin{bmatrix} \left(\sigma^{-1} + (1-\gamma_x)\varphi\omega\right)\left[\phi_H \widehat{c}_t^W + \phi_F \widehat{c}_t^{W*}\right] \\ + \gamma_x \varphi\omega \left[\phi_H \widehat{x}_t^W + \phi_F \widehat{x}_t^{W*}\right] - \left(\frac{(1-\psi)(1+\varphi)}{\psi}\right)\widehat{k}_t^W \\ + 2\phi_H\phi_F \widehat{rs}_t + (\phi_H - \phi_F)\eta\varphi\omega \widehat{t}_t^W \\ - \left(\frac{1+\varphi}{\psi}\right)\left[\phi_H \widehat{a}_t + \phi_F \widehat{a}_t^*\right] \end{bmatrix}, \tag{10.29}$$

$$\widehat{\pi}_t^* \approx \beta \mathbb{E}_t \left(\widehat{\pi}_{t+1}^*\right) + \Phi \begin{bmatrix} \left(\sigma^{-1} + (1-\gamma_x)\varphi\omega\right)\left[\phi_F \widehat{c}_t^W + \phi_H \widehat{c}_t^{W*}\right] \\ + \gamma_x \varphi\omega \left[\phi_F \widehat{x}_t^W + \phi_H \widehat{x}_t^{W*}\right] - \left(\frac{(1-\psi)(1+\varphi)}{\psi}\right)\widehat{k}_t^{W*} \\ - 2\phi_F\phi_H \widehat{rs}_t - (\phi_H - \phi_F)\eta\varphi\omega \widehat{t}_t^W \\ - \left(\frac{1+\varphi}{\psi}\right)\left[\phi_F \widehat{a}_t + \phi_H \widehat{a}_t^*\right] \end{bmatrix}, \tag{10.30}$$

where $\omega \equiv \left(\frac{\varphi\psi^2+(1-\psi)(1+\varphi)^2}{\varphi\psi+(1-\psi)\psi\varphi^2}\right)$ and $\Phi \equiv \left(\frac{(1-\alpha)(1-\alpha\beta)}{\alpha}\right)$ are two composite parameters, while the weighted averages for world capital are defined as $\widehat{k}_t^W \equiv \phi_H \widehat{k}_t + \phi_F \widehat{k}_t^*$ and $\widehat{k}_t^{W*} \equiv \phi_F \widehat{k}_t + \phi_H \widehat{k}_t^*$. The Calvo parameter $0 < \alpha < 1$ denotes the probability with which a firm is forced to maintain its previous period prices under the Calvo randomization assumption. Under home bias (i.e., if $\phi_H > \phi_F$), an additional equation is required to describe the dynamics of relative CPI inflation,

$$\widehat{\pi}_t^R \approx \beta \mathbb{E}_t \left(\widehat{\pi}_{t+1}^R\right) + \left[\Phi \widehat{rs}_t + \left(\frac{\phi_H - \phi_F}{\phi_H \phi_F}\right)\left(\beta \mathbb{E}_t \left(\widehat{t}_{t+1}^W\right) - \left(\frac{1+\beta\alpha^2}{\alpha}\right)\widehat{t}_t^W + \widehat{t}_{t-1}^W\right)\right], \tag{10.31}$$

where the relative CPI inflation is defined as $\widehat{\pi}_t^R \equiv \widehat{\pi}_t - \widehat{\pi}_t^*$. Equations (10.29) and (10.30) show that relative price adjustments through world terms of trade, $\widehat{t}_t^W$, and real exchange rates, $\widehat{rs}_t$, have a direct impact on inflation. Interestingly, (10.31) reveals that differences in CPI inflation across countries are explained by relative price effects only.

Monetary Policy Rules

We assume a cashless limit economy as in Woodford (2003). Monetary policy has an impact on inflation by regulating short-term nominal interest rates, and it has real effects because it interacts with the nominal rigidities. Since the Taylor (1993) rule has become the trademark of modern monetary policy, we assume that the monetary authorities set short-term nominal interest rates accordingly, i.e.,

$$\widehat{i}_t = \rho_i \widehat{i}_{t-1} + (1 - \rho_i) \left[\psi_\pi \widehat{\pi}_t + \psi_y \widehat{y}_t \right], \tag{10.32}$$

$$\widehat{i}_t^* = \rho_i \widehat{i}_{t-1}^* + (1 - \rho_i) \left[\psi_\pi \widehat{\pi}_t^* + \psi_y \widehat{y}_t^* \right]. \tag{10.33}$$

These symmetric policy rules target deviations of output and inflation from their long-run trends. The weights assigned to deviations of output and inflation are $\psi_y > 0$ and $\psi_\pi > 0$, respectively. In keeping with much of the literature, we augment the rule proposed by Taylor (1993) with an interest rate smoothing term regulated by the inertia parameter $0 < \rho_i < 1$, but we do not add discretionary monetary shocks.[7]

Investment, Trade and ToT

International Relative Prices

Domestic terms of trade, ToT_t, represents the value of the imported good (quoted in the domestic market) relative to the value of the domestic good exported to the foreign market, but expressed in units of the domestic currency. Similarly for the foreign terms of trade, ToT_t^*. This conventional definition of ToT measures the "foreign market" cost of replacing one unit of imports with one unit of exports of the locally-produced good, and can be formally expressed as,

$$ToT_t \equiv \frac{P_t^F}{S_t P_t^{H*}} = D_t \frac{P_t^F}{P_t^H}, \tag{10.34}$$

$$ToT_t^* \equiv \frac{S_t P_t^{H*}}{P_t^F} = D_t^* \frac{P_t^{H*}}{P_t^{F*}} = \frac{1}{ToT_t}, \tag{10.35}$$

where D_t and D_t^* capture deviations of the LOOP across countries, i.e.,

$$D_t \equiv \frac{P_t^H}{S_t P_t^{H*}}, \quad D_t^* \equiv \frac{S_t P_t^{F*}}{P_t^F}.$$

We also define a pair of international relative prices, T_t and T_t^*, as,

[7] The original Taylor (1993) rule can be seen as a special case of (10.32) and (10.33) where $\rho_i = 0$, $\psi_y = 0.5$ and $\psi_\pi = 1.5$.

$$T_t \equiv \frac{P_t^F}{P_t^H}, \tag{10.36}$$

$$T_t^* \equiv \frac{P_t^{H*}}{P_t^{F*}} = \frac{1}{D_t D_t^* T_t}, \tag{10.37}$$

The relative price T_t represents the value of the imported good (quoted in the domestic market) relative to the value of the domestic good sold in the domestic market. Similarly for the foreign relative price, T_t^*. The ratios T_t and T_t^* are the "local market" cost of replacing one unit of imports with one unit of the locally-produced good (not exported). The joint assumption of nominal rigidities and LCP implies that the LOOP fails, i.e., $D_t \neq 1$ and $D_t^* \neq 1$. Therefore, the distinction between ToT and other international relative prices becomes relevant for our understanding of the patterns of trade in a Q-INNS model.

After log-linearizing the definitions in (10.34)–(10.35) and (10.36)–(10.37), we get that,

$$\widehat{tot}_t = \widehat{d}_t + \widehat{t}_t,$$
$$\widehat{tot}_t^* = -\widehat{tot}_t = \widehat{d}_t^* + \widehat{t}_t^*,$$

and,

$$\widehat{t}_t = \widehat{p}_t^F - \widehat{p}_t^H,$$
$$\widehat{t}_t^* = -\left(\widehat{p}_t^{F*} - \widehat{p}_t^{H*}\right) = \widehat{p}_t^{H*} - \widehat{p}_t^{F*},$$

where $\widehat{d}_t \equiv \left(\widehat{p}_t^H - \widehat{s}_t - \widehat{p}_t^{H*}\right)$ and $\widehat{d}_t^* \equiv \left(\widehat{s}_t + \widehat{p}_t^{F*} - \widehat{p}_t^F\right)$ are the deviations of the LOOP. With this log-linear equalities, we define the world terms of trade as $\widehat{t}_t^W \equiv \widehat{p}_t^{F,W*} - \widehat{p}_t^{W*}$, where $\widehat{p}_t^{F,W*} \equiv \phi_F \widehat{p}_t^F + \phi_H \widehat{p}_t^{F*}$ and $\widehat{p}_t^{W*} \equiv \phi_F \widehat{p}_t + \phi_H \widehat{p}_t^*$. After some algebra, we find that $\widehat{t}_t^W$ is proportional to the difference between the two international relative prices, $\widehat{t}_t$ and $\widehat{t}_t^*$, i.e.,

$$\widehat{t}_t^W \approx (1 - \phi_F)\phi_F \left[\widehat{t}_t - \widehat{t}_t^*\right]. \tag{10.38}$$

We assume that CES aggregators are used to bundle up consumption and investment. Under standard results on functional separability, the corresponding CPIs can be approximated as,

$$\widehat{p}_t \approx \phi_H \widehat{p}_t^H + \phi_F \widehat{p}_t^F, \tag{10.39}$$

$$\widehat{p}_t^* \approx \phi_F \widehat{p}_t^{H*} + \phi_H \widehat{p}_t^{F*}. \tag{10.40}$$

The transformation of world terms of trade in (10.38) is based on this log-linearization of the CPIs.

Using the definition of $\widehat{t}_t$ and $\widehat{t}_t^*$ we can alternatively re-write $\widehat{t}_t^W$ as,

$$\widehat{t}_t^W \approx 2(1-\phi_F)\phi_F \widehat{tot}_t - \widehat{d}_t^W, \quad (10.41)$$

where $\widehat{d}_t^W \equiv (1-\phi_F)\phi_F\left[\widehat{d}_t - \widehat{d}_t^*\right]$ is our measure of world deviations of the LOOP. World terms of trade can be thought of as coming from fluctuations in $\widehat{d}_t^W$ or from fluctuations in a conventional measure of domestic ToT (i.e., $\widehat{tot}_t$). In a standard Q-IRBC model with flexible prices, $\widehat{d}_t = \widehat{d}_t^* = \widehat{d}_t^W = 0$ and ToT is proportional to world terms of trade. Otherwise, we must recognize that the relevant international relative price for expenditure-switching effects, $\widehat{t}_t^W$, does not exactly correspond to the data available on ToT.

Another important international relative price is the real exchange rate, which we define as $\widehat{rs}_t \equiv \widehat{s}_t + \widehat{p}_t^* - \widehat{p}_t$. Using the log-linearization of the consumption-price indexes in (10.39) and (10.40), it can be shown that,

$$\begin{aligned} \widehat{rs}_t &\approx \tfrac{1}{\phi_F}\widehat{t}_t^W - \widehat{tot}_t \\ &\approx (1-2\phi_F)\widehat{tot}_t - \tfrac{1}{\phi_F}\widehat{d}_t^W. \end{aligned} \quad (10.42)$$

This expression neatly shows that real exchange rate fluctuations arise from two channels: Compositional differences in the basket of goods due to home bias and deviations from the LOOP. In a flexible price model, the real exchange rate is purely proportional to conventional ToT, and that severely restricts the ability of the Q-IRBC framework (when it relies on home bias alone) to match the empirical features of both the real exchange rate and ToT. Equation (10.42) implies that world terms of trade are proportional to the real exchange rate plus the domestic ToT, i.e.,

$$\widehat{t}_t^W \approx \phi_F\left(\widehat{tot}_t + \widehat{rs}_t\right). \quad (10.43)$$

In other words, the world terms of trade is equivalent to a linear combination of domestic ToT and the real exchange rate, which are both observable in the data (unlike $\widehat{t}_t^W$ itself). Equation (10.43) suggests that in models with deviations of the LOOP real exchange rate is really crucial to help us account for the international relative price effects.[8]

Net Exports Share Over GDP

The home and foreign consumption bundles of the domestic household, C_t^H and C_t^F, as well as the domestic investment bundles, X_t^H and X_t^F, are aggregated by means of a CES index as,

[8] While the exploration of the dynamics of the real exchange rate goes beyond the scope of this paper, we refer the interested reader to Martínez-García and Søndergaard (2008b) for a deeper investigation of the issue in the Q-INNS model.

$$C_t^H = \left[\int_0^1 C_t(h)^{\frac{\theta-1}{\theta}} \mathrm{d}h\right]^{\frac{\theta}{\theta-1}}, \; C_t^F = \left[\int_0^1 C_t(f)^{\frac{\theta-1}{\theta}} \mathrm{d}f\right]^{\frac{\theta}{\theta-1}}, \quad (10.44)$$

$$X_t^H = \left[\int_0^1 X_t(h)^{\frac{\theta-1}{\theta}} \mathrm{d}h\right]^{\frac{\theta}{\theta-1}}, \; X_t^F = \left[\int_0^1 X_t(f)^{\frac{\theta-1}{\theta}} \mathrm{d}f\right]^{\frac{\theta}{\theta-1}}, \quad (10.45)$$

while domestic aggregate consumption and investment, C_t and X_t, are defined with another CES index as,

$$C_t = \left[\phi_H^{\frac{1}{\eta}} \left(C_t^H\right)^{\frac{\eta-1}{\eta}} + \phi_F^{\frac{1}{\eta}} \left(C_t^F\right)^{\frac{\eta-1}{\eta}}\right]^{\frac{\eta}{\eta-1}}, \quad (10.46)$$

$$X_t = \left[\phi_H^{\frac{1}{\eta}} \left(X_t^H\right)^{\frac{\eta-1}{\eta}} + \phi_F^{\frac{1}{\eta}} \left(X_t^F\right)^{\frac{\eta-1}{\eta}}\right]^{\frac{\eta}{\eta-1}}. \quad (10.47)$$

Given these aggregators and their foreign counterparts, we can easily characterize the system of demand equations underlying the model. These aggregators are also consistent with the CPIs log-linearized in (10.39) and (10.40). Then, the real exports and imports of domestic goods can be inferred as follows,

$$\begin{aligned} EXP_t &\equiv \int_0^1 \left(C_t^*(h) + X_t^*(h)\right) \mathrm{d}h \\ &= \left[\int_0^1 \left(\frac{P_t^*(h)}{P_t^{H*}}\right)^{-\theta} \mathrm{d}h\right] \phi_H^* \left(\frac{P_t^{H*}}{P_t^*}\right)^{-\eta} \left[C_t^* + X_t^*\right], \quad (10.48) \\ IMP_t &\equiv \int_0^1 \left(C_t(f) + X_t(f)\right) \mathrm{d}f \\ &= \left[\int_0^1 \left(\frac{P_t(f)}{P_t^F}\right)^{-\theta} \mathrm{d}f\right] \phi_F \left(\frac{P_t^F}{P_t}\right)^{-\eta} \left[C_t + X_t\right], \quad (10.49) \end{aligned}$$

under the symmetric home bias assumption (i.e., $\phi_H^* = \phi_F$).

In a two-country model, it suffices to determine the net exports share of the domestic country. A simple log-linearization of (10.48) and (10.49) allows us to obtain the following pair of equations,

$$\begin{aligned} \widehat{exp}_t &\approx -\eta\left(\widehat{p}_t^{H*} - \widehat{p}_t^*\right) + (1-\gamma_x)\,\widehat{c}_t^* + \gamma_x \widehat{x}_t^*, \\ \widehat{imp}_t &\approx -\eta\left(\widehat{p}_t^F - \widehat{p}_t\right) + (1-\gamma_x)\,\widehat{c}_t + \gamma_x \widehat{x}_t, \end{aligned}$$

where the relative price distortion at the variety level, captured by the terms within square brackets in (10.48) and (10.49), turns out to be only of second-order importance. The net exports share over GDP is defined as,

$$\begin{aligned}\widehat{tb}_t &\equiv \phi_F\left(\widehat{exp}_t - \widehat{imp}_t\right)\\ &\approx -\eta\left(\phi_F\left[\left(\widehat{p}_t^{H*} - \widehat{p}_t^{*}\right) - \left(\widehat{p}_t^{F} - \widehat{p}_t\right)\right]\right)\\ &\quad - (1-\gamma_x)\,\phi_F\left(\widehat{c}_t - \widehat{c}_t^{*}\right) - \gamma_x\phi_F\left(\widehat{x}_t - \widehat{x}_t^{*}\right).\end{aligned} \tag{10.50}$$

In steady state, ϕ_F is the domestic imports share over domestic GDP and, under symmetric home bias, also the foreign imports share over foreign GDP. Given that the steady state is symmetric, i.e., $\overline{Y} = \overline{Y}^*$, the weighted difference between real exports and imports in (10.50) can be reasonably interpreted as the net exports share over GDP.[9]

We define two measures of world price sub-indexes, $\widehat{p}_t^{H,W} \equiv \phi_H\widehat{p}_t^{H} + \phi_F\widehat{p}_t^{H*}$ and $\widehat{p}_t^{F,W*} \equiv \phi_F\widehat{p}_t^{F} + \phi_H\widehat{p}_t^{F*}$, and two measures of the relative price sub-indexes, $\widehat{p}_t^{H,R} \equiv \widehat{p}_t^{H} - \widehat{p}_t^{H*}$ and $\widehat{p}_t^{F,R} \equiv \widehat{p}_t^{F} - \widehat{p}_t^{F*}$. We already used $\widehat{p}_t^{F,W*}$ and $\widehat{p}_t^{W*}$ to define the world terms of trade before. Here, we use these definitions coupled with the log-linearization of the CPIs in (10.39) and (10.40) in order to express the relative prices embedded in (10.50) in the following terms,

$$\begin{aligned}\widehat{p}_t^{H*} - \widehat{p}_t^{*} &= \widehat{p}_t^{H,W} - \widehat{p}_t^{W} - \phi_H\left(\widehat{p}_t^{H,R} - \widehat{p}_t^{R}\right),\\ \widehat{p}_t^{F} - \widehat{p}_t &= \widehat{p}_t^{F,W*} - \widehat{p}_t^{W*} + \phi_H\left(\widehat{p}_t^{F,R} - \widehat{p}_t^{R}\right),\end{aligned}$$

where the relative CPI is $\widehat{p}_t^{R} \equiv \widehat{p}_t - \widehat{p}_t^{*}$.

The log-linearization of the CPI in both countries can be re-written as,

$$\begin{aligned}\phi_H\left[\widehat{p}_t^{H} - \widehat{p}_t\right] + \phi_F\left[\widehat{p}_t^{F} - \widehat{p}_t\right] &\approx 0,\\ \phi_F\left[\widehat{p}_t^{H*} - \widehat{p}_t^{*}\right] + \phi_H\left[\widehat{p}_t^{F*} - \widehat{p}_t^{*}\right] &\approx 0.\end{aligned}$$

Based on these relationships, we can infer that,

$$\begin{aligned}&\phi_F\left[\left(\widehat{p}_t^{H,W} - \widehat{p}_t^{W}\right) - \phi_H\left(\widehat{p}_t^{H,R} - \widehat{p}_t^{R}\right)\right]\\ &\quad + \phi_H\left[\left(\widehat{p}_t^{F,W*} - \widehat{p}_t^{W*}\right) - \phi_F\left(\widehat{p}_t^{F,R} - \widehat{p}_t^{R}\right)\right] \approx 0.\end{aligned} \tag{10.51}$$

Using the approximation derived in (10.51) and the definition of the world terms of trade, $\widehat{t}_t^{W} \equiv \widehat{p}_t^{F,W*} - \widehat{p}_t^{W*}$, we can write the relevant relative prices as follows,

$$\begin{aligned}\phi_F\left(\widehat{p}_t^{H*} - \widehat{p}_t^{*}\right) &\approx -\phi_H\left[\widehat{t}_t^{W} - \phi_F\left(\widehat{p}_t^{F,R} - \widehat{p}_t^{R}\right)\right],\\ \phi_F\left(\widehat{p}_t^{F} - \widehat{p}_t\right) &\approx \phi_F\left[\widehat{t}_t^{W} + \phi_H\left(\widehat{p}_t^{F,R} - \widehat{p}_t^{R}\right)\right],\end{aligned}$$

---

[9] A simple look at (10.41)–(10.42) and (10.50) suggests that there is a trade-off between quantities (net exports) and international relative prices which crucially depends on the parameterization of the steady state imports share ϕ_F.

which, after some algebra, implies that,

$$\begin{aligned}
&\phi_F\left[\left(\widehat{p}_t^{H*}-\widehat{p}_t^{*}\right)-\left(\widehat{p}_t^{F}-\widehat{p}_t\right)\right] \\
&\approx -\phi_H\left[\widehat{t}_t^{W}-\phi_F\left(\widehat{p}_t^{F,R}-\widehat{p}_t^{R}\right)\right]-\phi_F\left[\widehat{t}_t^{W}+\phi_H\left(\widehat{p}_t^{F,R}-\widehat{p}_t^{R}\right)\right] \\
&=-\left(\phi_H+\phi_F\right)\widehat{t}_t^{W}=-\widehat{t}_t^{W}.
\end{aligned}$$

Hence, replacing this expression into (10.50) we infer that the net exports share can be calculated as,

$$\widehat{tb}_t \approx \eta\widehat{t}_t^{W}-\left(1-\gamma_x\right)\phi_F\left(\widehat{c}_t-\widehat{c}_t^{*}\right)-\gamma_x\phi_F\left(\widehat{x}_t-\widehat{x}_t^{*}\right). \tag{10.52}$$

This expression for the net exports share illustrates the claim that the world terms of trade, $\widehat{t}_t^{W}$, is the model-consistent measure of international relative prices that explains the expenditure-switching across countries.

Adjustment in trade comes directly through movements in the world terms of trade, $\widehat{t}_t^{W}$, or from relative adjustments in consumption and investment across countries. This is the central equation in our analysis of the trade patterns. Our paper revisits the old question of what role does investment play in trade, but we do so with a two-sided strategy. On the one hand, we look at the role of adjustment costs in the accumulation of capital through investment. We recognize that adjustment costs have a role to play in determining the volatility of investment and consumption, and therefore can alter the implied trade dynamics. On the other hand, we recognize that Q-INNS models with deviations of the LOOP could lead to distortions in the allocation of expenditures across countries. We evaluate this additional channel and try to quantify the impact of those distortions on net trade flows.

Our previous discussion on the characterization of an appropriate international relative price measure allows us to re-write (10.52) as,

$$\widehat{tb}_t \approx 2\eta\left(1-\phi_F\right)\phi_F\widehat{tot}_t-\eta\widehat{d}_t^{W}-\left(1-\gamma_x\right)\phi_F\left(\widehat{c}_t-\widehat{c}_t^{*}\right)-\gamma_x\phi_F\left(\widehat{x}_t-\widehat{x}_t^{*}\right), \tag{10.53}$$

which mechanically shows the way in which the world relative price distortion, $\widehat{d}_t^{W}$, operates on the trade balance. In turn, (10.43) allows us to express net exports as a function of only observable international relative prices as,

$$\widehat{tb}_t \approx \eta\phi_F\left(\widehat{tot}_t+\widehat{rs}_t\right)-\left(1-\gamma_x\right)\phi_F\left(\widehat{c}_t-\widehat{c}_t^{*}\right)-\gamma_x\phi_F\left(\widehat{x}_t-\widehat{x}_t^{*}\right). \tag{10.54}$$

This characterization of the net exports share indicates that in a broad class of Q-INNS models the international relative price effects on expenditure-switching can only be accounted if we include domestic ToT and the real exchange rate simultaneously.[10]

The net exports share in (10.52) and the domestic ToT implicit in (10.43) do not constitute a trade model in themselves. All the other variables on the right- and left-hand side of both equations are endogenous, and their dynamics are determined by the full-blown model described in the previous section. However, the fact that the relationships in (10.52) and (10.43) hold (up to a first-order approximation) gives us a way to mechanically identify how the propagation of shocks

Table 10.2 Parameters used in the benchmark calibration

		Benchmark	CKM (2002)
Structural Parameters:			
Discount factor	β	0.99	0.99
Elasticity of intratemporal substitution	η	1.5	1.5
Elasticity of substitution across varieties	θ	10	10
Elasticity of intertemporal substitution	σ	1/5	1/5
(Inverse) Elasticity of labor supply	φ	3	5
Domestic goods bias parameter	ϕ_H	0.94	0.94
Foreign goods bias parameter	ϕ_F	0.06	0.06
Calvo price stickiness parameter	α	0.75	$N = 4$
Depreciation rate	δ	0.021	0.021
Capital/Investment adjustment cost	χ, κ	varies	varies
Labor share	ψ	2/3	2/3
Parameters on the taylor rule:			
Interest rate inertia	ρ_i	0.85	0.79
Weight on inflation target	ψ_π	2	2.15
Weight on output target	ψ_y	0.5	0.93/4
Exogenous shock parameters:			
Real shock persistence	ρ_a	0.9	0.95
Real shock correlation	$corr\left(\varepsilon_t^a, \varepsilon_t^{a*}\right)$	varies	0.25
Monetary shock correlation	$corr\left(\varepsilon_t^m, \varepsilon_t^{m*}\right)$	–	varies
Real shock volatility	$\sigma\left(\varepsilon_t^a\right) = \sigma\left(\varepsilon_t^{a*}\right)$	varies	0.007
Monetary shock volatility	$\sigma\left(\varepsilon_t^m\right) = \sigma\left(\varepsilon_t^{m*}\right)$	–	varies
Composite parameters:			
Steady state investment share	$\gamma_x \equiv \frac{(1-\psi)\delta}{\left(\frac{\theta}{\theta-1}\right)\left(\beta^{-1}-(1-\delta)\right)}$	0.203	(0.203)

This table summarizes our benchmark parameterization. Additional results on the sensitivity of certain parameters can be obtained directly from the authors upon request. The comparison is with CKM's (2002) model specification where monetary policy is represented by a Taylor rule.

[10] In fact, under complete international asset markets, (10.52) can be re-written more compactly. Using the *perfect international risk-sharing condition* in (10.3) we get that,

$$\widehat{tb}_t \approx \phi_F \left(\eta \widehat{tot}_t + (\eta - (1-\gamma_x)\sigma)\widehat{rs}_t\right) - \phi_F \gamma_x \left(\widehat{x}_t - \widehat{x}_t^*\right).$$

operates. Here, we exploit these relationships to focus our attention on the role of investment in trade, and how it is influenced by the presence of adjustment costs and/or large fractions of firms "unable" to update their prices in every period subject to LCP.

Quantitative Findings

Model Calibration

Our calibration is summarized in Table 10.2. For comparison purposes, we follow quite closely the parameterization of the Q-INNS model in CKM (2002). We refer the interested reader to their paper for a complete discussion of the calibration. Here, we only comment on those parameters that we calibrate differently. The Calvo price stickiness parameter, α, is assumed to be 0.75. This implies that the average price duration in our model is 4 quarters. Our choice is comparable to CKM (2002) since in their model a quarter of firms re-set prices every period and those prices remain fixed for a total of 4 periods. We also study the implications of the model under (quasi-) flexible prices. We do not simulate an exact solution for a comparable Q-IRBC model. Instead, we approximate that scenario by bringing the Calvo parameter, α, down to 0.00001 in our benchmark Q-INNS model. This implies that 99.999% of the firms are able to re-optimize their prices every period, and only a negligible fraction of them is subject to keeping the previous period prices.[11]

The inverse of the Frisch elasticity of labor supply, φ, is set to 3 instead of 5 as in CKM (2002). This is compatible with the available micro evidence (see, e.g., Browning et al. 1999, and Blundell and MaCurdy 1999), but not consistent with a balanced growth path. This choice is meant to reduce the sensitivity of the Phillips curve to consumption and investment fluctuations (see, e.g., Martínez-García and Søndergaard 2008b). The parameterization of the monetary policy rule is slightly different than in CKM (2002). The interest rate inertia parameter, ρ_i, equals 0.85, while the weight on the inflation target, ψ_π, equals 2, and the weight on the output target, ψ_y, is 0.5. Our Taylor rule targets current inflation, instead of expected inflation as in CKM (2002). The rule also includes interest rate smoothing and gives more weight to inflation than the one proposed by Taylor (1993).

We adapt the simulation strategy of CKM (2002) and set the parameters of the stochastic real shocks to approximate the features of US real GDP in the data. The aim is to investigate whether it is possible to account for consumption, investment,

[11] The (quasi-) flexible price experiment does not imply that $\widehat{d}_t^W$ is equal to zero. In fact, it will not be. Therefore, we should not view this experiment as if it were equivalent to a standard Q-IRBC model. The (quasi-) flexible price case merely reflects the limiting behavior of the Q-INNS model whenever the share of firms affected by the nominal rigidities becomes marginal (close to zero).

trade and ToT in a model that replicates key empirical moments of US real GDP with only real shocks.[12] We assume the persistence parameter of the real shocks, ρ_a, is set equal to 0.9. We choose the standard deviation of the real innovations to get the exact output volatility in the US data (i.e., 1.54%). In addition, we calibrate the cross-country correlation of the innovations to replicate the observed cross-correlation of US and Euro-zone GDP (i.e., 0.44). This calibration allows us to match exactly the volatility and cross-correlation of US real GDP, and also roughly approximates its persistence.

CKM (2002) select the adjustment cost parameter to match the empirical ratio of the standard deviation of consumption relative to the standard deviation of output in the data, while Raffo (2008) uses it to reproduce the volatility of investment relative to output. We select either the capital adjustment cost parameter, χ, or the investment adjustment cost parameter, κ, to ensure that investment volatility is as volatile as in the data (i.e., 3.38 times as volatile as US real GDP). This is consistent with the goal of adopting a Q theory extension that delivers the best possible fit for investment.

Model Exploration

From (10.52) we know that the net exports share must be linked to investment, consumption and the world terms of trade. From (10.42) we also know that a complex relationship exists between the world terms of trade, domestic ToT and world deviations of the LOOP. Based on the calibration described before, we are able to simulate the log-linearized model and gain further insight on trade. We are also able to assess the performance of the benchmark model relative to the observable data. The contemporaneous business cycle moments are summarized in Table 10.3.

We find that none of our experiments manages to generate a volatility of consumption above 55% of the observed volatility of US real consumption. Similar patterns can be found in BKK (1992, 1995), Heathcote and Perri (2002) and Raffo (2008). CKM (2002), however, match the consumption volatility, but do so by driving the adjustment cost parameter up at the expense of making investment significantly smoother than in the data. Although consumption is slightly more volatile under investment adjustment costs (IAC) than capital adjustment costs (CAC), this improvement is not sufficient to close the gap.

The trade off between investment and consumption volatility becomes particularly stark when we compare the IAC and CAC specifications against the no adjustment costs (NAC) case. Without adjustment costs, households take full advantage of capital accumulation as a mechanism to smooth consumption intertemporally. The

[12] CKM (2002) explore a combination of real and monetary shocks in their simulations.

consumption volatility produced by the model with sticky or (quasi-) flexible prices is less than 20% of the empirical volatility, while investment volatility is at least 67% higher. Overall, consumption volatility appears little affected by the choice of the Calvo price stickiness parameter.

The model also has difficulties matching the volatility of net exports. In the (quasi-) flexible price experiments, adding adjustment costs to the model impedes the ability of households to smooth consumption intertemporally. This leads to a higher reliance on trade for risk-sharing and, hence, a more volatile net exports share. The volatility of net exports is quite similar whether prices are (quasi-) flexible or sticky.

Turning to persistence, we observe that output persistence falls below the empirical numbers for US real GDP in the (quasi-) flexible price case with the CAC specification. The same is true for the persistence of consumption, investment and the net exports share. Using the NAC case does not substantially alter this conclusion, which is consistent with the results in BKK (1992, 1995). However, the findings are more mixed when we experiment with adjustment costs of the IAC type. The IAC specification produces higher persistence on output and investment. At the same time, it also generates counterfactually low first-order autocorrelations for consumption and net exports.

The results are somewhat different in the sticky price case, because adding adjustment costs helps us deliver persistence values for all variables that are roughly in line with the data. The differences between the CAC and IAC specifications are only marginal. The NAC case, however, cannot replicate sufficient persistence. Even when we look at a different calibration of the persistence of the real shock (i.e., $\rho_a = 0.75$) to enhance its odds on output persistence, the model cannot produce sufficient persistence in consumption, investment and net exports. In fact, with sticky prices and no adjustment costs we find a counterfactual, negative first-order autocorrelation for the net exports share. So far, our findings suggest that the Q-INNS model performs better (or certainly not worse) than a competing scenario with (quasi-) flexible prices.

Whether the model relies on sticky prices or (quasi-) flexible prices, the cross-country correlations of consumption and investment are very stable. It should be pointed out that all experiments generate very high cross-correlations of consumption, around twice as much as in the data. This finding is consistent with BKK (1992, 1995) and Heathcote and Perri (2002).[13] The difficulty to match the smaller cross-correlation of consumption relative to the cross-correlation of output found in the data is often known as the "quantity puzzle."

Most notably, we find that only models without adjustment costs can account (qualitatively at least) for the fact that the cross-country correlation of investment is lower than the cross-country correlation of output. Whether prices are (quasi-)

[13] In a complete asset markets model, this strong consumption cross-correlation has implications for the behavior of the real exchange rate through the *perfect international risk-sharing condition* in (10.3). We refer the interested reader to Martínez-García and Søndergaard (2008b) for additional insight on this issue.

Table 10.3 Selected business cycle moments of the baseline model

	US Data	Sticky prices IAC	Sticky prices CAC	Sticky prices NAC	Sticky prices NAC	(Quasi-) Flexible prices IAC	(Quasi-) Flexible prices CAC	(Quasi-) Flexible prices NAC
Std. Dev.								
GDP*	1.54	1.54	1.54	1.54	1.54	1.54	1.54	1.54
Investment*	5.21	5.21	5.21	7.08	7.09	5.21	5.21	6.62
Consumption	1.24	0.60	0.53	0.22	0.15	0.68	0.51	0.24
Net exports	0.38	0.17	0.14	0.10	0.07	0.20	0.13	0.04
Autocorrelation								
GDP	0.87	0.91	0.89	0.54	0.71	0.77	0.69	0.70
Investment	0.91	0.94	0.88	0.40	0.67	0.89	0.69	0.69
Consumption	0.87	0.82	0.83	0.75	0.76	0.48	0.70	0.76
Net exports	0.83	0.84	0.84	−0.12	−0.03	0.45	0.71	0.94
Cross-correlation								
GDP*	0.44	0.44	0.44	0.44	0.44	0.44	0.44	0.44
Investment	0.33	0.57	0.55	0.37	0.40	0.54	0.56	0.41
Consumption	0.33	0.65	0.63	0.69	0.66	0.68	0.62	0.62
Correlation								
GDP, net exp.	−0.47	0.49	0.49	−0.18	−0.11	0.41	0.52	−0.06
GDP, ToT	0.07	0.31	0.21	0.37	0.44	0.47	0.53	0.49
ToT, net exp.	−0.03	0.27	0.52	0.42	0.35	0.97	1.00	0.26
Parameterization								
$\sigma\left(\varepsilon_t^a\right) = \sigma\left(\varepsilon_t^{a*}\right) =$		2.07	1.89	1.27	1.785	1.43	1.34	1.15
$corr\left(\varepsilon_t^a, \varepsilon_t^{a*}\right) =$		0.4625	0.4475	0.4875	0.44	0.4775	0.465	0.457
$\rho_a =$		0.9	0.9	0.9	0.75	0.9	0.9	0.9
$\chi, \kappa =$		3.35	11.15	–	–	2.12	13.25	–

This table reports the business cycle moments given our benchmark parameterization. All theoretical statistics are computed after H–P filtering (smoothing parameter=1,600). NAC denotes the no adjustment cost case, CAC denotes the capital adjustment cost case, and IAC denotes the investment adjustment cost case. Sticky prices implies $\alpha = 0.75$, while (quasi-) flexible prices implies $\alpha = 0.00001$. We use Matlab 7.4.0 and Dynare v3.065 for the stochastic simulation

* We calibrate the volatility and cross-correlation of the real shock innovations to match the observed volatility and cross-country correlation of GDP. Whenever available, we calibrate the adjustment cost parameter to match the observed volatility of US investment

Data Sources: The Bureau of Economic Analysis and the Bureau of Labor Statistics. For more details, see the description of the dataset in the Appendix. Sample period: 1973q1–2006q4 (except for ToT, which covers only 1983q3–2006q4)

flexible or sticky seems to make little difference. BKK (1992, 1995) and Heathcote and Perri (2002) indicate that this stylized fact is not easy to match with a standard calibration of the IRBC model (without adjustment costs). This is, therefore, the first piece of evidence that comes out against the implementation of the Q theory extension by means of either the CAC or the IAC specifications.

On the Contemporaneous Correlations of ToT and Net Exports

The last three correlations reported in Table 10.3 are, however, the litmus test for each one of the experiments that we consider in this paper. The only models that can account qualitatively for the empirical evidence of countercyclical net exports are models without adjustment costs (NAC). BKK (1992, 1995) and Heathcote and Perri (2002) get a similar pattern in standard IRBC models without adjustment costs. Our model shows that it can deliver countercyclical trade patterns with either sticky or (quasi-) flexible prices, but the effects are weaker than in the data. Adding IAC or CAC adjustment costs increases the correlation and alters its sign (i.e., the trade balance is more likely to become procyclical).

Engel and Wang (2007) and Raffo (2008), using different models in the Q-IRBC tradition, are able to replicate the countercyclical trade patterns. The contemporaneous correlation between output and the net exports share is quite sensitive to the calibration of the model and the adjustment cost function. Even minor differences in the structure of the economy or the calibration could explain why they can account for this feature, while our model does not. For example, see BKK (1995, Fig. 11.4). Raffo (2008, p. 21) notes that: "Higher substitution between intermediates translates into lower response of the terms of trade. At this value, net exports are already procyclical. In the limiting case of perfect substitute intermediates, this economy resembles a one-good economy and net exports are systematically procyclical."

The elasticity of intratemporal substitution, η, plays an analogous role in our model as suggested by (10.52). We leave the exploration of this and other structural parameters for future research. It suffices to say that while including adjustment costs in the model reduces the volatility of investment and increases the volatility of consumption (and net exports), it may also push the contemporaneous correlation between output and net exports up. The effect can be strong enough to make net exports procyclical. This finding suggests that the Q theory extension to an open economy setting has to be undertaken with great care.

Consistent with the results of Raffo (2008), the model produces high and positive contemporaneous correlations between output and ToT. This is true for all variants of the model. However, we find that the model with sticky prices tends to generate lower correlations closer to the data. Adding adjustment costs helps further on this front. Therefore, based on the contemporaneous correlations alone, the Q-INNS model appears to offer a better fit for the data. However, as we shall see shortly, the interpretation becomes more complex when we look at the shape of the cross-correlation function.

The experiment with (quasi-) flexible prices and no adjustment costs (NAC) generates a contemporaneous correlation of 0.26 between ToT and net exports, which is far away from the value of −0.03 observed in the data. Adding adjustment costs makes matters even worse. In turn, adding adjustment costs in a sticky price scenario helps reduce the correlation. Even though no model does better than the (quasi-) flexible price one without adjustment costs (NAC), the Q-INNS model with IAC adjustment costs also does well. Once again, the interpretation is less straightforward when we look at the entire cross-correlation function.

BKK (1994, p. 94) point out that "the contemporaneous correlation between net exports and the terms of trade is weaker, moving from −0.41 in the benchmark case to −0.05" with a higher elasticity of intratemporal substitution between foreign and domestic goods. When discussing the countercyclical nature of net exports, we already quoted a similar argument by Raffo (2008). Indeed, recalling our previous discussion we could say that there are other structural parameters that do matter, as (10.52) indicates, but the importance of the adjustment cost parameter cannot be discounted.

On the Cross-Correlations of ToT and Net Exports

Figures 10.1 and 10.2 plot the cross-correlations between real GDP and the real net exports share. The data reveals the same type of S-shaped pattern that Engel and Wang (2007) emphasize in their paper. We show that only models without adjustment costs (NAC) can generate countercyclical trade patterns. We also find that only the (quasi-) flexible price scenario with no adjustment costs (NAC) can qualitatively approximate the S-shaped pattern of the cross-correlation function. The sticky price scenario without adjustment costs (NAC) moves us away from the empirical evidence.

As Fig. 10.2 demonstrates, adding IAC or CAC adjustment costs alters the shape of the cross-correlations in a fundamental way. The cross-correlation function becomes shaped like a tent, with its peak around the contemporaneous correlation. The dominant effect comes from having adjustment costs embedded in the model, but the contribution of sticky prices is also noticeable. Engel and Wang (2007) have a model that also matches qualitatively this cross-correlation function, and they do so with adjustment costs. Our models are not immediately comparable, but their paper is encouraging. It suggests that there is still room to reconcile the Q theory extension with the empirical evidence.

Our reading of these results is that the (quasi-) flexible price scenario without adjustment costs (NAC) brings back the flavor of the BKK (1992, 1995) model, where investment resources are being shifted across countries in search of (temporarily) higher productivity and higher returns. Adding adjustment costs caps the size of these effects because we set the adjustment cost parameter high enough to ensure that investment flows are not too volatile. The side-effect is that the trade balance becomes procyclical and the cross-correlation function peaks contemporaneously.

Figures 10.3 and 10.4 plot the cross-correlations between real GDP and ToT. Raffo (2008) argues that the IRBC framework delivers a contemporaneous correlation between GDP and ToT that is counterfactually too high. We confirm that the contemporaneous correlation between GDP and ToT is well-above its value in the data (i.e., 0.07). However, we also note that all the experiments display a tent-shaped pattern which is inconsistent with the S-shaped empirical cross-correlation function. Combining price stickiness with adjustment costs (preferably of the CAC

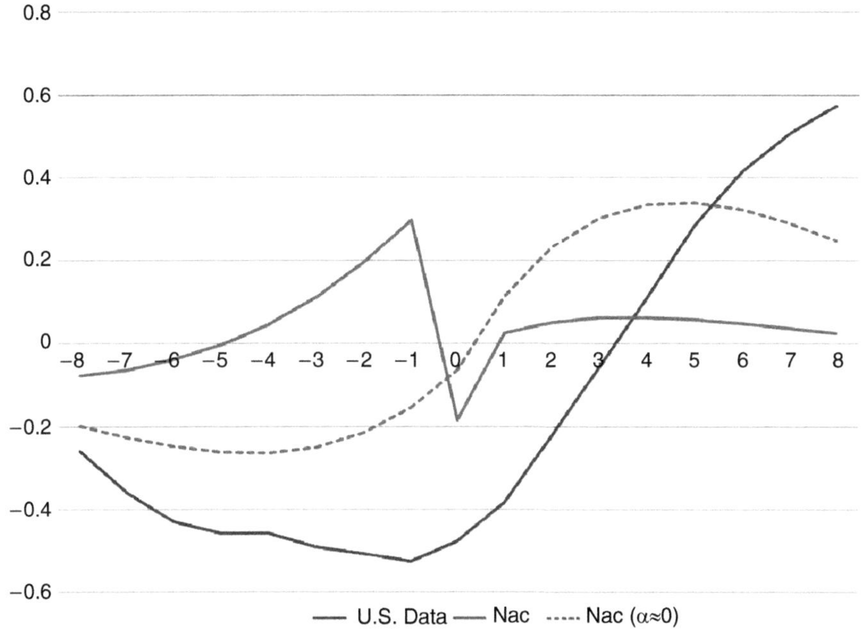

Fig. 10.1 Cross-correlations of output with net exports (without adjustment costs)
This figure plots the cross-correlation of output at t and net exports at t+s given our parameterization. All theoretical cross-correlations are computed after H–P filtering (smoothing parameter = 1,600). NAC denotes the no adjustment cost case, while $\alpha \approx 0$ indicates the experiment with (quasi-) flexible prices. We use Matlab 7.4.0 and Dynare v3.065 for the stochastic simulation. Data sources: The Bureau of Economic Analysis and the Bureau of Labor Statistics. For more details, see the description of the dataset in the Appendix. Sample period: 1973q1–2006q4

type) allows us to qualitatively fit the cross-correlations of real GDP with current and lagged ToT, but the leads are significantly different than in the data (specially 3 − 4 periods ahead). These features are a challenge for the IRBC literature (see, e.g., Raffo, 2008) as well as for the INNS/Q-INNS model.

The J-curve has been extensively discussed in the IRBC literature, specially since BKK (1994) showed that the standard framework was powerful enough to replicate this stylized fact. We still find evidence of a J-curve effect in the data, as reported in Figs. 10.5 and 10.6, although the strength of the correlation diminishes beyond a 4 period lead (1 year ahead). Our quantitative findings are consistent with the intuition of BKK (1994) given that our best qualitative fit for the cross-correlations between ToT and the net exports share comes from the (quasi-) flexible price scenario without adjustment costs (NAC). Adding adjustment costs and/or sticky prices not only alters the shape of the cross-correlation function, it also shifts its peak from leads to either contemporaneous or lagged cross-correlations.

A consistent message emerges from Figs. 10.1 through 10.6. Our experiment with (quasi-) flexible prices and no adjustment costs (NAC) approximates the good

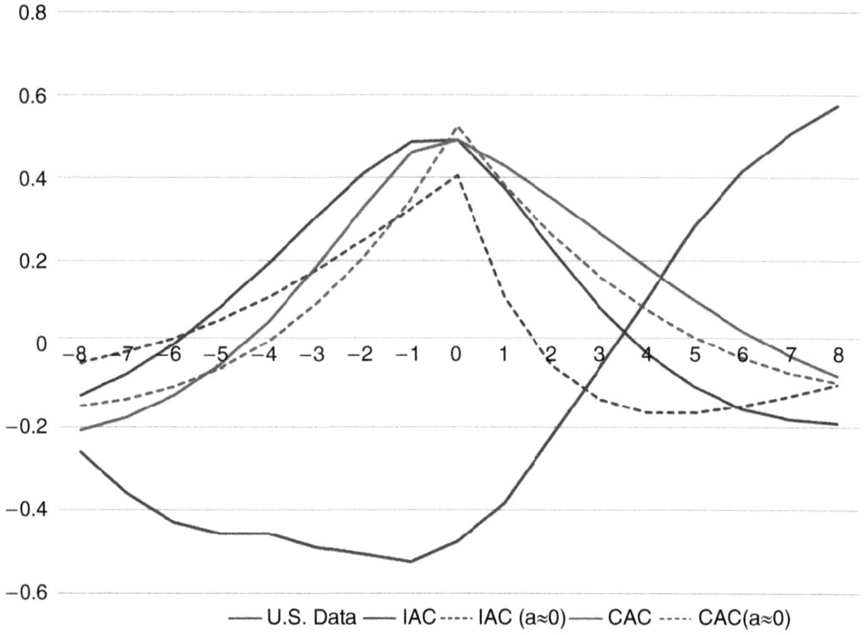

Fig. 10.2 Cross-correlations of GDP with net exports (with adjustment costs)

This figure plots the cross-correlation of output at t and net exports at t+s given our parameterization. All theoretical cross-correlations are computed after H–P filtering (smoothing parameter = 1,600). CAC denotes the capital adjustment cost case, IAC denotes the investment adjustment cost case, while $\alpha \approx 0$ indicates the experiment with (quasi-) flexible prices. We use Matlab 7.4.0 and Dynare v3.065 for the stochastic simulation. Data sources: The Bureau of Economic Analysis and the Bureau of Labor Statistics. For more details, see the description of the dataset in the Appendix. Sample period: 1973q1–2006q4

and the bad features of the IRBC model. It qualitatively tracks the J-curve effect and the S-shaped pattern of the cross-correlation between GDP and net exports. It also produces an excessively high correlation between output and ToT, and cannot track the S-shaped pattern of the cross-correlations between these two variables at different leads and lags. Whenever we try to pull the model closer to our Q-INNS benchmark by making price stickiness or adjustment costs a more relevant factor in the dynamics, we end up worsening the trade predictions along some of these dimensions.

Concluding Remarks

The findings in this paper suggest that a Q theory extension of the standard INNS model has important, although conflicting implications for our ability to replicate observed international business cycle patterns. On the one hand, adding adjustment

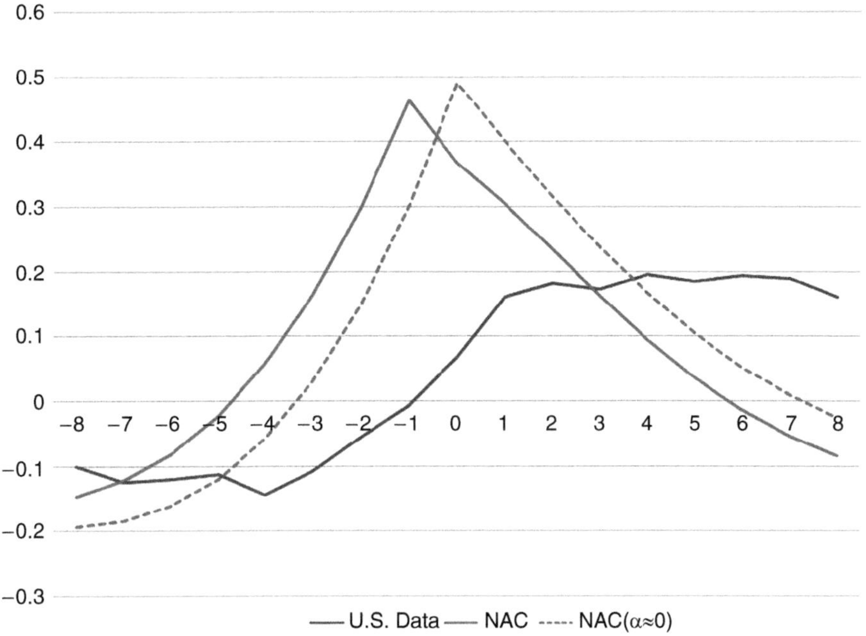

Fig. 10.3 Cross-correlations of GDP with ToT (without adjustment costs)

This figure plots the cross-correlation of output at t and terms of trade (ToT) at t+s given our parameterization. All theoretical cross-correlations are computed after H–P filtering (smoothing parameter = 1,600). NAC denotes the no adjustment cost case, while $\alpha \approx 0$ indicates the experiment with (quasi-) flexible prices. We use Matlab 7.4.0 and Dynare v3.065 for the stochastic simulation. Data sources: The Bureau of Economic Analysis and the Bureau of Labor Statistics. For more details, see the description of the dataset in Appendix. Sample period: 1983q3–2006q4

costs makes investment costlier and, therefore, results in a smoother investment series and a more volatile consumption series. At the same time, the net exports share becomes more volatile. While the model does not perfectly match the properties (on volatility, persistence and cross-country correlations) of consumption, investment and net exports, adding adjustment costs appears to lead us in the right direction overall.

On the other hand, we see that the model with adjustment costs cannot replicate well-known features of the trade data such as the J-curve (see, e.g., BKK 1994), the S-shaped cross-correlation of GDP and net exports (see, e.g., Engel and Wang 2007), and the weak and S-shaped cross-correlation between GDP and ToT (see, e.g., Raffo 2008). Furthermore, our analysis suggests that a full-blown INNS model with sticky prices and LCP does not do any better than an alternative variant with (quasi-) flexible prices. In fact, the (quasi-) flexible price scenario without adjustment costs delivers similar results to those documented in the standard IRBC

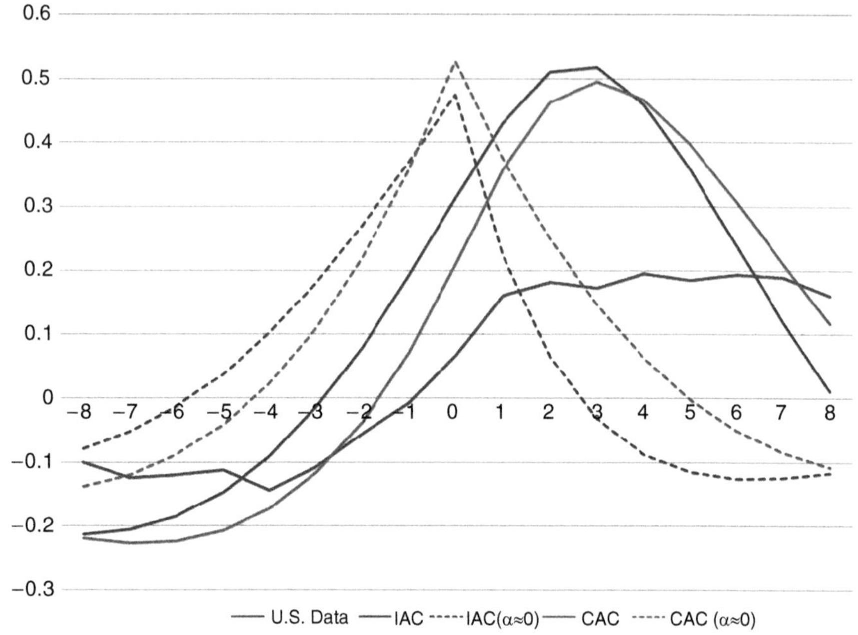

Fig. 10.4 Cross-correlations of GDP with ToT (with adjustment costs)

This figure plots the cross-correlation of output at t and terms of trade (ToT) at t+s given our parameterization. All theoretical cross-correlations are computed after H–P filtering (smoothing parameter = 1,600). CAC denotes the capital adjustment cost case, IAC denotes the investment adjustment cost case, while $\alpha \approx 0$ indicates the experiment with (quasi-) flexible prices. We use Matlab 7.4.0 and Dynare v3.065 for the stochastic simulation. Data sources: The Bureau of Economic Analysis and the Bureau of Labor Statistics. For more details, see the description of the dataset in the Appendix. Sample period: 1983q3–2006q4.

literature and tracks qualitatively the S-shaped cross-correlation of GDP and net exports and also the J-curve.

An open question is what role monetary policy plays in all of this. In the standard INNS model, with or without the adjustment costs, the size and effect of the relative price distortion resulting from nominal rigidities (price stickiness and LCP) depends on the path of inflation and, by extension, on the choice of monetary policy. We have taken as given a version of the Taylor rule with interest rate inertia and used a very specific calibration. The predictions of the model for trade are conditional on that calibration of the Taylor rule, and are likely to be different for alternative policy rules or parameterizations. We leave the close examination of the interplay between monetary policy and trade dynamics for future research.

We interpret the findings of the paper mainly as a cautionary tale, and not as a final word on the subject. To sum up: We need to be mindful of the fact that adjustment costs together with nominal rigidities can have unintended consequences for the trade dynamics of the standard Q-INNS model. Therefore, we have to think

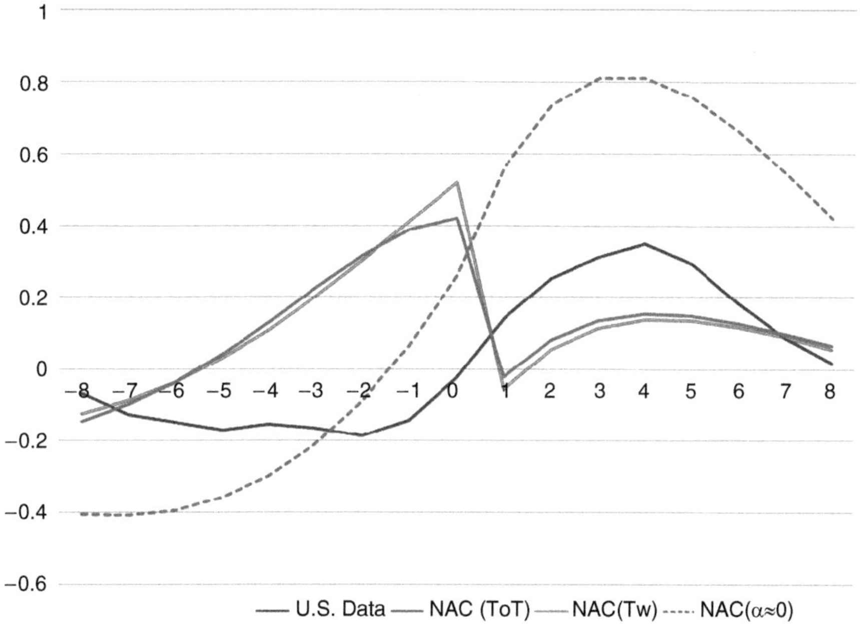

Fig. 10.5 Cross-correlations of ToT with net exports (without adjustment costs)

This figure plots the cross-correlation of terms of trade at t and net exports at t+s given our parameterization. We distinguish between conventional terms of trade, ToT, and world terms of trade, T_W. World terms of trade captures the relative price effects in the net exports share. All theoretical cross-correlations are computed after H–P filtering (smoothing parameter = 1,600). NAC denotes the no adjustment cost case, while $\alpha \approx 0$ indicates the experiment with (quasi-) flexible prices. We use Matlab 7.4.0 and Dynare v3.065 for the stochastic simulation. Data sources: The Bureau of Economic Analysis and the Bureau of Labor Statistics. For more details, see the description of the dataset in the Appendix. Sample period: 1983q3–2006q4

deeply about how to reconcile the Q-INNS model with the empirical evidence on trade.

Appendix: Dataset

We collect US quarterly data spanning the post-Bretton Woods period from 1973q1 through 2006q4 (for a total of 136 observations per series). The US dataset includes real output (rgdp), real private consumption including durables and nondurables (rcons), real private fixed investment (rinv), real exports (rx), the export price index (px), real imports (rm), the import price index (pm), and population size (n). The US import price index and the US export price index cover only the sub-sample between 1983q3 and 2006q4 (for a total of 94 observations). All data is seasonally adjusted.

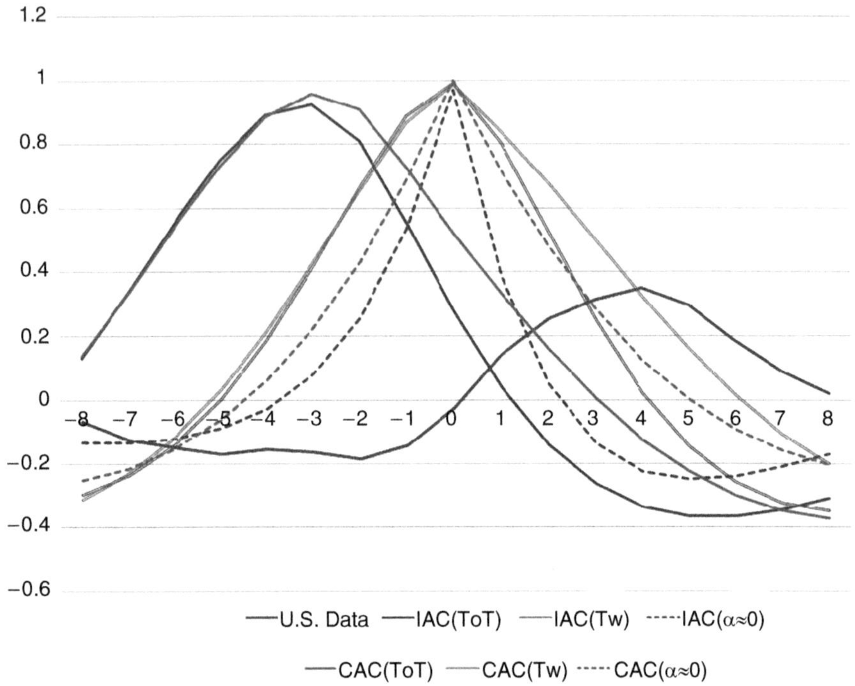

Fig. 10.6 Cross-correlations of ToT with net exports (with adjustment costs)

This figure plots the cross-correlation of terms of trade at t and net exports at t+s given our parameterization. We distinguish between conventional terms of trade, ToT, and world terms of trade, T_W. World terms of trade captures the relative price effects in the net exports share. All theoretical cross-correlations are computed after H–P filtering (smoothing parameter = 1,600). CAC denotes the capital adjustment cost case, IAC denotes the investment adjustment cost case, while $\alpha \approx 0$ denotes the experiment with (quasi-) flexible prices. We use Matlab 7.4.0 and Dynare v3.065 for the stochastic simulation. Data sources: The Bureau of Economic Analysis and the Bureau of Labor Statistics. For more details, see the description of the dataset in the Appendix. Sample period: 1983q3–2006q4

– Real output (rgdp), real private consumption (rcons) and real private fixed investment (rinv): Data at quarterly frequency, transformed to millions of US Dollars, at constant prices, and seasonally adjusted. Source: Bureau of Economic Analysis.
– Real exports (rx) and real imports (rm). Data at quarterly frequency, transformed to millions of US Dollars, and seasonally adjusted. Source: Bureau of Economic Analysis.
– Import price index (pm) and export price index (px). Data at quarterly frequency, indexed (2000=100), but not seasonally adjusted. Source: Bureau of Labor Statistics. (We compute a conventional measure of terms of trade, tot = pm/px, based on the data for the import and the export price indexes. We seasonally-adjust the resulting series with the multiplicative method X12.)
– Working-age population between 16 and 64 years of age (n): Data at quarterly frequency, expressed in thousands, and seasonally adjusted. Source: Bureau of Labor

Statistics. (We compute working-age population as the difference between civilian non-institutional population 16 and over and civilian non-institutional population 65 and over. We also seasonally-adjust the resulting series with the multiplicative method X12.)

The real output (rgdp), real private consumption (rcons), real private fixed investment (rinv), real exports (rx), and real imports (rm) are expressed in per capita terms dividing each one of these series by the population size (n). We compute the terms of trade ratio (tot) and the real net export share over GDP, rnx = ((rx - rm)/rgdp)*100, based on the data for real imports (rm), real exports (rx), the import price index (pm), the export price index (px), and real GDP (rgdp). We express all variables in logs and multiply them by 100, except the real net export share (rnx) which is already expressed in percentages. Finally, all series are Hodrick–Prescott (H–P) filtered to eliminate their underlying trend. We set the H–P smoothing parameter at 1,600 for our quarterly dataset.

Acknowledgements We would like to thank Mark Wynne, Roman Sustek, Finn Kydland and Carlos Zarazaga for many helpful discussions. We also acknowledge the support of the Federal Reserve Bank of Dallas and the Bank of England. However, the views expressed in this chapter do not necessarily reflect those of the Federal Reserve Bank of Dallas, the Federal Reserve System or the Bank of England. All errors are ours alone.

References

Abel AB (1983) Optimal investment under uncertainty. Am Econ Rev 73(1):228–233

Backus DK, Kehoe PJ, Kydland FE (1992) International real business cycles. J Polit Eco 100(4):745–775

Backus DK, Kehoe PJ, Kydland FE (1994) Dynamics of the trade balance and the terms of trade: the J-curve? Am Econ Rev 84(1):84–103

Backus DK, Kehoe PJ, Kydland FE (1995) International business cycles: theory and evidence. In: Cooley TF (ed) Frontiers of business cycle research. Princeton University Press, Princeton

Blundell R, MaCurdy T (1999) Labor supply: a review of alternative approaches. In: Ashenfelter O, Card D (eds) Handbook of labor economics, vol 3. Elsevier Science BV, Amsterdam

Browning M, Hansen LP, Heckman JJ (1999) Micro data and general equilibrium models. In: Taylor JB, Woodford M (eds) Handbook of macroeconomics, vol 1. Elsevier Science BV, Amsterdam

Calvo GA (1983) Staggered prices in a utility-maximizing framework. J Monetary Econ 12(3):383–398

Chari VV, Kehoe PJ, McGrattan ER (2002) Can sticky price models generate volatile and persistent real exchange rates? Rev Econ Stud 69(3):533–563

Christiano LJ, Eichenbaum M, Evans CL (2005) Nominal rigidities and the dynamic effects of a shock to monetary policy. J Polit Econ 113(1):1–45

Engel C, Wang J (2007) International trade in durable goods: understanding volatility, cyclicality, and elasticities. GMPI Working Paper 3, Federal Reserve Bank of Dallas

Ghironi F, Melitz MJ (2007) Trade flow dynamics with heterogeneous firms. Am Econ Rev Papers Proc 97(2):356–361

Heathcote J, Perri F (2002) Financial autarky and international business cycles. J Monetary Econ 49(3):601–627

Justiniano A, Primiceri GE (2008) The time-varying volatility of macroeconomic fluctuations. Am Econ Rev 98(3):604–641

Lucas RE Jr, Prescott EC (1971) Investment under uncertainty. Econometrica 39(5):659–681
Martínez-García E, Søndergaard J (2008a) Technical note on the real exchange rate in sticky price models: does investment matter? GMPI Working Paper 16, Federal Reserve Bank of Dallas
Martínez-García E, Søndergaard J (2008b) The real exchange rate in sticky price models: does investment matter? GMPI Working Paper 17, Federal Reserve Bank of Dallas
Raffo A (2008) Net exports, consumption volatility and international business cycle models. J Int Econ 75(1):14–29
Taylor JB (1993) Discretion versus policy rules in practice. Carnegie-Rochester Conference Series 39:195–214
Warnock FE (2003) Exchange rate dynamics and the welfare effects of monetary policy in a two-country model with home-product bias. J Int Money Finance 22(3):343–363
Woodford M (2003) Interest and prices. Foundations of a theory of monetary policy. Princeton University Press, Princeton

Chapter 11
The Anticompetitive Effects of the Antitrust Policy

David Bartolini and Alberto Zazzaro

Abstract Few scholars have seriously considered the possibility that the very existence of an antitrust law might make markets less competitive. In this chapter, we provide a selective review of this thought-provoking literature. The focus of our analysis is on contributions within the limits of the neo-classical theory of firms and markets, pointing out that antitrust legislation can hinder price/output competition. Following this literature, the introduction of antitrust penalties or leniency programmes can have the perverse effect of stabilizing cartels and increasing their size, as these policies may raise the costs of deviating and/or renegotiating a collusive agreement.

Introduction

Economists, legal scholars and historians have consistently alerted policy makers to the difficulty of establishing the anticompetive nature of cartels and other agreements among firms, to the welfare costs of "too-much" antitrust regulation and the risk of its misapplication. Since enforcing antitrust policies is costly, it might be optimal for society (consumers and producers) to tolerate some degree of collusion

[1] See Posner (1976), Bork (1978), Sproul (1993), Crandall and Winston (2003), and Levenstein and Suslow (2006). A broad, updated review of the economic theory of competition policy is provided by Motta (2004).

D. Bartolini
Università Politecnica delle Marche, Ancona, Italy and Osservatorio per le Politiche Economiche Regionali (OPERA), Ancona,
e-mail: d.bartolini@univpm.it

A. Zazzaro
Università Politecnica delle Marche, Ancona, Italy; Money and Finance Research Group (MoFiR) and CFEPSR,
e-mail: a.zazzaro@univpm.it

G. Calcagnini and E. Saltari (eds.), *The Economics of Imperfect Markets*, Contributions to Economics,
DOI: 10.1007/978-3-7908-2131-4_11, © Springer Physica-Verlag Berlin Heidelberg 2010

among firms, while saving on investigation, prosecution and compliance costs and reducing the probability of erroneously acting against non-colluding firms (Besanko and Spulber 1989; Souam 2001; Frezal 2006; Martin 2006). However, few scholars have seriously considered the possibility that the very existence of an antitrust law might make markets less competitive, stimulating rather than deterring collusive practices. In this chapter, we provide a selective review of this thought-provoking literature.

Among those who have underlined the anticompetitive effects of laws prohibiting explicit collusive agreements we can distinguish two broad groups. The former consists of scholars in the libertarian, anarchy-capitalist tradition who totally reject the antitrust legislation as violating property rights, hindering free competition and damaging people's individual interests. They typically argue that as long as access to the market is free, we cannot speak of monopoly, even for goods and services currently served by only one producer. Similarly, to the extent that agreements of any sort are voluntarily subscribed by individuals, and consumers are not coerced by force to acquire a certain product, we cannot speak of conspiracy against competition. As Murray Rothbard, the undisputed champion in the libertarian tradition, strikingly claimed: "The only viable definition of monopoly is a grant [or privilege] from the government. It is therefore quite clear that it is impossible for the government to *decrease* monopoly by passing punitive laws."(Rothbard 1970, p. 60).[2] In this view, cartels are simply a form of organization alternative to markets that, like firms in the Coase's celebrated *Nature of firms* (Coase 1937), allows better coordination of decisions and effort among cartel members, reducing transaction costs and creating value for members and others (Rothbard 1962; Salin 1996).

A second group of contributions moves within the limits of the neo-classical theory of firms and markets, pointing out that antitrust legislation can hinder price/output competition. Following this literature, the introduction of antitrust penalties or leniency programmes can have the perverse effect of stabilizing cartels and increasing their size, as these policies may raise the costs of deviating and/or renegotiating a collusive agreement (McCutcheon 1997; Ellis and Wilson 2001; Harrington 2004; Bartolini and Zazzaro 2008).

In this chapter, we focus exclusively on the latter strand of literature, restricting our attention to models of static competition. The rest of the chapter is organized as follows: in the next section, we consider the effects of antitrust penalties on competition; then, we extend the analysis to leniency programmes and draw some concluding remarks.

[2] The absolute irreconcilability between free capitalism and antitrust legislation in the libertarian tradition is well summarized by Walter Block: "The premise underlying laissez-faire capitalism is that the only actions which should be illegal are those which involve an initiation of aggression against another person or his property. Antitrust law is clearly in violation of this principle, because it prohibits business practices no one even alleges constitute such depredations." (Block 1994, p. 35).

Antitrust policy I: Monetary Fines

The need for a public authority to combat practices restrictive of competition is unanimously claimed by the economic literature on static competition. Absent innovation, collusive agreements among firms for restricting output or increasing prices reduce consumer surplus and social welfare, as they reduce the number of rival sellers in the market. Economists classify collusive behavior in two types: *tacit*, when firms coordinate without communicating with each other; *explicit*, when firms communicate to reach an agreement. Antitrust authorities, however, can prosecute collusive agreements only in the presence of hard evidence of conduct violating competition laws. This makes collusion very difficult to detect and combat. The main instrument at the disposal of authorities to inhibit cartel formation is monetary fines, levied against firms found guilty of collusion in front of a court of law.

In this section we show that fines do not always hit their target, and in some circumstances they can even favor collusion. Specifically, we discuss four recent contributions that highlight the possibility that the introduction of an antitrust monetary fine adversely affects competition by making collusive agreements tougher to break up. These contributions differ in the modeling approach and in the stage of the cartel's life they focus on. The first two papers consider the case of tacit collusion sustained through price strategies; the third contribution considers explicit collusion where sustainability is threatened by the possibility to renegotiate the collusive agreement; the fourth focuses on the process of cartel formation, rather than on its sustainability, which is warranted by the assumption of binding agreements.

Antitrust Fines and the Cost of Deviating

Ever since Stigler (1950), industrial economists have recognized that cartels are characterized by a fundamental instability due to the incentives each member has to deviate from the collusive agreement by increasing output or reducing prices. Therefore, in order to sustain a collusive cartel, firms need to devise a strategy to *punish* deviations from the agreement. For instance, coalition members could agree to decrease (increase) prices (output) so as to eliminate possible gains from deviation. The implementation of this punishment strategy, however, involves a sudden change in either prices or quantities, which can be seen as a signal of collusion by the antitrust authority. This would raise the probability of members being fined, and increase the cost of cheating on the collusive agreement.

Cyrenne (1999)

The signaling effect of the punishment phase was first investigated by Cyrenne (1999) who considered a non-cooperative model of collusion with uncertain demand based on Green and Porter (1984). In this model, collusive behavior is sustained through a finite reversion trigger strategy, where firms punish a deviation by supplying the Cournot–Nash quantity for $T - 1$ periods, and then revert to the collusive quantity. Firms, however, do not directly observe deviations; they only observe a "common market price," p_t, which depends on the industry output Q_t, and a zero-mean-value stochastic part θ:

$$p_t = p(Q_t) + \theta_t \tag{11.1}$$

Therefore, when a firm observes a market price lower than the reference price $p(Q_t)$, it does not know whether such a price is the result of a deviation from collusion (an increase in Q_t) or an adverse demand shock (a decrease in θ_t). In this context, firms engage in punishment only if the price goes below a certain threshold, p^*, which represents the rule of punishment firms agreed upon, that is, only if $\theta < p^* - p(Q_t)$. The probability that this event happens is $\gamma = G(p^* - p(Q_t))$ where $G(\cdot)$ is the distribution function of θ. Whenever a trigger strategy is initiated, firms are placed under investigation by the antitrust authority and bear a penalty F, which can be thought of as the fine times the probability of being convicted of collusion, plus the costs of mounting a defence.

The expected discounted value of producing the collusive output q is given by the current profit, plus the expected profits for the next periods which vary with probability γ, the trigger strategy adopted, and the antitrust penalty:

$$\begin{aligned} V_i(q) &= \pi_i(q) + (1-\gamma)\,\delta V_i(q) + \gamma\left(\sum_{\tau=1}^{T-1} \delta^{\tau}\pi^{n} + \delta^{T} V_i(q) - F\right) \\ &= \frac{\pi^n}{1-\delta} + \frac{\pi_i(q) - \pi^n - \gamma F}{1 - \delta + \gamma(\delta - \delta^T)} \end{aligned} \tag{11.2}$$

where $\delta > 0$ is the discount factor and π^n indicates the Nash profits from the punishment strategy.

When deciding on the level of p^* and the length of punishment $(T - 1)$, firms must balance the need to sustain the cartel with the risk of starting a price war, simply because a demand shock has occurred. Green and Porter show that the output chosen collusively by firms exceeds the joint profit maximizing output, because firms prefer to reduce gains from a deviation, so as to reduce the severity of the punishment. When collusion is considered illegal, firms are also aware that any deviation may trigger an antitrust investigation and a penalty F. As a result, the equilibrium collusive output is still lower (and market less competitive), as "the gains from deviating from the collusive strategy have been reduced exogenously" by the introduction of the antitrust fine (Cyrenne 1999, p. 265).

Harrington (2004)

The anticompetitive result in Cyrenne's model is based on the assumption that the output strategy of competitors is unobservable and the probability of being audited does not actually depend on the magnitude of price variation. Harrington (2004), provides a richer analysis of cartel pricing behavior that considers the whole pricing path. Contrary to Cyrenne, in Harrington's model the pricing strategy of the other firms is observable, hence each firm can immediately detect deviation from the collusive price tacitly agreed upon. Firms, of course, would prefer to collude on high prices, but in doing so they face two types of constraints: internal stability and antitrust auditing policy. The former concerns the incentive of deviating from the collusive agreement: the higher the collusive price, the greater the incentive to break up the cartel. The latter refers to the risk of attracting the attention of the antitrust authority, for the probability of auditing increases with the variation in the level of prices.

Harrington compares the steady-state collusive price when collusion is legal with the steady-state price in the presence of an antitrust law and demonstrates that in some cases the introduction of an antitrust penalty might increase the long-run collusive price. In particular, a price p sustains collusion if:

$$\frac{\pi(p)}{1-\delta} \geq \bar{\pi}(\psi(p), p) + \delta\left(\frac{\pi^n}{1-\delta}\right) \tag{11.3}$$

where the left hand side represents the discounted flow of collusive profits,[3] which must be higher than the deviation payoff $\bar{\pi}$, plus the discounted payoff from punishment π^n – which is the profit firms earn when they play the Nash equilibrium strategy.[4] Denote by $\tilde{p}$ the highest price which supports collusion. If condition (11.3) holds for all $p \in [p^n, p^m]$, where p^m is the monopolistic price, then $\tilde{p} = p^m$; otherwise $\tilde{p}$ is the price that makes firms indifferent between colluding and cheating, i.e., the price for which condition (11.3) holds as equality.

In the presence of an antitrust authority, colluding firms have to consider the probability of being investigated and convicted by a court to pay a penalty. Harrington assumes this probability to be exogenous and dependent on the observed variation of prices between the current and the previous period:

$$\phi(p^t, p^{t-1})$$

The function $\phi(\cdot,\cdot)$ assumes a value of zero when $p^t = p^{t-1}$, and is weakly increasing with respect to price increments. The penalty in the case of successful prosecution is characterized by a fixed fine F.[5] Let $\bar{\Lambda}(p)$ be the maximum payoff

[3] The collusive profit does not necessarily derive from monopoly pricing; it depends on the price level firms in the cartel decide to enforce.

[4] The function $\psi(p)$ defines the deviating price which maximizes the firm's profit given that all the other firms' price is p.

[5] In the original model, Harrington (2004) assumes that the penalty also consists of a compensative part X^t, proportional to the social welfare losses produced by collusion, which increase with the current collusive price and the duration of the cartel.

of deviation from the collusive price p:

$$\bar{\Lambda}(p) = \arg\max_{p_i} \bar{\pi}(p_i, p) + \delta\phi(p_i, p)\left(\frac{\pi^n}{1-\delta} - F\right) + \delta[1 - \phi(p_i, p)]\left(\frac{\pi^n}{1-\delta}\right) \tag{11.4}$$

and p^* be the highest price sustaining collusion in the presence of antitrust penalty, which is defined by:

$$\frac{\pi(p)}{1-\delta} \lesseqqgtr \bar{\Lambda}(p) \text{ as } p \gtreqqless p^* \qquad \forall\, p \in [p^n, p^m] \tag{11.5}$$

In words, p^* is the price that makes firms indifferent between continuing to collude and deviating. The question is whether p^* is greater than $\tilde{p}$. In order to prove that the collusive price under antitrust legislation can be higher than the collusive price without antitrust, Harrington shows that the payoff of cheating is greater in the absence of antitrust penalties, that is

$$\bar{\pi}(\psi(p), p) + \delta\left(\frac{\pi^n}{1-\delta}\right) > \bar{\pi}(p_i, p) + \delta\phi(p_i, p)\left(\frac{\pi^n}{1-\delta} - F\right) + \delta[1 - \phi(p_i, p)]\left(\frac{\pi^n}{1-\delta}\right) \tag{11.6}$$

Considering that $\bar{\pi}(\psi(p), p) \geq \bar{\pi}(p_i, p)$ for all p, condition (11.6) becomes:

$$\frac{\pi^n}{1-\delta} > \phi(p_i, p)\left(\frac{\pi^n}{1-\delta} - F\right) + [1 - \phi(p_i, p)]\left(\frac{\pi^n}{1-\delta}\right) \tag{11.7}$$

and, after some computation, we have:

$$\frac{\pi^n}{1-\delta} > \frac{\pi^n}{1-\delta} - \phi(p_i, p)F \tag{11.8}$$

which is satisfied, as $F > 0$.

Therefore, the antitrust penalty reduces the gains from deviation. As a consequence, we have:

$$\frac{\pi(\tilde{p})}{1-\delta} \geq \bar{\Lambda}(\tilde{p}) \tag{11.9}$$

From condition (11.5), this implies that $\tilde{p} \leq p^*$. Now we have two possible cases: either $\tilde{p} = p^m$, and therefore the antitrust fine cannot produce any perverse effect, or $\tilde{p} < p^m$ and the collusive price in the presence of an antitrust fine is higher than the collusive price without such a policy.[6]

[6] The result that the antitrust penalty reduces competition only when the original price is lower than the monopolistic price, is mirrored by a similar condition in Bartolini and Zazzaro (2008), where in order to have the perverse effect the market structure without antitrust should not be a monopolistic cartel. We postpone further discussion on this point after the introduction of Bartolini and Zazzaro's model.

Antitrust Fines and Cartel Formation

In both Cyrenne's and Harrington's models the perverse effect of the antitrust fine is the result of the relaxation of the internal stability constraint. The intuition is that by decreasing the gains from deviation, the antitrust policy may lead to a higher (lower) collusive price (output). While focusing on the effect of the antitrust penalty upon the strategy which sustains collusion, both models only consider the case of tacit collusion and leave unexplored firms' incentives to sign explicit collusive agreements.

In this section we focus on the formation of cartels. Two theoretical models are considered: the first one is in line with the traditional non-cooperative approach, while the second one applies a cooperative approach to cartel formation.

McCutcheon (1997)

When we consider the formation of an explicit cartel, the collusive agreement should specify, besides prices and output, a punishment strategy to deter cartel members' deviations from the agreement. In this setting, cartels are sustained as an equilibrium of a repeated game under the implicit assumption that the punishment strategy is credible, and that the cartel's members can commit to it. However, this cannot be taken for granted, as typically the punishment strategy damages not only the deviators, but also the members that enforce the punishment. Therefore, cartel members might be willing to renegotiate the initial agreement once a firm deviates. The point is that when firms form a cartel or renegotiate their rules they need to meet to set the details of the agreement. These meetings are likely to leave some evidence, which the antitrust authority can exploit in order to prove the existence of the collusive agreement in front of a court of law.

McCutcheon (1997) considers a setting in which firms need to meet, at least once, to set up the collusive agreement, and, then, they *may* meet again for renegotiating the terms of the original agreement. She shows that in a standard Bertrand duopoly model with homogeneous products, the possibility of renegotiaing the original agreement and the costs of renegotiation affect the equilibrium outcome and the effectiveness of an antitrust fine.

In a repeated game version of this model, absent renegotiation, a collusive monopolistic price can be sustained by a trigger strategy whenever:

$$\frac{\pi^m}{2(1-\delta)} \geq \pi^m + \frac{\delta}{1-\delta}\pi^n \tag{11.10}$$

where $\delta > 0$ is the discount factor, while π^m and π^n indicate as usual the profits from monopolistic collusion and the profit arising from playing the Nash equilibrium at any stage after deviation.

Now, let us assume that renegotiation is possible and *costless*. A collusive agreement would hardly be sustained in this scenario. For instance, in the above example firms would have an incentive to meet with the deviating firm and renegotiate another collusive agreement, the reason being that by punishing the deviating firm they also punish themselves. If this is so, the punishment strategy is not credible and the cartel cannot be sustained. This opens the quest for punishment mechanisms that are renegotiation-proof, i.e., punishment strategies whose payoffs are not Pareto-inferior to other available alternatives. McCutcheon, however, shows that in a repeated game where the stage game is a Bertrand duopoly with pure strategies, the only renegotiation-proof equilibrium is the one-shot Nash equilibrium of the game. Hence, if renegotiation is costless, firms cannot collude.

Although there might be other oligopoly games and renegotiation procedures which do not destroy the possibility of forming cartels, the message is that renegotiation is bad for collusion and good for competition. Now, if an antitrust penalty is introduced, firms have to compare the cost of renegotiating the agreement, in terms of the expected fine, with the benefits of doing so. Suppose that in every meeting the cartel incurs a probability $\theta \in [0, 1]$ of being detected and being punished with a monetary fine f. Therefore the expected cost of each meeting is $F = \theta f$. The benefit of such meetings is the discounted value of collusive profits net of the profits earned when a collusive agreement (or renegotiation) is not achieved. Therefore, in the initial meeting, where the decision to form a cartel is taken, these gains are equal to:

$$\frac{\pi^m}{2(1-\delta)} - \frac{\pi^n}{1-\delta} \tag{11.11}$$

If, for simplicity, we normalize the Nash equilibrium profit to zero, the first meeting would not take place, and the cartel would not form, if:

$$F \geq \overline{F} = \frac{\pi^m}{2(1-\delta)} \tag{11.12}$$

In the following meetings, where the original agreement may be renegotiated, the net gains depend on the punishment strategy. For example, with a trigger strategy the benefits are the same as for the initial meeting, implying no possibility either to form or sustain the collusive agreement. Specifically, when $F \geq \overline{F}$, no meeting takes place, while when $F < \overline{F}$ renegotiation is always profitable and therefore collusion is not sustainable.

When the punishment phase lasts for a given number of periods T, say the minimum number of punishment periods that satisfy internal stability, the benefit from renegotiation will be lower than the benefit from the first agreement

$$\tilde{F} = \frac{\pi^m}{2}\left(\frac{1-\delta^T}{1-\delta}\right) < \overline{F} \tag{11.13}$$

and a renegotiation meeting will take place only if $F < \tilde{F}$. In this case, we have three cases:

1. The actual antitrust fine is low, that is $F < \tilde{F}$. Thus the expected cost of a meeting is low too and renegotiation will always take place, preventing the formation of a collusive cartel.
2. The antitrust fine is at an intermediate level, that is $\tilde{F} \leq F < \overline{F}$. Thus the expected cost is high enough to prevent renegotiation, but not so high to prevent the initial meeting, hence leading to a stable cartel.
3. The antitrust fine is large, that is $F \geq \overline{F}$. Thus the expected cost of the initial meeting is so high that no collusive agreement takes place.

Finally, it is worth noting that the "perverse" effect of the antitrust penalty depends on the discount factor. In particular, for a given punishment strategy of length T, the possibility of $F \in [\tilde{F}, \overline{F}]$ increases with δ: the more firms care about future payoffs the wider is the range of anticompetitive expected fines.

Bartolini and Zazzaro (2008)

Although the need for meeting qualifies McCutcheon's model as an explicit collusion model, once again the mechanism through which antitrust fines might reduce competition in the market is by providing sustainability of cartels of a given size. In Cyrenne (1999) and Harrington (2004) the existence of an antitrust penalty increases the cost of cheating on the implicit agreement, while in McCutcheon (1997) the presence of (not very large) antitrust fines increases the cost of renegotiating the punishment strategy, enhancing the sustainability of the cartel. However, a question left almost unanswered by the literature on collusion is the process of cartel formation. How many firms enter a cartel? What happens if more than one cartel forms?

In order to address these issues, a change in the methodological approach is needed. A natural candidate for this change is the theory of coalition formation, recently extended by Bloch (1996) and Ray and Vohra (1997, 1999) by considering a partition function approach with externalities.[7] This literature focuses on the formation of coalitions across a given number of players, and it is directly applicable to the case of collusion, providing a characterization of a generic industry into coalitions of firms (cartels).

Bartolini and Zazzaro (2008) build on this literature to consider the role of the antitrust penalty on cartel formation: they provide a general result showing that if the firms' payoff structure is characterized by grand coalition superadditivity (GCS) and coalitional symmetry (CS), and if the equilibrium structure of the industry, in the absence of the antitrust policy, is not a monopolistic cartel, then there exists a range of antitrust penalties which would lead to the formation of the monopolistic cartel (the grand coalition), reducing market competition.

Grand coalition superadditivity and coalitional symmetry are the basic ingredients of many cartel formation models. For GCS, industry profits reach their highest

[7] See Ray (2007) for an introduction to this literature.

level in the grand coalition.[8] CS requires that industry profits are equally shared among coalitions, regardless of the coalition structure (e.g., regardless of the number of members per coalition). It is worth noting that CS implies symmetric players, the absence of synergy among cartel members and the presence of positive externalities in cartel formation. Put together, GCS and CS are sufficient to show that there exists a range of values of the expected antitrust fine that break any partial cartel but do not deter the formation of the grand coalition.[9]

Formally, consider a symmetric game of coalition formation $\Gamma(N, \Omega, \pi)$, where N is a finite number of firms, Ω is the set of all possible partitions of these firms into cartels (coalitions), and π is the set of firms' payoff (partition function).[10] Define F as the expected antitrust penalty, which is equal to the monetary fine times the probability of being convicted. Let F_1 be the penalty level above which firms in the monopolistic cartel prefer to deviate to the singleton structure, where all firms compete individually, and, analogously, let $F_{\mathcal{P}}$ be the minimum antitrust penalty which breaks up a coalition structure $\mathcal{P} \in \Omega$. Then it can be proved that if π satisfies grand coalition superadditivity and coalitional symmetry, $F_1 \geq F_{\mathcal{P}}$ for all $\mathcal{P} \in \Omega$ (Bartolini and Zazzaro, 2008, Proposition 3).

In other words, in the class of games that are characterized by GCS and CS there always exists a range of penalties, F, such that all coalition structures but the grand coalition are broken up. Therefore, if the market structure in the absence of an antitrust law consists of more than one monopolistic cartel, it exists a level of antitrust penalty that would lead firms to form the grand coalition. The intuition is that as the antitrust penalty increases the cost of forming a cartel, it reduces the possibility of firms in the industry free riding on the decisions of others to restrict competition. Given the assumptions of GCS and CS, in any coalition structure $\mathcal{P}$ there is at least one cartel in which the *per-member* payoff is lower than in the grand coalition. As a consequence, any coalition structure $\mathcal{P}$ is destabilized by a smaller fine than the grand coalition. Obviously, as in McCutcheon (1997), if the expected penalty is set at a level higher than F_1, even the monopolistic cartel is unprofitable and no cartel forms in the industry.

To illustrate, consider the case of five symmetric firms with constant marginal cost c, competing *à la* Cournot in a market characterized by homogeneous goods and a linear inverse demand $p = a - bQ$.[11] Before competing, firms can decide whether to form a cartel. Once formed, cartels compete non-cooperatively in the

[8] GCS is a weaker version of superadditivity, as it only requires the firms' payoff vector in the grand coalition (the monopolistic cartel) to be larger than the payoff vector of firms in any other coalition structure. Formally, given N players, for every state $x = (\pi, \mathcal{P})$, there is $x' = (\pi', \{N\})$ such that $\pi' \geq \pi$, where $\{N\}$ is the grand coalition, $\mathcal{P}$ is any coalition structure, and π is the firms' payoff vector (Ray 2007, p. 192).

[9] Under stricter conditions, this result can be extended to the case of asymmetric firms (Bartolini and Zazzaro 2008).

[10] For a definition of coalition games, see Ray (2007).

[11] This example was first studied by Ray and Vohra (1997) and then revisited in Bartolini and Zazzaro (2008).

Table 11.1 Structure of the game $\Gamma(5, \Omega, \pi)$

coalition structure	π_1	π_2	π_3	π_4	π_5
$\mathcal{P}_1$ {1,2,3,4,5}	$\frac{1}{20}$	$\frac{1}{20}$	$\frac{1}{20}$	$\frac{1}{20}$	$\frac{1}{20}$
$\mathcal{P}_2$ {1,2,3,4} {5}	$\frac{1}{36}$	$\frac{1}{36}$	$\frac{1}{36}$	$\frac{1}{36}$	$\frac{1}{9}$
$\mathcal{P}_3$ {1,2,3} {4,5}	$\frac{1}{27}$	$\frac{1}{27}$	$\frac{1}{27}$	$\frac{1}{18}$	$\frac{1}{18}$
$\mathcal{P}_4$ {1,2,3} {4} {5}	$\frac{1}{48}$	$\frac{1}{48}$	$\frac{1}{48}$	$\frac{1}{16}$	$\frac{1}{16}$
$\mathcal{P}_5$ {1,2} {3,4} {5}	$\frac{1}{32}$	$\frac{1}{32}$	$\frac{1}{32}$	$\frac{1}{32}$	$\frac{1}{16}$
$\mathcal{P}_6$ {1,2} {3} {4} {5}	$\frac{1}{50}$	$\frac{1}{50}$	$\frac{1}{25}$	$\frac{1}{25}$	$\frac{1}{25}$
$\mathcal{P}^*$ {1} {2} {3} {4} {5}	$\frac{1}{36}$	$\frac{1}{36}$	$\frac{1}{36}$	$\frac{1}{36}$	$\frac{1}{36}$

Firms' payoffs are normalized by imposing $\frac{(a-c)^2}{b} = 1$

market. In this game, a coalition structure $\mathcal{P}$ consists of $m(\mathcal{P})$ cartels, S_j, of size s_j. The per-member payoff is given by

$$\pi_i(S_j, \mathcal{P}) = \frac{1}{s_j} \frac{(a-c)^2}{b[m(\mathcal{P})+1]^2} \qquad \forall\, i \in S_j, \quad \forall S_j \in \mathcal{P} \quad \text{and} \quad \forall\, \mathcal{P} \in \Omega \tag{11.14}$$

Since firms are symmetric, we assume that the profit generated by a coalition is equally shared among members.[12] The incentive which drives firms to form a cartel is clearly reducing $m(\mathcal{P})$, which increases the payoff of the cartel. However, as the number of participants in the cartel increases, s_j, the per-member profit decreases. Hence, each firm has an incentive to stay out of the cartel, hoping that the rest of the firms form a cartel. The structure of this game is summarized by Table 11.1,[13] where we impose $\frac{(a-c)^2}{b} = 1$.

The equilibrium (or equilibria) of the coalition game $\Gamma(5, \Omega, \pi)$ depends on the assumptions on how coalitions actually form. To be specific, we consider the concept of *equilibrium binding agreement* (EBA), introduced by Ray and Vohra (1997). A coalition structure $\mathcal{P}$ is an EBA if it is not *blocked* by any other finer coalition structure. Put differently, a coalition structure is stable only if firms have no incentive to deviate to another structure that can be formed via disintegration of existing coalitions. According to this concept, it is easy to show that the monopolistic cartel

[12] This is not a restriction as Ray and Vohra (1997) show that the equal division of the coalition worth arises in any equilibrium of a coalition formation game with symmetric players.

[13] Since players are symmetric, we can omit coalition structures that are just a permutation of players in the same coalition structure.

is not stable because firm 5 has an incentive not to sign a monopolistic collusive agreement, for its payoff in $\mathcal{P}_2$, is higher than in $\mathcal{P}_1$. The only EBA is the coalition structure $\mathcal{P}_5$, where two cartels form and one firm stays alone.[14] Here no firm has an incentive to split into finer coalitions, whether $\mathcal{P}_6$ or $\mathcal{P}^*$.[15]

Now, let us introduce a perturbation of the game Γ by an antitrust penalty F imposed on firms found guilty of restricting competition. Consider the coalition structure $\mathcal{P}_5$. If the penalty announced by the antitrust authority is sufficiently high to make the payoff of firms in cartels $\{1,2\}$ and $\{3,4\}$ lower than the payoff they can gain competing as singletons, i.e., if $F \geq F_5 = \left(\frac{1}{32} - \frac{1}{36}\right) = \frac{1}{288}$, then $\mathcal{P}_5$ is no longer sustainable as an EBA. If, however, $F < F_3 = \left(\frac{1}{27} - \frac{1}{36}\right) = \frac{1}{108}$ firms would find it optimal to partition themselves as in $\mathcal{P}_3$. In fact, firms in the two-member cartel receive a higher individual expected payoff than in the grand coalition, hence blocking $\mathcal{P}_1$; at the same time, firms in the three-member cartel have no incentive to split because in $\mathcal{P}_3$ they receive a profit higher than in $\mathcal{P}^*$. However, for firms in the three-member cartel the individual payoff is lower than in the grand coalition $\mathcal{P}_1$. This implies that if $\frac{1}{108} \leq F < F_1 = \left(\frac{1}{20} - \frac{1}{36}\right) = \frac{1}{45}$ the penalty would dissolve $\mathcal{P}_3$, but not the monopolistic cartel which, due to GCS, is still more rewarding than competition in $\mathcal{P}^*$.

Summing up, the effect of an increase in the expected fine on competition is *not* monotone; at first, we have a decrease in competition, and only when the fine hits the highest threshold is there an increase in competition. When the authority cannot observe the level of market demand (or firms' costs) and, hence, the threshold above which the penalty induces atomistic competition, it is possible that the (non-distortionary and socially costless) penalty which maximizes the social welfare is lower than F_1 and, in some circumstances, even zero.

Antitrust policy II: Leniency Programmes

In the previous section, we actually abstracted from the fact that the antitrust authority does not directly apply any penalty to firms, and that it is only a court of law that, after hearing the alleged colluders and the authority, and evaluating the bevidence, can impose and enforce a penalty. The main purpose of leniency programmes is precisely to reduce the costs of the auditing process and, more importantly, to facilitate the collection of legal evidence of collusion. This is achieved by granting a penalty reduction to firms which self-report the existence of a cartel and facilitate the collection of evidence.

[14] Actually the singleton coalition structure, $\mathcal{P}^*$, is always an EBA by definition; firms should not select this equilibrium, however, if there is another which gives all of them a higher payoff.

[15] Obviously, if we apply a different concept of stability the coalition structure prevailing in equilibrium can be different. For example, using the sequential formation model proposed by Bloch (1996), the equilibrium of the game is coalition structure $\mathcal{P}_2$, that still consists of a partial cartel, leaving unaltered the possibility of the antitrust penalty generating anticompetitive effects.

In the United States, the Department of Justice introduced the possibility to grant immunity from criminal sanctions to self-reporting firms in 1978.[16] The leniency programme was radically revised in 1993, providing for the "automatic" granting of (monetary and criminal) leniency to the first firm reporting the existence of a cartel, while it remains discretionary for the other firms. Moreover, the possibility of applying for leniency is granted even after an investigation process has begun. These features have contributed to the success of the "revised" leniency programme. According to data reported by the OECD (2002), on average, 20 companies per years have applied for leniency, with respect to one per year with the old programme. Since the US leniency programme was revised, cooperation from applicants resulted in a dramatic increase of convictions and in over USD 4 billion in criminal fines (Hammond, 2008). The European Commission introduced its first leniency programme in 1996 and revised it in 2002, increasing the size of the fine abatement and reducing the discretionality of its application.

Apart from helping the antitrust authority to detect cartels and gain information on price-fixing agreements, leniency programmes can also be designed so as to discourage the formation of cartels or encourage their breakdown. In particular, while the leniency granted *after* an investigation has started aims at facilitating the provision of evidence in the trial, the leniency granted to whistleblowers *before* their cartel is placed under scrutiny by the authority affects firms' incentives to enter a collusive agreement or break up the existing ones.

Leniency During Investigation

In this subsection, we consider the effect of leniency programmes when firms can apply (for leniency) even after an investigation has started.

Motta and Polo (2003)

The relationship between leniency programmes and antitrust law enforcement was first studied by Motta and Polo (2003), who pointed out that the effectiveness of the programme depends on the possibility of cartel members applying for leniency even after a formal investigation has started. To illustrate, assume that firms face an expected penalty from colluding equal to μF, where $\mu = \alpha\theta$ consists of two parts, the probability of being audited $\alpha \in [0, 1]$, and the probability of being convicted $\theta \in [0, 1]$. Assume also that the leniency programme reduces the monetary fine to reporting firms, $R < F$, but without rewarding them $R \geq 0$.

In this setting, Motta and Polo (2003) consider two possible scenarios. In the first scenario, firms can apply for leniency *only* before the authority has begun

[16] In the US, unlike Europe, price fixing is a criminal offense.

an auditing process. In the second, self-reporting firms can apply for leniency *also* after an investigation has started. The time structure of the sequential game is the following:

- At date 0, the antitrust agency announces the policy, $\{\alpha, \theta, F, R\}$.
- At date 1, firms decide whether to collude or deviate, and the corresponding profits are realised.
- At date 2, firms decide whether to report and apply for leniency.
- At date 3, an investigation may take place, and according to the leniency programme firms can collaborate and apply for a reduction of the fine, or not.
- At date 4, (1) if cartels have been punished the Nash equilibrium is played; (2) if cartels have been investigated but not found guilty no further investigation can take place, finally; (3) if cartels have not been investigated the game is repeated from date 1 onwards.

As usual, let π^m be the profit in the case of collusion, π^d the profit from deviation, π^n the Nash equilibrium profit and δ the discount factor. The ex-ante payoff of firms at date 1 is given by the following equations,

$$V_{cnr} = \pi^m + \delta \left\{ \alpha \left[\theta \left(\frac{\pi^n}{1-\delta} - F \right) + (1-\theta) \left(\frac{\pi^m}{1-\delta} \right) \right] + (1-\alpha) V_{cnr} \right\} \tag{11.15}$$

$$V_{cr} = \pi^m + \delta \left[\alpha \left(\frac{\pi^n}{1-\delta} - R \right) + (1-\alpha) V_{cr} \right] \tag{11.16}$$

$$V_r = \pi^m + \delta \left(\frac{\pi^n}{1-\delta} - R \right) \tag{11.17}$$

$$V_d = \pi^d + \frac{\delta}{1-\delta} \pi^n \tag{11.18}$$

Since all the subgame perfect equilibria involve symmetric strategies, these equations describe all possible sets of equilibrium strategies. V_{cnr} represents the present value of colluding at date 1 and then not applying for leniency either before or after an investigation has taken place. In this case, the cartel is sentenced to pay a fine F with probability $\alpha\theta$. V_{cr} is the present value of colluding at stage 1 and then applying for leniency if an investigation has started. In this case the probability of punishment has increased to α, but the penalty is lower, $R < F$. When the firm self-reports before being investigated, the payoff is V_r equal to the discounted flow of Nash equilibrium profits minus the reduced penalty R. Finally, the expected value from deviation is V_d, where a firm gets the deviation profit in the first period and the Nash equilibrium payoff subsequently.

When the leniency programme does not allow firms under investigation to apply for a reduced fine, V_{cr} cannot be an equilibrium strategy, as firms receive no benefit by reporting. As a consequence, since $V_r \leq V_d$ for any $R \geq 0$, the leniency policy has no effect on the collusive behaviour of firms. In this case, if the level of the expected penalty, F, is not high enough to deter the formation of a cartel, i.e., to make $V_{cnr} < V_d$, the introduction of a leniency programme does not affect the sustainability of the agreement, as no firm has an incentive to apply for leniency.

On the contrary, if the leniency programme allows firms report after the investigation has started, the programme might influence the collusion strategy by making V_{cr} greater than V_{cnr}. Therefore, even if firms find it optimal to form a cartel, $V_{cnr} > V_d$, once they are placed under scrutiny by the authority they might prefer to desist from colluding and apply for leniency. However, if at the outset $V_{cnr} < V_d$, the introduction of a very generous fine rebate for whistleblowers could have the perverse effect of favouring the formation of collusive agreements, because, while the antitrust fine would not be high enough to discourage firms from colluding, the possibility of being relieved of the penalty once the cartel is detected can make collusion profitable, $V_{cr} > V_d$.

Leniency (Only) before Investigation

We now consider leniency programmes in which the possibility to apply for leniency is allowed only before a firm is audited.

Ellis and Wilson (2001)

The idea that in order to be effective in deterring cartels, leniency has to be extended to firms under investigation is challenged by Ellis and Wilson (2001), who show that leniency may break up collusive agreements even when firms can apply for leniency only before any formal investigation has started. Their main argument is that the firm which applies for leniency not only avoids the fine, but may also gain in terms of market competition with respect to the other members of the cartel which are affected by the antitrust penalty. As they argue (Ellis and Wilson 2001, pp. 9–10), "the damage [to the other firms] might arise from the jailing of key executives, as well as the costs of rebuilding lost reputation. Furthermore, once convicted of antitrust abuses a firm is often made to introduce costly internal mechanisms that ensure future compliance with the antitrust laws."

Ellis and Wilson consider Bertrand competition among n firms producing differentiated products. In this set-up, the share of market captured by each firm depends on the cost structure of the other firms. The antitrust penalty works as an extra cost which forces firm to change their optimal strategy. As a result, the Nash equilibrium favors the firm which has applied for leniency, whose cost structure has not changed.

This intuition can be easily incorporated into Motta and Polo's model, by changing the expected value of reporting:

$$V_r' = \pi^m + \delta(\bar{\pi}^n - R) + \frac{\delta^2}{1-\delta}\pi^n \qquad \text{with } \bar{\pi}^n > \pi^n \tag{11.19}$$

In the first period, the firm gains the monopoly profit, π^m. In the second period, the firm reports, incurring a fine R but gaining $\bar{\pi}^n$ which is higher than the Nash Equilibrium profit without the fine. Then in the subsequent periods the usual Nash equilibrium is played. Clearly, the gains from deviating may be smaller than the gains from reporting, $V_r' > V_d$. In particular, assuming $R = 0$, a necessary condition for the firm to report is:

$$\delta > \frac{\pi^d - \pi^m}{\bar{\pi}^n - \pi^n} \tag{11.20}$$

Ellis and Wilson (2001) push this argument even further, arguing that the leniency programme can actually reinforce the stability of the cartel. In the event that no firm self-reports the cartel, the sole presence of the leniency programme may act as a punishment mechanism that makes deviations less profitable and a cartel with a higher pricing strategy sustainable. The feasibility of this argument relies on the assumption that all firms but the deviant can actually apply and benefit from the leniency programme. In this situation the benefit from deviation becomes:

$$V_d' = \pi^d + \delta(\underline{\pi}^n - F) + \frac{\delta^2}{1-\delta}\pi^n \qquad \text{with } \underline{\pi}^n < \pi^n \tag{11.21}$$

In conclusion, leniency programmes make the punishment more bitter for the deviating firm, but also less costly for the firms that enforce it, and this can make collusive agreement stronger.

Spagnolo (2000)

Motta and Polo (2003) show that when leniency is also granted to firms reporting after an investigation has started, it can create a perverse incentive to form new cartels, as the punishment is actually reduced.

This argument is further pursued by Spagnolo (2000), who shows that even a leniency programme which does not allow applications to be filed when the cartel is under investigation, can adversely affect competition in the market. This is because it reduces the net benefit from deviation and, therefore, facilitates the formation of cartels.[17] Here, we present a simplified version of Spagnolo's model which captures the essential ingredients of his analysis:

- At date 0, the antitrust authority announces its policy $\{\alpha, F, R\}$, where we assume that $\theta = 1$, i.e., if audited, a firm is always fined.
- At date 1, firms decide whether to collude or deviate on prices.
- At date 2, firms observe the strategies played in the previous stage, and decide whether to report (and, if possible, apply for leniency R); buyers observe the prices and the sale takes place.
- At date 3, if no firm has reported in the previous stage, the investigation is started with probability α, and colluding firms must pay F.

[17] This perverse effect is also discussed by Buccirossi and Spagnolo (2006), who apply a similar framework to a model of illegal trade.

The punishment inflicted at date 3 consists of a monetary fine F, plus a damage equal to the profits made so far, so that, after a cartel is detected and colluders have paid back profits to the authority, their payoff is negative.

Notice that the structure of the game is essentially one-shot, as firms choose either prices or output[18] only once, at date 1. However, the game has some elements of sequentiality as the strategy of the firm consists in both setting the price (or quantity) and deciding whether to report the existence of the cartel.

In this setting, if no antitrust policy is in place, it is well known that collusion strategies cannot be supported as an equilibrium. Similarly, in the absence of a leniency programme, i.e., $R = F$, no collusive strategy can be sustained in equilibrium. Consider the case in which firms have an incentive to form a cartel, i.e., $(1-\alpha)\pi^m - \alpha F > \pi^n$. Firms could enforce this agreement by threatening to report, at date 2, the existence of the cartel if some firm deviates; this strategy, however, would enforce a collusive agreement only if credible. At date 2, a firm which observes a deviation by another firm can either go along with it or report the existence of the cartel, receiving the following payoffs,

$$\begin{aligned} V_{nr} &= (1-\alpha)\pi^{md} - \alpha F && \text{(if it does not report)} \\ V_r &= -F && \text{(if it does report)} \end{aligned}$$

where π^{md} is the payoff a firm that played the collusive strategy receives if some other firm deviates. Clearly, the strategy to report the cartel if somebody deviates is credible only if $V_{nr} < V_r$ and $\pi^{md} < -F$, which *never* holds as long as $\pi^{md} \geq 0$. Therefore, the simple implementation of an antitrust penalty does not induce a collusive equilibrium.

Things change when the law provides for a partial or complete penalty exemption for firms that reveal the existence of the cartel to the Authority, i.e., $R \in [0, F)$. Firms now incur a different (lower) penalty if they report the cartel, so the punishment strategy is credible if

$$\begin{aligned} (1-\alpha)\pi^{md} - \alpha F &< -R \\ R &< \alpha F - (1-\alpha)\pi^{md} \end{aligned} \tag{11.22}$$

If $\pi^{md} \geq \frac{\alpha}{1-\alpha} F$, then a leniency programme that does not provide any reward to whistleblowers cannot affect the collusive agreement, and we are back to Motta and Polo's result. However, as long as $\pi^{md} < \frac{\alpha}{1-\alpha} F$ and the leniency programme consists in a large penalty rebate – small R – the antitrust policy provides the incentive to sustain collusive agreements, that were impossible had the leniency policy not been introduced. In particular, Spagnolo (2000) considers the case of competition à la Bertrand, where $\pi^n = \pi^{md} = 0$, and shows that a strong leniency programme, with $R = 0$, induces the formation of a cartel for any level of collusive prices, p^c, such that $(1-\alpha)\pi(p^c) - \alpha F \geq 0$.

[18] In Spagnolo's model only duopolistic Bertrand competition is considered.

It is worth noting that an increase in the monetary fine F or in the probability of auditing α, would increase *ex-ante* deterrence, but, making condition (11.22) easier to satisfy, would increase the sustainability of the cartel. However, as Spagnolo notes, the key ingredient of his model is the impossibility of the deviating firm to fine tune the negative effect of deviation on the other firms. Otherwise, a firm could choose a deviating strategy that makes firms indifferent between reporting and not reporting, hence making collusion always unsustainable.

Given the objective of our analysis, we conclude by drawing attention to a variation of Spagnolo's model that can provide further interesting insights in terms of perverse effects of antitrust monetary fines. In the sequential model proposed by Spagnolo (2000), firms' payoffs are realized only at the end of the game. In this way, a report of a collusive cartel would lead to the repetition of the entire game. This can be a natural set-up for the analysis of procurement auctions, where the whole procedure can be subject to annulment, even after the auction has taken place. However, it is a less realistic assumption when considering antitrust trials in which it is in practice very difficult to take the profits firms accumulated during the life span of the cartel away.[19] Accordingly, let us consider Spagnolo's model with an antitrust policy consisting only in the enforcement of a fixed fine F with probability α, i.e., colluding firms can retain their past profits if the cartel is detected. In this case, it is easy to show that even in the absence of a penalty discount, $R = F$, if the antitrust penalty is not very high, the threat to reveal the existence of the collusive agreement to the authority can be credible enhancing the sustainability of the cartel. Assume that the antitrust fine is not sufficiently high to deter firms from forming a cartel:

$$\begin{aligned} \pi^m - \alpha F &< \pi^n \\ F &< \frac{\pi^m - \pi^n}{\alpha} = F^* \end{aligned} \tag{11.23}$$

The strategy to punish deviators by reporting evidence on the collusive agreement is now credible if:

$$\begin{aligned} \pi^{md} - \alpha F &< \pi^n - F \\ F &< \frac{\pi^n - \pi^{md}}{1-\alpha} = \widetilde{F} \end{aligned} \tag{11.24}$$

When condition (11.24) holds, firms would find it more profitable to pay a fine rather than let somebody deviate and break up the cartel. Under Bertrand competition this condition in never satisfied, as $\pi^n = \pi^{md} = 0$ (consistent with Spagnolo's model). However, if we consider other types of competition, say Cournot competition, one cannot exclude that there exist some strategies for which $\pi^n > \pi^{md}$. In this case, if $F < \widetilde{F} < F^*$ the presence of an antitrust monetary fine makes the punishment strategy credible and, once more, it proves an unintentional device to sustain collusive cartels.

[19] In antitrust laws, however, it is common to introduce some elements of proportionality in penalty schemes.

Concluding Remarks

A common theme in the industrial organization literature is that in the in presence of market imperfections competition should be regulated and protected by law. However, the same market imperfections could cause antitrust interventions to be detrimental of market competition.

Although the models presented in this chapter span different methodological approaches, they all show that the introduction of antitrust fines and leniency programmes may have undesirable, anticompetitive effects.

As regards monetary fines, contributions in the standard framework of noncooperative repeated games Cyrenne (1999); Harrington (2004); McCutcheon (1997) demonstrate that a monetary fine tends to reduce competition by making the collusive agreement easier to sustain, because the fine increases the costs of deviation and/or the cost of renegotiating the original agreement. Bartolini and Zazzaro (2008) focus on the formation of cartels within the approach of coalition formation games. They show that a monetary fine, discouraging the formation of partial cartels, reduces the possibility of some firms exploiting the positive externality generated by collusive agreements and increases the incentives to form a monopolistic coalition.

Albeit using different approaches, these models reach similar conclusions. For instance, in both Bartolini and Zazzaro's and McCutcheon' s models, the perverse effect arises only for intermediate values of the monetary fine, while a "sufficiently" large penalty would prevent the formation of any cartel. Furthermore, Harrington's model predicts that the perverse effect does not arise should the cartel adopt a monopolistic price strategy. Analogously, Bartolini and Zazzaro's model predicts a perverse effect of the antitrust penalty only if firms are not colluding as a monopolistic cartel.

In the same vein, a generous leniency programme can break collusive agreements, as it makes the threat of self-reporting more credible. In general, leniency policies reduce the duration of collusive agreements, which is good for markets where a cartel would have formed anyway. We cannot exclude, however, the formation of cartels in industries where a cartel would not have formed had the leniency programme not been in place.

Finally, it is important to stress that the general message coming from this literature does not point to the abrupt elimination of any antitrust policy. Rather, it is a note of caution for the policy maker in devising penalty schemes that may produce opposite effects to the desired ones. On the one hand, only very strong monetary and nonmonetary sanctions can discourage firms from colluding. On the other, in a world of uncertainty, where the exact penalty levels which induce more collusion are not known to the authority, a large penalty makes cartel deterrence more likely, but it also increases the risk of fostering broader and tougher collusive agreements.

Acknowledgements We would like to thank participants of the conference "The Economics of Imperfect Markets," held in Rome (May 2008), for useful comments on an earlier draft of this work. Usual disclaimer applies.

References

Bartolini D, Zazzaro A (2008) Are antitrust fines friendly to competition? An endogenous coalition formation approach to collusive cartels. SSRN elibrary

Besanko D, Spulber DF (1989) Antitrust enforcement under asymmetric information. Econ J 99(396):408–425

Bloch F (1996) Sequential formation of coalitions in games with externalities and fixed payoff division. Games Econ Behav 14:90–123

Block W (1994) Total repeal of antitrust legislation: A critique of bork, brozen, and posner. Rev Aust Econ 8(1):35–70

Bork RH (1978) The antitrust paradox: a policy at war with itself. Basic Book, New York

Buccirossi P, Spagnolo G (2006) Leniency policies and illegal transactions. J Publ Econ 90(6–7): 1281–1297

Coase RH (1937) The nature of the firm. Econ 4(16):386–405

Crandall RW, Winston C (2003) Does antitrust policy improve consumer welfare? Assessing the evidence. J Econ Perspect 17(4):3–26

Cyrenne P (1999) On antritrust enforcement and the deterrence of collusive behaviour. Rev Ind Organ 14(3):257–272

Ellis CJ, Wilson WW (2001) What doesn't kill us makes us stronger: An analysis of corporate leniency policy. University of Oregon, Oregon

Frezal S (2006) On optimal cartel deterrence policies. Int J Ind Organ 24(6):1231–1240

Green EJ, Porter RH (1984) Noncooperative collusion under imperfect price information. Econometrica 52(1):87–100

Hammond SD (2008) Recent developments, trends and milestones in the antitrust division's criminal enforcement program. Available at http://usdoj.gov/atr/public/speeches/232716.htm

Harrington JE Jr (2004) Cartel pricing dynamics in the presence of an antitrust authority. RAND J Econ 35(4):651–673

Levenstein MC, Suslow VY (2006) What determines cartel success? J Econ Lit 44(1):43–95

Martin S (2006) Competition policy, collusion, and tacit collusion. Int J Ind Organ 24:1299–1332

McCutcheon B (1997) Do meetings in smoke-filled rooms facilitate collusion? J Polit Econ 105(2):330–350

Motta M (2004) Competition policy: theory and practice. Cambridge University Press, Cambridge

Motta M, Polo M (2003) Leniency programs and cartel prosecution. Inter J Ind Organ 21:347–379

OECD (2002) Fighting hard core cartels: harm, effective sanctions and leniency programmes. OECD, Paris

Posner RA (1976) Antitrust law: an economic perspective. University of Chicago Press, Chicago

Ray D (2007) A game-theoretic perspective on coalition formation. The Lipsey Lectures, Oxford University Press, NY

Ray D, Vohra R (1997) Equilibrium binding agreements. J Econ Theor 73:30–78

Ray D, Vohra R (1999) A theory of endogenous coalition structures. Games Econ Behav 26: 286–336

Rothbard MN (1962) Man, economy and state. William Volker Fund and D. Van Nostrand, NJ

Rothbard MN (1970) Power and market: government and the economy. Institute for Human Studies, Menlo Park, California

Salin P (1996) Cartels as efficient productive structures. Rev Aust Econ 9(2):29–42

Souam S (2001) Optimal antitrust policy under different regimes of fines. Int J Ind Organ 19(1–2): 1–26

Spagnolo G (2000) Self-defeating antitrust laws: How leniency programs solve Bertand's paradox and enforce collution in auctions. FEEM

Sproul MF (1993) Antitrust and prices. J Polit Econ 101(4):741–754

Stigler GJ (1950) Monopoly and oligopoly by merger. Am Econ Rev Proc 40:23–34

GPSR Compliance

The European Union's (EU) General Product Safety Regulation (GPSR) is a set of rules that requires consumer products to be safe and our obligations to ensure this.

If you have any concerns about our products, you can contact us on ProductSafety@springernature.com

In case Publisher is established outside the EU, the EU authorized representative is:

Springer Nature Customer Service Center GmbH
Europaplatz 3
69115 Heidelberg, Germany

Batch number: 10725802

Printed by Printforce, the Netherlands